BRIAN F. STELCK

D0743984

M I S S I O N
I N
B O L D
H U M I L I T Y

MISSION
IN
BOLD
HUMILITY

DAVID BOSCH'S WORK CONSIDERED

WILLEM SAAYMAN AND KLIPPIES KRITZINGER
EDITORS

ORBIS BOOKS
Maryknoll, New York 10545

The Catholic Foreign Mission Society of America (Maryknoll) recruits and trains people for overseas missionary service. Through Orbis Books, Maryknoll aims to foster the international dialogue that is essential to mission. The books published, however, reflect the opinions of their authors and are not meant to represent the official position of the society.

Library of Congress Cataloging-in-Publication Data

Mission in bold humility : David Bosch's work considered / Willem
    Saayman and Klippies Kritzinger, editors.
        p.   cm.
    Includes bibliographical references.
    ISBN 1-57075-087-4 (alk. paper)
    1. Mission – Theory – History of doctrines – 20th century.
    2. Bosch, David Jacobus.   I. Saayman, W. A. (Willem A.)
    II. Kritzinger, J. J.
    BV2063.M56174   1996
    266'.001–dc21
                                          96-46650
                                          CIP

...we regard our involvement in dialogue and mission as an adventure, are prepared to take risks, and are anticipating surprises as the Spirit guides us into fuller understanding. This is not opting for agnosticism, but for humility. It is, however, a **bold humility** — or a humble boldness. We know only in part, but we do know. And we believe that the faith we profess is both true and just, and should be proclaimed. We do this, however, not as judges or lawyers, but as witnesses; not as soldiers, but as envoys of peace; not as high-pressure salespersons, but as ambassadors of the Servant Lord.

– David Bosch
Transforming Mission

CONTENTS

ABBREVIATIONS

ABRECSA	Association of Black Reformed Christians in South Africa
CWME	Commission for World Mission and Evangelism
DEIC	Dutch East India Company
DRC	Dutch Reformed Church
EATWOT	Ecumenical Association of Third World Theologians
ETHOS	Evangelical Theological House of Studies
IIMO	Interuniversity Institute for Missiological and Ecumenical Research
NGK	Nederduitse Gereformeerde Kerk
NHK	Nederduitsch Hervormde Kerk
NIR	National Initiative for Reconciliation
SACC	South African Council of Churches
SACLA	South African Christian Leadership Assembly
SAMS	Southern African Missiological Society
SVD	Society of the Divine Word
UNISA	University of South Africa
VSB	Vrouesendingbond
WCC	World Council of Churches

DAVID BOSCH, THE SOUTH AFRICAN

Willem Saayman and Klippies Kritzinger

The date was July 1979. In Pretoria, notorious capital of apartheid South Africa, more than 5,000 Christians had gathered for the South African Christian Leadership Assembly (SACLA). It was the biggest such gathering ever attempted up to that time. Christians representing all the spectrums of the Christian community in South Africa were there: ecumenicals and evangelicals; Protestants and Roman Catholics; straitlaced Presbyterians and exuberant Pentecostals and Charismatics; Black and White; supporters of the extra-parliamentary political movements, as well as supporters of the government and the various homeland systems. The only significant group of Christians that was not represented were the African Initiated Churches. This gathering was more than two years in the making, and to anyone with experience of the Christian divisions in South Africa, it was nothing less than a miracle that it could happen at all. It was the fruit of two years of planning by an executive committee that represented the whole spectrum of the Christian community in South Africa. It was formed under the leadership of David Bosch. Indeed, it would not be too much to say that even the executive committee would not have been able to hold together had it not been for the leadership of David Bosch.

Even so, the very fact that the meeting was taking place was considered by many to be miraculous. There had been all kinds of opposition against it. The Afrikaans Reformed Churches did not appreciate the attempt and took various decisions in its governing bodies to prevent its members from participating. Conservative Evangelicals regarded with great suspicion the involvement of such as Bishop Desmond Tutu and muttered darkly about "communist plots" behind the gathering. Supporters of the extra-parliamentary political movements reacted angrily against the legitimacy ascribed to people who worked within the Homeland system. Small wonder, then, that the final decision by the Minister of Justice, on the advice of the Security Police, to allow the meeting to go ahead was taken only 24 hours before the start of the meeting. The executive committee was very much aware of all the contradicting influences and all the

Willem Saayman is professor and head of the Missiology Department at the University of South Africa and the General Secretary of the Southern African Missiological Society. He has missionary experience in Namibia, Zimbabwe, and South Africa. Klippies Kritzinger is professor of missiology at the University of South Africa, editor of *Missionalia,* and an ordained minister of the Uniting Reformed Church in Southern Africa.

various centrifugal powers which threatened to tear the gathering apart. For this reason, they had decided not to appoint in advance the preacher for the rally on the closing day of the assembly. Actually, quite a few of us on the executive committee did not expect the assembly to last until the closing rally! But the assembly was taking place and experiencing unexpected success. The executive committee therefore had to decide on appointing the speaker for the closing rally. After a lengthy period of moving prayer and reflection on what had happened so far, and what we expected to happen in the future, the committee came to a unanimous decision — the only person who could address this closing rally was David Bosch. In a moving ritual, the thirty-odd members of the executive committee gathered around David, who was kneeling on the cold cement floor of one of the rooms at the Pretoria showgrounds where the assembly took place. Solemnly we laid our hands on his head, while a few of the church leaders present led us in prayer and in supplication that God anoint David for this very important gathering. As one stood among the members of the executive committee, it was clear that if, at this specific stage in South African history, a single leader of the Christian church had to be appointed, the only person who could fill the bill would be this humble Afrikaner of Dutch Reformed origin, David Bosch. How was it possible that this man — a representative of the Afrikaner people, founders of the hated apartheid system, a member of the Dutch Reformed Church (DRC), a church regarded by many other churches as a heretical Christian community, a white man — could be considered for this eminent position?

There is no simple answer to this question. Certainly it was possible because of this man's sincere pastoral concern, a concern which made him able to listen intently and to hear the hurt and the joy of others. An answer was to be found partly too in his brilliant theological capabilities, especially the ability to cut to the core of an argument and lay out a case in such a way that everybody could understand what the real issue was. The answer lay partly in his patent humility, which always made him a simple son of Africa. But above all, perhaps, the answer can be found in his undoubted integrity. Here was a person trusted (albeit grudgingly) even by his most vociferous opponents. Neither the leadership of the DRC, who considered him with great suspicion, nor the leadership of any extra-parliamentary political movement, nor the leadership of any other church or Christian group, could ignore the fact that this was a man of total integrity. The preeminent concern in any decisions which he took, and in any advice that he gave, was never the position of any specific group or above all of David Bosch himself, but always the signs of the reign of God. That was what moved him more than anything else: the passion to erect signs of the coming shalom, of the rivers of peace and justice which would one day flow over the land. None of us agreed with him all the time on the way to bring this about; but we did agree that David Bosch was a credible and trustworthy disciple of Jesus Christ. And it was for this reason that all the various groups together on that day in July 1979, whatever might have been the hidden agendas at the back of their minds, were unanimous in their decision that there was only man who could deliver the closing address.

Many words have been written about the theological contribution of David Bosch. And *Transforming Mission* will always stand as his chief theological legacy. We have worked with David Bosch over a long period as his colleagues and friends. We therefore felt it necessary to include in this *Festschrift* a personal reflection on David Bosch, because we feel that one is better able to understand and evaluate his immense theological contribution if one is better acquainted with who and what he was as a human being. In this contribution we are therefore going to bring into relief a few qualities that marked his fruitful and interesting life. We highlight aspects from the "oral tradition" of those who lived and worked with David on a daily basis in order to portray his character as a Christian leader, as a friend, and as a human being.

We have already referred to David Bosch's integrity. Few among his worst enemies seldom doubted that it was a sense of rectitude and integrity that guided his thinking and action. It was one of the reasons why he was elected as Dean of the Faculty of Theology at the University of South Africa (UNISA), the largest theological faculty in South Africa. He served as Dean during very difficult times, when difficult decisions had to be made. It was a time when all kinds of government interventions against academic freedom had to be vigorously resisted. It was at a time when non-racialism was totally rejected in most spheres of life. Within these difficult circumstances, members of the Faculty of Theology were often considered to be troublemakers. As a result, David was often criticized from various sides for the positions which he vigorously defended. Indeed, there were times when principals of UNISA expressed the desire to get rid of this troublesome faculty. Yet, in times of great crisis, it was to David that the Rectors and Management Committee of the University turned often for guidance and help. The fact that eventually non-racialism was established as the guiding principle in all the practices of UNISA can be attributed to a large extent to the intervention of David Bosch. And his efforts were successful only because people trusted in his integrity and rectitude.

One aspect of David's life about which little is known outside a small circle of friends was his tireless advocacy for colleagues and associates who got entangled in the racist bureaucracy of apartheid's civil service. He was approached by many black South Africans whose passport applications had not been approved one or two days before their intended departure for conferences or periods of study overseas. This occurred, also, in the case of many overseas academics and activists whose visas were being delayed. He would doggedly appeal to a suppressed sense of fair play and humanity within the minds of the apartheid bureaucrats. He did not always succeed, and when he did, it was not because he had some hidden apartheid connections, but because of the residual respect among rank and file civil servants for a church minister and (even more) for a professor of theology that allowed his entreaties to bear fruit. But it was also his quick and incisive thinking that enabled him to unmask false arguments and half-truths in the reasoning of the bureaucrats and to turn these to the advantage of his friends.

Still, in all these bureaucratic battles, Bosch succeeded in steering clear of paternalism and of the desire to control people by exacting debts of gratitude.

In this respect his relationships with people were remarkably non-manipulative. His painful childhood experiences of dire poverty in rural Western Transvaal undoubtedly contributed to his down-to-earth approach to people and his obvious solidarity with people oppressed by history's unforgiving tides.

The most moving moment in David's funeral service was when Dr. Takatso Mofokeng, his colleague at UNISA and his friend for many years, spoke about the way in which David had died. He pointed out that David died waiting — like so many black South Africans — for an ambulance. Mofokeng observed that David died the way he had lived — in solidarity with black people. There is perhaps no greater tribute that can be paid to a white Afrikaner by a black theologian. It takes away nothing from the tragedy of David's death or from the deaths of those thousands of his black compatriots, but it situates him where he wanted to be and where he was clearly perceived to be by many black people who knew him. David tried to live as one who knew that the value of a theologian's life will be judged not in terms of intellectual rigor and academic originality, but in terms of what the least of Jesus' sisters and brothers experienced in their contact with that scholar.

Another important dimension of his person and character was his ecumenical spirit. The incident to which we referred above, occurring around the creation of SACLA, already illustrates the wide acceptance that he enjoyed across the spectrum of the Christian community in South Africa. This is not something which came naturally to a person from the DRC. When David started out as a young missionary in the Eastern Cape (Transkei), the ethos of the DRC was marked by a strict sense of separation from other Christian groups. Early on David rejected this ethos and grew in an ecumenical spirit. He was one of the leaders in the creation of the Transkei Council of Churches, a Council within which, for the first time, the DRC was represented. He was also a valued adviser and resource person for the South African Council of Churches (SACC), even when there was no contact whatsoever between SACC and the DRC. In the dark days of the state of emergency of the middle 1980s, when the National Initiative for Reconciliation (NIR) was launched, David was the obvious choice as its leader. And although many of us, especially from the "younger" black churches, did not wish to become involved with the NIR, none doubted his integrity or his ecumenical inclination. For David it was always patently obvious that one could only know the length and breadth and height and depth of the love of Christ in communion with *all* God's people.

Not all South Africans were favorably impressed by David's ecumenical theology. Something that is not widely known is that a charge of insubordination was laid against him in 1982 by a minister of the (white) DRC of which he was a member and a minister. This was as a result of the paper he had read at the 1982 "Church in the 1980s" conference held at UNISA. In that paper he spoke of "blind spots" that churches develop in their reading of the Bible:

> I observe a similar veil preventing the Afrikaans Reformed Churches from really hearing what the Bible says about the unity of the Church.... [T]his particular form of blindness is not part of the true Reformed tradition.

The Afrikaans Reformed Churches have only to return to their roots to discover that what they now cherish is nothing but a heresy that strikes at the very foundation of the Church. Because of this heresy the Afrikaans Reformed Churches have designed a missiology tailor-made "for Churches and institutions whose main function in society is to reinforce the status quo," where the Church becomes little more than a pale reflection of its environment. (Bosch 1983b: 36)

David's use of the term "heresy" for apartheid theology was not original at the time (January 1982), for it had been given prominence by the Association of Black Reformed Christians in South Africa (ABRECSA) at their founding meeting in October 1981. It had been used also by Dr. Manas Buthelezi (1976), when he called apartheid in the church a "damnable heresy." Through the decision of the World Alliance of Reformed Churches in Ottawa (1983) to suspend the membership of the Afrikaans Reformed Churches, the expression "apartheid is heresy" soon became an important cry in the final phase of the theological struggle against apartheid. But in January 1982, when David read his paper to a (largely white) academic audience, it came as a great shock to those Afrikaner theologians who were loyal to their church leadership and were not in touch with the thinking of black theologians. It was therefore hardly surprising that a minister of the DRC lay a charge against him with the presbytery in which he resided.

He was accused of contravening that part of his oath of ministerial office in which he (like all other ministers of the DRC) had to declare that he would not publicly disagree with the policies or doctrines of the church, but instead follow "proper channels" to raise the issue with the appropriate bodies within the church. But it was also clear that the charge was laid against him by right-wing colleagues because he dared to attack the racial policy of the DRC. When David appeared before the presbytery session where the charge was to be investigated, he was well prepared. He handed out his defense to each of the ministers present and then read it to them. When he left the meeting, the committee discussed the matter and eventually pronounced him not guilty. Even his three accusers agreed with the verdict.

One of the members of the committee, who in no way agreed with David's substantive views, made a strong point of the fact that his integrity was beyond question and that no one could doubt his loyalty to the gospel or to the local congregation which he and his family attended.

An essential part of David's wide ecumenical outlook was a firm commitment to the local church. It was a loyalty which many of his friends, who knew his stand on apartheid, could not fathom, because for a number of years beginning in the 1970s he was never invited to preach from the pulpit of any Dutch Reformed Congregation. He was frequently invited to preach in congregations of the Presbyterian, Anglican, Methodist and many other churches, but he was simply frozen out by his own church. And yet he remained a critically loyal DRC member until his death, trying his best to bring about change from within the church itself. It is a sad comment on the ideological blindness of the DRC and of the Afrikaner community at large that it did not recognize or honor one of their greatest sons.

A final episode from David's long and fruitful career that merits mention was his intervention during the 1980 Melbourne conference of the Commission for World Mission and Evangelism (CWME) of the World Council of Churches. There was a tension-filled discussion in the conference plenary when human rights violations were being debated. Some delegates argued that the conference had to condemn the Russian invasion of Afghanistan by name, in the same specific terms that it censured South Africa for its apartheid policy. These delegates were not satisfied with the general terms in which the report of Section II addressed this issue:

> During recent years many countries have used their military capability to intervene in the internal affairs of other nations. It has deprived nations of their right to determine their own future and inflicted further suffering on the people. The result is a new critical escalation of world tensions.
>
> As Christian individuals and as churches responsibly working within our societies, we are called to advocate that our governments respect and uphold the freedom of peoples and nations, and avoid the use of military or economic intervention to gain sovereignty over other nations. (CWME 1980:185J)

The delegates of the Russian Orthodox Church attending the conference objected strongly to the suggestion that their government be singled out for censure. There were a number of reasons why they did so, ranging from possible support for the Soviet government to fear that the state would institute further repressive measures against the church if it were seen to be participating in a conference that condemned Soviet foreign policy. Within that tense situation, David got up to propose a resolution which was subsequently accepted by the conference. It read:

> We wish to state that the mentioning of specific countries and situations in the resolutions of this conference is partly to be attributed to current events in those countries. We recognize, however, that there are other countries where foreign powers are intervening militarily, and governments which oppress, exploit, imprison and kill innocent people. We may be able to identify some of those countries and peoples. Others, however, we dare not identify for the simple reason that such a specific public identification by the Conference may endanger the position — even the lives — of many of our brothers and sisters, some of whom are participating in this Conference. We therefore confess our inability to be as prophetic as we ought to be, as that may, in some instances, entail imposing martyrdom on our fellow believers in those countries — something we dare not do from a safe distance. We know that many of them suffer under different regimes for their faith in Jesus Christ and urge that freedom of conscience be respected as well as other human rights. At the same time, we want to assure our unnamed brothers and sisters in many unnamed countries that

we have not forgotten them; we identify strongly in their suffering for the kingdom of God. (CWME 1980:251)

Was this a cheap compromise that allowed the World Council to practice double standards? Was it pandering to the Soviet state by not being brave enough to censure them by name for their atrocities? Did it bring cold comfort to the suffering Christians in Pakistan and other states neighboring on Afghanistan? Or was it a positive attempt to reconcile opposing factions that stemmed from Christian compassion? Opinions will vary, but the fact that this suggestion was made by a person coming from South Africa, who was willing to identify with the strong criticism expressed by the conference against his own country, must give it at least some credibility.

What emerges from the style of this intervention brings into relief certain fundamental features of David's life and theology:

- a sharp, logical mind that saw the heart of the issue at stake;
- a consistent and disarming honesty;
- a deep empathy with people who suffer;
- a refusal to impose suffering on others;
- a "catholic" commitment to defuse tension and facilitate reconciliation between different Christians groups.

This proposal was vintage Bosch, both in content and in style.

Finally, one cannot talk about David Bosch, the human being, without mentioning his incisive theological acumen. His many articles and books stand as monuments to this ability, and the articles in this book celebrate that acumen. From within our South African perspective, though, we feel it necessary to mention especially the influence David had on the definition of Christian mission as it is widely understood in South Africa today. His holistic, encompassing understanding of the *missio Dei*, in which the church is privileged to participate as God's servant, forms the basis of missiological consensus in South Africa today. The respectability which missiology enjoys as a theological discipline in South Africa, the flourishing of its study — especially on the post-graduate level — should be mainly ascribed to the labors of David Bosch over many years. To a large extent the true value of David's legacy will only become visible in the missiological endeavors of his younger colleagues and especially of his many post-graduate students. We hope that the various contributions in this volume, by many of his international friends and colleagues, will serve as a worthy first building block to a monument that will be a fitting memorial for the human being, our friend, David Bosch.

– 2 –

AFRICA IN DAVID BOSCH'S MISSIOLOGY

SURVEY AND APPRAISAL

Frans J. Verstraelen

The Man and His Missiology

We realize increasingly today that to understand the intellectual production of a scholar — especially when the work requires existential involvement, as is the case in producing theology — knowledge of an author's biography and history are not only helpful but even necessary. In what follows, I attempt to do this. I do not, however, seek to repeat David Bosch's "story," which has been told several times by his friends and colleagues (see, for example, Verkuyl 1992 and the first chapter of this volume). I merely seek to highlight aspects of his life and work that elucidate the theme of this contribution.

Reflection on Bosch's Missionary Experience in Transkei (1957–71)

If mission is crossing frontiers, then it is important for a missiologist who has to reflect systematically on the foundation, history, and praxis of Christian mission within differing social, economic, cultural, political and religious contexts, to have missionary experience outside his or her own culture and context. David Bosch did practical missionary work among the Xhosa in Transkei (1957–66). This was followed by a lectureship at the theological school in Umtata through 1971. How Bosch performed as a missionary is reflected in a series of articles in Afrikaans on the life of a missionary (Bosch 1973a). These reflections were originally presented during a course meant for white members of the Dutch Reformed Church involved in missionary activities. It is a very touching report which shows respect for the humanity of "the other," the black brother and sister, with their own cultural and religious background. It is also a report that shows David's sensitivity for black people's position and predicament:

Frans J. Verstraelen is professor of Christian Theology at the University of Zimbabwe. He has served as director the Interuniversity Institute for Missiological and Ecumenical Research (IIMO) and as general secretary of the International Association of Mission Studies (IAMS).

I gratefully acknowledge assistance in collecting and/or photocopying much of the material used in this contribution from Dr. Leny Lagerwerf, Interuniversity Institute for Missiological and Ecumenical Research (IIMO), Leiden, the Netherlands, and from Mrs. Monica Strassner and Ms. Saretha Botha, Library — University of South Africa (UNISA), South Africa.

All translations of quotations in Afrikaans, Dutch, or German are by myself.

their experience of white people cursing them, pushing them aside, or paying them hunger-wages. As a result of this, in Bosch's view, black people commonly see in white missionaries, even the most friendly and positive ones, a representative of the ruling class in South Africa; they have more possessions and more privileges. In sum, black people knew and experienced whites primarily in a boss-servant relationship, and this pattern held also for relations with white missionaries (Bosch 1973a: I:9–10).

Bosch, on the other hand, knows also his white customers, the addressees of his lecture/article: Whites look at blacks either as servants or as criminals, who are always regarded as objects of mission even if they are already Christians (Bosch 1973a: II:15; III:11). Mission in this "white" view must be concerned with "lost souls." Reference to such needs of black people as poverty, hunger, and so forth, runs a risk of identification with communism, and a missionary showing such a concern risks becoming a toy of communism (Bosch 1973a: IV:18–19).

Against such stereotypical ideas, fruit of a longstanding indoctrination program under the South African apartheid system, Bosch offers his own understanding of missionary work. He undergirds his views with references to biblical texts, which are often given fresh interpretation. Characteristic for a missionary, according to Bosch, is the development of empathy in humility and modesty, not pity. This empathy applies also to their "pagan" beliefs, since the religion of the others is "holy ground" (Bosch 1973a: II:13–14,16). Such attitudes lead to acknowledging the common humanity of both blacks and whites. As regards the question of salvation, mission has nothing to do with being superior, because — in the words of D. T. Niles quoted by Bosch — being a missionary "is like a beggar who tells another beggar where to find bread" (Bosch 1973a: II:14).

For Bosch the missionary's glorious age has ended, as has a "one-way" understanding of mission. It is therefore time to get rid of the idea that "we" [he is addressing whites] can always do something for "them" (because they are black), assuming that we shall give and they shall receive. Mission, in his view, will more and more consist in a two-way process in which peoples build each other up spiritually (Bosch 1973a: III:11). A missionary therefore cannot look at a black person with the eyes of a boss. A missionary relationship is characterized by being a servant (2 Cor 4:5; cf. 6:4), a beggar vis-à-vis other beggars (Bosch 1973a: II:12).

The symbol of a balanced understanding of mission, in Bosch's view, is the cross. The cross keeps two lines together: the vertical one directed toward God and eternal salvation, and the horizontal one directed toward human beings and all their needs, bodily and spiritual. One who merely concentrates on the vertical line finds the biblical message condemning rather than praising him, in Bosch's opinion. Basing himself on the message of both the Old and New Testaments, Bosch warns against the danger that missionaries try to be more spiritual than the Bible itself. For him the whole message and aim of mission can be summarized by the text of John 10:10: "I have come that they may have life, and have it to the full" (Bosch 1973a: V:21–24).

We may conclude that the missionary experience of David Bosch among and with the Xhosa in Transkei gave him precious insight into mission as service and partnership, as well as attitudes of empathy, humility, and modesty vis-à-vis people of cultural and religious backgrounds different from his own. I have paid attention to David Bosch's reflection on his own missionary experience, because what is convincingly shown is his integrity as a human being and as a Christian, as a missionary, and as a missiologist. I wish to state clearly my belief in David Bosch's personal and professional integrity before embarking on a survey and sometimes critical evaluation of his missiology in relation to Africa. My criticism, though serious, is never intended to be judgmental of his person.

Some Remarks on Bosch's Missiology

It is not my intention to present an evaluation of David Bosch's missiology as a whole. I limit myself to remarks which can throw light on our theme. For that purpose I look closely at the sources and the method of his missiology. Luckily Bosch himself has given us some clues. *The Journal of Theology for Southern Africa,* celebrating its first ten years (1972–82), invited a number of people to reflect on the development of their theological thinking during the past decade. Under the general heading "How My Mind Has Changed" (Bosch 1982c), Bosch asked himself whether his mind had indeed changed. His conclusion is, somewhat surprisingly, negative. In his own words: "I have come to the conclusion that the major changes in my theological thinking took place during the previous decade (the sixties), and not to the same extent during the seventies" (6). Bosch continues: "Perhaps, for me, the seventies were, rather, a decade of clarification and consolidation of a theological position that had already developed reasonably clear contours before that time" (6). Bosch indicates a threefold impetus that assisted him in gaining a greater conceptual clarity in the 1970s: attending a variety of local and international conferences on mission (1975a); reading more widely in connection with the foundation of *Missionalia;* and increased involvement in the South African scene.

This threefold missionary and missiological impetus contributed to a "current view of mission as being a more comprehensive concept than I would have thought a decade ago" (Bosch 1982c:7). From Bosch's own words, it can be deduced that the formative years of his theological insights and convictions must be located in the sixties, roughly coinciding with his missionary period in Transkei (1957–71). Nevertheless, Bosch does not mention his missionary experience as having contributed to his missiological understanding but merely clarifying and consolidating his theological options and position. Paraphrasing Bosch's own words: after he had turned forty in 1969, he did not change his views radically (Bosch 1982c:6).

One should recall that in the 1970s a veritable Copernican revolution took place in the way theology was done. This revolution did not occur in the North but in the South. I speak, of course, of the emergence of the "theology of liberation," which also implied a "liberation of theology" (see Segundo 1976). This new theology found supporters not only in Latin America, but also among other third world groups (for example, blacks in the United States and South Africa). It achieved organizational structure in the foundation of the Ecumenical Association of Third World Theologians (EATWOT), which held its first Intercontinental Conference in Dar es Salaam, Tanzania, August 1976, and produced its report, "The Emergent Gospel: Theology from the Developing World" (Torres and Fabella 1978).

In line with an understanding of the task of theology to be contextual and relevant in specific situations, it soon became clear that there could not be only one form of third world theology. A new methodology was needed. This new way stressed the importance of praxis — a seamless web linking the experience and reflection by women and men who found inspiration in the good news of the Gospel of Jesus Christ. This led inevitably to a variety of theologies, each with its own emphasis and focus. There was, however, common agreement that contextual theology, whatever its concrete forms, needed a liberative thrust geared toward fullness of life for all. The specific character of liberation theology consists in "critical reflection on Christian praxis in the light of the Word.... Confronted with an unjust society, Christians feel keenly that they cannot claim to be Christians without a commitment to liberation" (Gutiérrez 1973:13, 145).

In this perspective, commitment comes first as "a transforming activity marked and illuminated by Christian love.... Theology is a reflection, a critical attitude. Theology follows: it is the second step" (Gutiérrez, quoted in McGovern 1989:32). Liberation theology and third world theologies in general, by introducing an inductive or empirical element into their conception of the theological process, not only elicited controversy and criticism but also challenged Western theologians to review their way of doing theology.

One of those who felt himself challenged was the white South African theologian Albert Nolan, a member of the Dominican Order. In an interview I had with him in Johannesburg in 1985, Nolan explained that a stay of six weeks in Latin America in 1975 occasioned a breakthrough from his previous rational method of theologizing toward conceiving of theology as at the service of liberation. Nolan became convinced that there were no questions too radical to ask. This was quite different from traditional theology, which consisted largely in systematizing answers to questions from the past and adapting answers to past questions to today's questions. Nolan's visit to Latin America, where he met important representatives of liberation theology, such as Gustavo Gutiérrez and José Míguez Bonino, convinced him that a similar type of theology was necessary for South Africa. His commitment at that time was in relation to the Young Christian Student movement in the Soweto region. Nolan, as a white theologian, came to identify himself with and was converted to the cause of this struggling people.

David Bosch was, of course, aware of the theological developments we have been discussing. But they apparently did not convince him to alter a theological approach that he had developed in the 1960s. It can, therefore, safely be concluded that the 1970s, during which third world theologians reinterpreted and reappropriated the Christian message on their own terms and during which period third world theologies challenged many Western theologians, did not significantly change Bosch's missiology. At any rate, I find nothing in his writings that indicates that the development of third world theological interpretations of Christianity really affected his way of theologizing. Indeed, in 1982, Bosch indicated two things that anchored his orientation: first, acknowledgment that, "I myself — for better or for worse — stand in this Western tradition" (Bosch 1982c:6); and second, his option to minister to Afrikaner Christians: "In my own ministry my concern is particularly with the White Afrikaans Reformed Churches" (9).

In addition, his last work, *Transforming Mission* (1991a), contains a rich inventory of all that encompasses a "comprehensive concept of mission," and in drawing it up, Bosch remains consistent with his theological stance. If any development can be discerned it is not to incorporate empirical analysis as an essential part of theological method. For a more adequate understanding of mission, Bosch notes that perhaps one cannot do this by means of *theoria*... but only by means of *poiesis*, which involves imaginative creation or representation of evocative images (Bosch 1991a: 512). Sensitized by a theology of liberation approach, one would expect that theory should start from praxis, which in the cries of the oppressed and the poor goes far beyond any creative imagination.

Africa in Bosch's Major Missiological Works

Bosch's bibliography contains twelve different publications in book form. Four are written in Afrikaans and two are in Dutch. Of the books in English, two were published in South Africa and three in the United States, and one of those was copublished in Britain. Bosch's doctoral dissertation was written in German and published in Switzerland.

In his first major work, a reflection on the future of mission in the view of Jesus (1959), Africa is not featured. *A Spirituality of the Road* (1979a) functions only marginally in *Transforming Mission* (see 1991a: 177). In this section, therefore, I will use only *Witness to the World* (1980a) and *Transforming Mission* (1991a).

Witness to the World

This book is dedicated "To the Church in South Africa — 'ecumenical' and 'evangelical,' Protestant and Roman Catholic, Black and White." This looks promising, but when one scrutinizes the contents, one looks in vain for any connection with concrete African contexts. Africa as a whole, South Africa, African theology, and black theology do not feature in the index. Three Africans are mentioned — John Gatu (because he was the first to suggest a moratorium on missions and missionaries from the West, p. 5); John Mbiti (because he belongs to a category of missiologists who refuse to be categorized simply as "evangelical" over against "ecumenical," p. 29); and Burgess Carr (classified as typical "ecumenical," p. 29) who, as Secretary General of the All Africa Conference of Churches, at a meeting in Lusaka, May 1974 stated, "we must give our unequivocal support to the liberation movements" (p. 37). There is no reference to non-white theologians of his own country, such as Manas Buthelezi, Allan

Boesak, and G. M. Setiloane, who were already heralding a new analysis and evaluation of Christianity and its mission in so-called "Christian" South Africa.

Adrio König, a colleague at the University of South Africa, in his review of *Witness to the World*, took Bosch to task. Bosch summarizes König's criticism and then responds:

> König laments the fact that my illustrations derive exclusively from overseas and that one searches in vain for examples "from the ecclesiastical, social, or political life in South Africa." This is not entirely fair — cf. for instance, pp. 206 and 223. On the whole, however, König is correct. As "excuse" I could mention that *Witness to the World* has in view a wider readership than that of South Africa — it has been published simultaneously in England, the U.S.A., and South Africa. Moreover, I was of the opinion that the type of person who would read the book, would have no difficulty in recognizing the consequences of my views for his particular situation. "Those who have ears to hear...." (Bosch 1980b:20)

Here Bosch candidly reveals his way of theologizing: developing ideas. It is a method based, of course, on divine revelation as expressed in the biblical message and on the theological tradition of his own tradition (Calvinism), which applies theological doctrine to particular situations. This is not, one readily sees, a liberation theology method.

Transforming Mission

In the foreword to his *opus magnum*, Bosch writes that his original idea was to revise *Witness to the World*, but that he soon discovered that he had "outgrown his previous book," and that "in any case, a book for the early eighties would not address the challenges of the early nineties. Too much had happened in the eighties, in respect of theology, politics, sociology, economics" (Bosch 1991a:xv–xvi). Still, Bosch also indicates that between the two books there are "essential continuities" and important "discontinuities."

A major innovation is the attention paid to mission as contextualization, as liberation, and as inculturation (420–57). Bosch even concludes his explanation of contextual theology by saying that "the best models of contextual theology succeed in holding together in creative tension *theoria, praxis* and *poiesis*" (431). Nevertheless, there is scarcely any reference in *Transforming Mission* to concrete contexts. South Africa in particular is absent. For the Bosch of *Transforming Mission*, the principal interlocutors are established Western theologians and missiologists, many of whom already figured in *Witness to the World*.

It is true that a good number of third world theologians make appearances in *Transforming Mission*: seven from Asia, ten from Africa, and eleven from Latin America. On closer inspection, one discovers that these theologians are referred to marginally — with the exception of Gutiérrez and Segundo, who had been recognized by the Western theological establishment as theologians to be reckoned with.

An examination of the African theologians referred to substantiates my evaluation. Ten (black) Africans are mentioned, three of them from South Africa.

Of the seven African theologians outside South Africa, only four are listed in the bibliography — Appiah-Kubi, Mbiti, Pobee, and Ukpong. The rest are merely mentioned in the corpus of the book (Gatu, Sanneh, and Tshibangu). There is no reference to theologians such as F. Eboussi Boulaga and Jean-Marc Éla. The three black South African theologians mentioned are Boesak, Mosala, and Bishop Alpheus Zulu, who is quoted but without bibliographical mention. The reason for these omissions cannot be that African or black theologies have nothing to do with mission. The reason, in my opinion, is that Bosch has diffi-culty in giving "context" a central place in his way of theologizing. This appears to be the case when one considers his methodology (which, as we have indicated above, assumed its basic form in "pre-contextual" modes of doing theology in the 1980s). I believe that Bosch, in the final analysis, continued to belong to the cat-egory of theologians who theologize *from above* rather than *from below*. Bosch is aware of these two types of theologizing (see 1991a:423), but his orientation is not "from below." Bosch, in term of social sciences, is a "Weberian" rather than a "Marxian" intellectual, following an idealist approach "that attempts to deal with ideas and feelings as if they are independent entities that have a life of their own" (Mofokeng 1990:170). Minimally, one must say that analysis of Bosch's two major missiological works shows that he above all seeks to clarify theolog-ical and missiological concepts and ideas; he leaves the practical application of these ideas to his readers.

Africa and South Africa in Other Writings

In this section we shall examine how David Bosch's missiological articles, es-says, and contributions to collective works relate to Africa and, in particular, what his stated involvement in the South African scene entails missiologically. Here we shall see Bosch often to be highly "contextual," though in his own characteristic way.

Africa (aside from South Africa) in Bosch's Thought

I use the word "Africa" consistently here to distinguish between the Republic of South Africa and the rest of this huge continent; nonetheless, some overlap and ambiguity will occur.

First we should realize that South Africa was relatively isolated from the rest of the world, including Africa, for some years after it left the United Nations. This hampered South Africans, blacks and whites, from maintaining normal social contacts, as well as cultural and scientific exchange. Nevertheless, Bosch regularly obtained missiological and theological materials from around the world. His journal *Missionalia* shows what abundant good use he was able to make of it.

In January 1970, the Southern African Missiological Society held a confer-ence in Johannesburg on the theme, "Church and Culture Change in Africa," a report of which was published under the same title. Bosch, at the time General Secretary of the Society, wrote the preface of the report. In it he states:

In a changing world, of which Africa has become a mere province, it becomes increasingly necessary to make the message of the Cross relevant in
a new way to the lives of people, especially those who are caught up in the
whirlwind of change which is at present sweeping over the continent of
Africa. (Bosch 1971:7)

As editor of the report, Bosch also selected comments made by Eugene A.
Nida of the American Bible Society, who had participated as a guest speaker.
Herein attention was given to, for instance, the role of the ancestors and the
Holy Spirit, a major African preoccupation that is of scant interest in the West
and North.

As an author of many articles and essays, Bosch made valuable contributions to three themes: God in Africa (1973b and 1973c), Evil in Africa (1987a),
and Renewal of Christian Community in Africa (1978). He also wrote three
substantive essays on theology in Africa (1975b, 1984a, and 1987b). I present
below a short summary and evaluation of these six themes and essays.

God in Africa. "God through African Eyes" (Bosch 1973b) was an im-
promptu presentation at a Consultation at Mapumulo in 1972; it was published
without references because the editor of the report did not allow rewriting, anxious as he was to get the report published as soon as possible. Bosch had to rely
on his memory, a memory that contained a rich reservoir of names and functions
of God among various African ethnic groups. In this piece, Bosch demonstrates
the same sensitivity and humility that we saw above in his reflections on the life
of a missionary (1973a).

He is aware that some of the participants in the Consultation "may regard it
presumptuous on the part of a White man to attempt to say something about
traditional African beliefs and the relevance of Scripture to them," as if — with
reference to a critical remark of the Nigerian theologian E. Bolaji Idowu —
Europeans think they have a clear concept of God (Bosch 1973b:68). Bosch,
on the contrary, says that he considers himself as a fellow-Christian "believing
that God has encountered you and me, and who now together with you attempts to stammer out something of what this encounter ought to mean to us
all, Blacks and Whites" (68). In addition, Bosch gives a short testimony: "My
fellowship with African Christians over a period of sixteen years has enriched
me immensely. And my study of and encounter with African traditional religions has contributed very much to this enrichment" (72). But he is quick to
add that, when attempting to interpret the meaning of certain aspects such as
the idea of the goodness of God, "I do not simply make use of my own limited and inadequate observations. I rather refer to what Africans themselves say
about this, people like Mbiti, Danquah, Idowu, Sawyer and others" (74). Having thus explained himself, Bosch assumes the confidence of a theologian who,
on the basis of his understanding of the Bible, concludes that a choice must be
made between "indigenization" and "syncretism" in regard to the concept of God
in Africa. In that context, "Indigenization means clothing the God of Scripture
in the cultural robes of a specific people. Syncretism means redecorating the traditional God in Christian robes" (77). The least one can say to this is that, on

the one hand, it seems missiologically sound; while, on the other hand, it is not immediately clear whether there is a clearcut difference between indigenization and syncretism.

The essay "God in Africa: Implications for the Kerygma" (1973c) is a richly documented essay which also makes use of a good number of African scholars. Basically it is a comparative theological study of the traditional concepts of God and the God of Scripture. Bosch is aware that "Africa displays an immense variety of customs and beliefs," and that "no such thing as *the* religion of Africa exists" (4). He also is informed about theories on "God" in African traditional religion propounded by non-theologians like Okot p'Bitek and Robin Horton, but he addresses his ideas to fellow theologians. Bosch asks whether — as the majority of African theologians seem to accept — the God of Scripture is the same as the traditional God. In his conclusion Bosch warns against merely trying to discover similarities or dissimilarities between the two concepts:

> This process of comparison and contrast tends to be rather superficial; it easily gets stuck in the area of religious phenomena, images, myths, systems, etc., without reaching down to the existential realities at the root of these phenomena. Then no real encounter takes place but at best a kind of shallow adaptation. (20)

Instead of "shallow adaptation" Bosch proposes meeting on a deeper level, a meeting between the uncovered "heart" of the African idea of God with the "heart" of God's self-revelation according to Scripture. He observes that, "It is on this deeper level — not on the level of the conceptual or the purely ontological — that we shall discover the elements of both continuity and discontinuity between African religions and the Gospel" (21). Bosch's stress on both continuity and discontinuity is very valid, but he does not venture clues as to how this meeting can take place.

Evil in Africa. In "The Problem of Evil in Africa" (1987a), Bosch gives a survey of African views on witchcraft and of the response of the Christian Church. This is a remarkable and enlightening contribution to solving a problem that still haunts many Africans (Christian Africans included). He observes, first, that, while in the Hebrew and Christian Scriptures there is the figure of Satan, regarded as intrinsically and irreversibly evil, such a concept of Satan seems to be foreign to traditional Africa. There is the tendency to interpret this figure (*uSathana* in an Africanized form in Xhosa) "in relation to the Supreme Being ... as a manifestation of God, his dark side with which we have to remain on friendly terms. Many Xhosa Christians conceive Satan as a son of God, indeed his elder son ... therefore, in the final analysis, harmless" (40–41).

Second, he observes that in traditional African society the author of evil par excellence is not Satan but a human figure: the witch. Bosch presents witchcraft within a broad historical context and notes parallels elsewhere, for instance by referring to witchcraft and witch hunting in Europe (41–42). Third, Bosch tries to understand the phenomenon of witches and witchcraft from an African traditional perspective (42–49), *before* any attempt at a theological evaluation. Bosch refers also to secular "witch hunting," and asks himself "whether South African society is not currently experiencing a witch hunt craze of grotesque proportions," for example, in "the bizarre crimes that are perpetrated by people from both the right and the left," which are, according to him, "phenomenologically speaking, manifestations of witchcraft beliefs and scape-goating."

Before trying to answer how the church should respond to the scourge of witchcraft in Africa, Bosch first addresses the question of what constitutes an authentic Christian understanding of sin and evil. This encompasses both moral evil (sin) and physical evil (everything that purposely affects the physical and social well-being and dignity of human beings).

Bosch's is an empathic and lucid exposition of the problem of witchcraft in Africa. It offers a balanced Christian perspective and practical suggestions for combatting this evil. Though Bosch himself favors a position that seeks to help people change their overall interpretive framework, he nevertheless respects attempts undertaken to combat witchcraft and witchcraft beliefs by accepting, in essence, the traditional African interpretive framework. This essay on evil in Africa has retained its value over time and can be recommended to people concerned with pastoral care and training.

Renewal in Africa. At a conference held in Nairobi, in December 1976, Bosch addressed the issue of "Renewal of Christian Community in Africa Today" (1978). In that address, he puts the question whether the deepest need of the church in Africa does not lie in the fact that, "by and large, we have failed to create that new community, that really is a different community, which should be an alternative to all other communities on earth. Have we really understood what it means to be the church in the world?" (92). Bosch especially criticizes evangelical churches for trying "to keep the Christian message pure from all earthly things such as politics, social programs, and the like," with the result being accommodation "to the existing structures of the societies to which we belong," because that would have been "incompatible with the Church's 'purely religious' task" (92). The examples given are, however, not that convincing for challenging societal structures. They refer to the apparent inability of the churches to unite black and white in common faith and overcome tribalism. The least one can say in this connection is that there are many non-theological factors at work, and they differ in South Africa and the rest of Africa. As long as such factors are not addressed (for instance, in South Africa, the economic factor of injustice between whites and blacks), mere unity in faith becomes a farce. For Bosch the church as a "truly alternative community" implies, of necessity, a tension between church and state. It also means that "the church therefore stands neither to the right nor to the left. In fact, she does not stand at all; she is on the move, she has no fixed and unalterable position" (99). Bosch explains this thesis saying that "the Church as the truly alternative community should never identify with any empirical state or any suggested political solution" (99). One can ask if such a position is tenable. How does it apply in regard to political choices that affect the lives and the well-being of people? Can the church never support any suggested solution?

Bosch's rationale for this concept of the church as a truly alternative community is the imperative of following Jesus (100). He stresses in this respect compassion, but also liberation, but this understood as "true liberation." To make his understanding clear, Bosch contrasts the aims of the Zealots with the aim of Jesus: "They wanted a mere change of government, Jesus wanted a total and radical change" (100). Bosch leaves vague what such a total and radical change entails, except to say that "Jesus preached a solution that was absolutely contrary to any human thinking," with reference, for instance, to love of enemies (Lk 6: 27–28).

In the context of discussing theologizing in Africa, we find further insights into how Africa fit into Bosch's thought. To these three sources (1975b, 1984a, and 1987) we now turn.

Theologia Africana. The first source we turn to was a contribution to a volume of collected essays entitled on *Teologie en Vernuwing* ("Theology and Renewal") Bosch's contribution is "En route to a *Theologia Africana*" (1975b), a reflection on "indigenization" or "localization" of Christianity in a biblical and historical perspective. It weighs the question whether the church or theology is ever really indigenous. He states that indigenization can never be a closed process and argues that it is not fundamentally a question of *indigenous* theology but of *relevant* theology for a certain socio-cultural context that counts. A possible term for this is "local" theology or *theologia in loco*, concepts which, he shows, must never be separated from *theologia oecumenica*, a danger present in the use of the concept "indigenous" theology (1975b:162–63).

Nevertheless, Bosch was looking forward to a *theologia Africana* which would be relevant not only for Africa, but which would also contribute to the *ecclesia universalis*, keeping both in creative tension. Bosch concludes on a revealing personal note: "The meeting and longtime contact with the church in Africa has opened for me as Westerner new perspectives without which I would have been poorer theologically and spiritually" (179).

Missionary Theology in Africa. Ten years after "En Route to a *Theologia Africana*," Bosch shows that he has kept abreast of the turbulent development of African theology. In his "Missionary Theology in Africa" (1984a), he offers a rich survey of missiological developments in Africa. He is aware of the fact that many African authors would not classify their own work under the rubric "missiology" because of negative connotations of that term as it relates to the experience of Africans with "mission." Bosch, nevertheless, says "I believe, nonetheless, that what most African theologians are involved in, is missionary theology" (15). This presupposes, however, that the word mission and its cognates must be rehabilitated: "If it is true that 'the Church is missionary by its very nature' (*Ad Gentes*, 2), then it follows that mission is at the heart of any authentic theology" (15).

In his survey Bosch concentrates on theological contributions by Africans, and only occasionally refers to writings of expatriates. The literature is surveyed under seven aspects: historical studies; African theology; reflections on African religious heritage; theology of communication; pastoral theology; the church and its selfhood; and theologies of liberation and political theology. Under "African theology," Bosch first·states that "African theology and Black theology represent two distinct though by no means unrelated approaches to the theological scene on the African continent," and that all relevant theologizing in Africa moves "between culture and politics" (19).

Bosch traces the use of the term "African theology" back in the 1950s and mentions *Des prêtres noirs s'interrogent* (published in 1956) as "a book that was to have much influence in Catholic circles" (19). Bosch introduces, in addition to John Mbiti, a number of African theologians: Tshibangu, Mulago, and Bimwenyi-Kweshi from Zaire; Nyamiti of Tanzania; Pobee and Dickson of Ghana; and Adoukono of Benin. These are followed by fifteen names of other African theologians.

Under the heading "Theologies of Liberation and Political Theology," Bosch refers mainly to black theology, which we will discuss below. Bosch discerns a trend toward political theology broadly represented throughout Africa. But he correctly observes a difference in the position of churches in the colonial period when compared with their positions in the post-independent period. While the Christian faith in the colonial era played a crucial role in the awakening and development of African self-esteem, and while, later on, the church served as an incubator of African nationalism, "after independence, the African church seemed to have given up its prophetic role" (34). Christopher Mwoleka with Joseph Healy, Peter Alute S. Kijanga and Laurenti Magesa, all from Tanzania, are criticized for affirming the policy in vogue in their country, and for endorsing socialism virtually without reservation. The same is said of Canaan S. Banana's 1982 book, *Theology of Promise: The Dynamics of Self-Reliance,* as "an attempt to reconcile the Socialist revolution with the Christian faith" (34).

Bosch ends his article positively. On the credit side he mentions the fact that "the African Church is alive and growing, that the number and the quality of African theologians increase annually, and that the African Church is well aware that it lives in a missionary context" (37).

This 1984 essay shows how much deeper David Bosch had entered into new theological developments taking place in Africa, as compared with earlier work. Still, though he was well informed, Bosch did not really take seriously the remark made by Andrew Walls that "in future Third World theologies would be the only theologies worth bothering about, since the majority of Christians live there" (quoted by Bosch in 1984a:14). Admiration of Western thought was apparently too deeply ingrained in Bosch for him to consider third world theologies and theologians, as having the same value as Western. He therefore assumed that Walls had made the above remark "perhaps with tongue in the cheek" (14).

A Missiology for Africa? In *Reflecting on Mission in the African Context,* Bosch indicates why this handbook was being published:

> The reader interested in mission in the African context searches in vain for a systematic treatment of how missiology addresses this particular milieu. Most reflections on mission...are written from a Western vantage point, reflecting mainly for example a German, Dutch or North American approach. It is from this absence of a genuinely relevant handbook

for missiology that the idea was born to produce a missiological reflection locally, not only *in* but also *for* the African context. (1987b, vii)

After this declaration, the reader might expect that a number of African theologians and material produced by Africans would form part of this publishing initiative. On study, however, it turns out that only Afrikaner theologians — all professors associated with one of the seven theological institutions of the family of the white Dutch Reformed churches — have contributed reflections. The bibliography reveals the names of only one Latin American, one Asian, one African, and eight black South African theologians, from a total of about 175 authors. Names of black South African theologians who had developed new approaches to the mission of the church in the South African scene (such as Bishop Desmond Tutu and Allan Boesak) are painfully absent.

Bosch was an integral part of this project and wrote chapter 3, "Theologies of Mission." (1987b). After his ground-breaking article "Missionary Theology in Africa" (1984a), this piece is disappointing, partly because of Bosch's understanding of the relationship between theology and missiology. He puts theology of mission in biblical and historical perspective, but when dealing with contemporary models of mission Bosch remains completely captive to Western discussions on issues such as the relationship between ecumenical and evangelical Protestants. This is a problem that, I suspect, vexes African Christians and theologians, mainly when they depend on expatriate purses. Third world Christians, including Africans, do tend to be evangelical in their piety but ecumenical in their understanding that religion must be of help in day-to-day problems.

Bosch's Missiological Involvement in South Africa

Bosch has stated, following Martin Kähler, that "the early Church, because of its missionary encounter with the world was forced to theologize," further, "that theology had no reason to exist other than critically accompany the church in its mission to the world" finally, "that theology was, therefore, by definition the product of an emergency situation" (1984a: 15). In his reflection on how his mind had changed (1982c:7), he had indicated that his involvement in the South African scene had contributed to a comprehensive concept of mission.

Indeed, his bibliography shows that living and participating in the emergency situation that characterized South Africa forced Bosch to reflect on mission at the spot where church meets world. He was aware that understanding mission as "the ministry of crossing frontiers" encompasses "geographical, ideological, cultural, religious, or social" frontiers. He, however, does not mention economic factors in such lists, though economics is of central importance, since it determined the apartheid system in a most fundamental way. Though his broad understanding of mission brings missiology close to theological ethics, Bosch sought to address the issues facing Christians and churches in South Africa as a missiologist. Hence the title of this subsection.

Because Bosch's missiological reflection on South African issues and challenges produced over twenty publications, I limit myself drastically in my analysis and evaluation of these writings. In order to somehow cope with this task I will present these writings under four main headings: theologies, races, churches, and reconciliation. This is, of course, somewhat artificial, and some overlap is unavoidable.

Involvement in Theological Developments

In this section I will discuss the publications of Bosch concerned with missiology (1975a) and with black theology (1972a, 1974a, and 1984a) in the South African context.

Missiology

Bosch's article "Missiological Developments in South Africa" (1975a) was read at the meeting of the International Association for Mission Studies in Frankfurt in July 1974. It is so compact that it can scarcely be summarized; I therefore limit myself to a few remarks.

Bosch begins by saying that considerable developments have taken place in the field of mission studies in South Africa since the early 1960s. New chairs of missiology and four organizations concerned with missiological research had been established. Bosch sees South Africa as a fertile ground for developing missiology because "South Africa is not merely a laboratory of the world in general, but specifically also of the Church." Furthermore, "the missiologist is ... often the only [one] who tackles the hot issues of the Third World ... the relationship between the Christian faith and other faiths, the problem of poverty, of the relationship between the races, of development, of culture, of industrialization and secularization, and many others" (13). Bosch seems, however, to be naïve regarding the first part of the statement, "Perhaps nowhere else has the Church been doing more to meet these challenges, but equally perhaps nowhere else has it been as evident that all the Church's efforts have not been enough" (13–14).

Bosch perceives increasing interest in socio-ethical and socio-political factors affecting the church's missionary task. However, he considers race and race relations more important than problems related to urbanization and industrialization "which South Africa shares with the whole world" (26). Especially revealing is his remark, "that contributions on this issue from Afrikaner theologians, with a few exceptions, tend to be little more than a barely concealed justification of the status quo. Non-Afrikaners have been unanimous in their condemnation of the so-called 'South African' way of life" (26).

When evaluating the South African contributions to missiology, Bosch remarks that missiology in South Africa is still, to a very large extent, dependent on missiology elsewhere — and is almost exclusively a white enterprise. G. Setiloane and Lukas de Vries are mentioned as having made contributions from the ranks of the "younger" churches, but Bosch does not list their publications, though he notes that in the area of black theology, black theologians have begun to contribute meaningfully to missiological discussions (29).

Black Theology

In four articles, Bosch paid explicit attention to black theology. Though he acknowledged, in an early stage of black theology in South Africa, that it had begun to contribute meaningfully to missiological discussion (Bosch 1975a: 29), Bosch did not follow later developments as closely as he did its beginning. This criticism has been made by his younger colleague Klippies Kritzinger, who also mentions that David Bosch was one of the first white theologians in South Africa to take black theology seriously (Kritzinger 1990: 34).

Bosch wrote a review (1972a) of *Essays on Black Theology,* edited by Mokgethi Motlhabi, soon after that book's publication. Since the book was banned by the South African government, all quotations from these "essays" in Bosch's review had to be deleted. With its many open white spaces, the review is a reflection of the pathological situation in South Africa at the time.

Bosch's review showed that he considered black theologians' understanding of salvation as "total liberation" as "justified and relevant in many ways" (6). But he also sees black theologians "in danger of seriously underestimating the reality of the power of sin in human life." Their ideal of a just society without oppression and selfishness brings Bosch to say, "the dreams these black brethren are dreaming are utopian." It is clear that Bosch considers such ideals to be unattainable, though this, in his view, does not mean that they should not be pursued (7).

In 1974, Bosch published an article on various interpretations of what black theology is or ought to be, "Currents and Crosscurrents in South African Black Theology" (1974a). Since this article was published outside South Africa in the *Journal of Religion in Africa,* Bosch could now freely quote from *Essays on Black Theology.* In his introductory remarks Bosch states that black theology was born 270 years ago with the Congolese girl Kimpa Vita, baptized Béatrice, and appearing in public as a prophetess. He discusses also the situation in American black theology, especially the contribution of James Cone.

Bosch discerns currents in this newly born theology, sums up its major elements, and, finally, evaluates South African black theology in three points. This article has been published in *Black Theology: A Documentary History, 1966–1979,* edited by Gayraud S. Wilmore and James Cone in 1979, though it did not make it into the revised, two-volume edition of that book. Cone introduces Bosch's article as "important because it compares Black theology in the United States with Black theology in South Africa from the perspective of a White South African theologian" (Wilmore and Cone 1979: 142).

Ten years later, in 1984, Bosch refers to black theology, now in the context of theologies of liberation and political theology (Bosch 1984a: 32–33). There are references to recent books like Allan Boesak's *Farewell to Innocence* (1976) and also to four consultations of the Umpumulo Missiological Institute. Still, as regards his understanding of the character and subject matter of black theology, Bosch returns to ideas found in *Essays on Black Theology,* which we have already discussed. It appears that Bosch had not followed closely the developments taking place in black theology. It had, in the meantime, entered into its second phase. The relationship between praxis and theological reflection had become more apparent. Black theologians became aware of their own class-based character: male, academic, and clerical. They declared that black theology cannot be a theology of liberation unless feminist theology constitutes an essential part of a broad movement of black liberation theology. Above all, a sharper analysis showed that the South African realities consist of the double bondage of racial and economic oppression, also that the apartheid system is buttressed both by racial and class contrasts and constituted a form of "racial capitalism" (see Verstraelen-Gilhuis 1992: 29–32).

Issues of Race

Bosch gave much thought to race relations in South Africa. He tried, in particular, to provide insight into the self-understanding and position of the Afrikaners, the "White tribe of Africa," to which he not only belonged, but with which he identified himself loyally, though not uncritically. In this section I will try to explicate Bosch's views on the Afrikaners and on race relations in South Africa.

Afrikaners

The attitudes and position of the Afrikaners vis-à-vis other races cannot be properly understood without entering into their history or without trying to understand them from their own perspective. Bosch wrote several essays that throw light on this history; on the close link between the Afrikaners and the Dutch Reformed Church (see 1984b, 1986a and b, 1991b); and also on relationships of Afrikaners with other races in South Africa (see 1979c, 1983d).

It is important to understand why there has been a peculiar combination of religion and racial prejudice in Afrikaner history. Bosch observes that "It would be correct to say that during the 1940s and 1950s virtually all Afrikaner intellectuals subscribed to apartheid as an ideology firmly underpinned with a theological rationale" (1984b: 14). However, contrary to a generally accepted interpretation, Bosch, with other contemporary scholars, rejected the "Calvinist paradigm" as an explanation of early Afrikaner history and thinking. He notes:

> Most of the early Afrikaners were unsophisticated and, in fact, barely literate. The Bible was often the only book they had, and they tended to interpret it literally, not only as the revealed Word of God, but also as the final source of knowledge.... Religious fundamentalism is, however, not the same as Calvinism. (1986b: 205)

Afrikaner history goes back to the founding of a Dutch colony at the Cape of Good Hope in 1652. But it is only in reaction to the adversities experienced in their dealings with British imperialism that the Afrikaners gradually developed their brand of nationalism and identity, captured by the phrase, "laager mentality." The Anglo-Boer War (1899–1902) in particular, and the subsequent vigorous policy of Anglicization, which banned the use of the Dutch language from schools, immensely strengthened this laager mentality. Having lost their political freedom on the battlefield, Afrikaners were now fated to lose their identity as well. In this, the Afrikaners' darkest hour, it was above all the Afrikaans churches that rallied to the people's aid. Church and people became virtually indistinguishable (207). Concluding an analysis of the religious roots of the history of the Afrikaners and their churches, Bosch says that this history — at least from their perspective — is

> the history of the 200 year struggle of a small nation against its destruction. . . . The Afrikaner has the feeling [of being] left alone all the time. In such a condition the natural, human instinct emerges to survive, an instinct which ignores all rational arguments. One cannot reason with emotions [nor] with fear. Thus many Afrikaners retreat into the "laager," preparing themselves to the utmost. (1983d: 104–5)

The Dutch Reformed Church became more and more the church for and of the Afrikaners, and the Afrikaner-Broederbond (Brotherhood), "the watchman on Zion's walls." Eventually,

> After 1948 the church . . . enthusiastically put its theological seal on the policy of apartheid. Everything should be put into operation to guarantee the survival of the Afrikaner. Even mission should be employed for that purpose. (1991b: 89)

For a long time, the National Party (which was founded in 1914 and obtained its electoral victory in 1948) has been the pure and unadulterated expression of classical Afrikaner religio-political thinking. The party entrenched racial separation and discrimination. Certain dramatic events in the 1970s led to a rupture of that unity. Such events, including the violence in Soweto on June 16, 1976; the death of Steve Biko, murdered in a police cell, on September 12, 1977, which was followed by the banning of several anti-apartheid organizations, including the Christian Institute, in October 1977; and black pressure, had led by 1985 to "more fundamental political reform than in the total preceding period" (1986b: 214). Bosch substantiates this by referring to: restoration of citizenship to blacks, scrapping of Influx Control and the passbook system, abolition of the Mixed Marriages Act, and assurances to include blacks in decision making processes at the highest level. But Bosch carefully adds that all these changes (real and promised) did not mean that the white minority was willing to jeopardize, even theoretically, its position of power and privilege.

We recite this history because it helps us to understand that Bosch's being an Afrikaner is part of his biography. Thus, when writing on Afrikaners, Bosch is not only writing *about them* but as *one of them*. But Bosch was also a sincere Christian and theologian and, therefore, could not identify himself completely with the cause of the Afrikaners. Still Bosch remained close to his people and their church as a theological pastor: "In my own ministry my concern is particularly with the White Afrikaans Reformed churches" (1982c:7). A pastor, if he does not want to lose his flock, does not take radical steps. And this sometimes makes him look ambiguous in the eyes of those who suffer from the position taken by the group of the pastor's special concern. This reservation was felt by many in regard to Bosch's Afrikaner identification, as we shall see below.

Race Relations

In "Racism and Revolution" (1979c), Bosch analyzed the response of the churches in South Africa. He subdivided the South African ecclesiastical scene into five categories: (1) the Afrikaans Reformed Churches; (2) the member churches of the South African Council of Churches (SACC); (3) the Roman Catholic Church; (4) the conservative Evangelical churches; and (5) the African Independent Churches. Bosch starts by analyzing the development of racial thinking in the Dutch Reformed Church, and moves from there to a brief discussion of the attitudes and responses in other churches. He believed that every other response to racism and revolution was largely a reaction to what was happening in the Dutch Reformed Church (DRC). He summarized the factors that account for the ethos of the DRC's response to racism and revolution as a conviction of a "manifest destiny"; as an identification with the people of Israel; as a missionary calling to evangelize and uplift the blacks and to defend "White Christian civilization"; as the maintenance of the purity of the Afrikaans people, leading to their separateness as a condition for enjoying the blessing of God, and lastly, as a positive attitude to law, a tendency to regard prevailing circumstances as inevitable because they have been willed by God. In this connection Bosch refers to a recent report of the General Synod of the Dutch Reformed Church on human rights which contains a devastating diagnosis of some of the fruits of racial segregation — job reservation, homelands policy, the black townships, the position of the "Coloreds" and "Indians." Still, he shows, the report does not in any way suggest that the cause of all this is to be found, even partially, in the laws themselves. The report states: "As institution the Church submits itself to the authority and law of the state ... provided the legal order does not conflict with the Word of God." Bosch then adds the remark "but no such conflict is registered anywhere."

In the face of all this, Bosch also considered the image that most outsiders had of the DRC — as being "entirely doctrinaire and completely incapable of seeing the plight of other people" — as an oversimplification. First, he notes that there were numerous dissident voices and factors which partly explain the situation. Still, Bosch states explicitly, "they do not mitigate the wrongs committed in the name of the Christian faith."

Turning to white, English-speaking churches, Bosch states that they have always responded differently from the DRC to the issue of race. But this difference, in his view, was not primarily due to theological reasons. The true difference lays in the socio-psychological sphere. The Afrikaner Christian, belonging to a minority group, felt threatened and developed a laager mentality; the English-speaking Christian, member of a dominant language and culture group within the British empire, did not feel threatened until the revolution was far along. Consequently "Afrikaners emphasized their cultural distinctiveness from the Blacks (and from the English, for that matter), while the English embarked on a program of Anglicizing the Blacks (and, of course, the Afrikaner)" (1979c: 18).

In dealing with the response of black Christians to issues of race and racism, Bosch makes some of his most interesting observations when he observes "an amazing degree of parallelism in the response of Afrikaners and Blacks to the dynamics of the South African situation" (18–19). In another article he indicates three fundamental motives operative in Afrikaners' outlook on life and society: "the Exodus motif, as reaction to British imperialism; the suffering motif, especially during and after the Anglo-Boer War; and the eschatological motif in anticipating a return to a republican government in which the Afrikaner would exercise state power" (1983d:105). Bosch seeks to show that exactly the same three motifs operate in black societies in South Africa (105).

The motifs, I would observe, may indeed run parallel, but the contexts in which Afrikaners and blacks found themselves were quite different. Bosch speaks of two contextual theologies in contradiction to one another, but the way in which Bosch concludes this article is puzzling. He merely asks two questions: "What do we do in such a situation? Is only one model legitimate? This in my view is the decisive question." However, in his earlier article (1979c) Bosch had stressed the dissimilarities between the situation of Afrikaners and blacks. Sharpeville (March 1960) marked a watershed. "Before Sharpeville the Africans dreamed that it was possible to establish a non-racial society. The concept of non-racialism would be the very foundation of a more genuine, cross-cultural nationalism" (1979c:19, quoting Mphahlele 1977:24). After Sharpeville, the mood of black nationalism became increasingly militant and uncompromising. Bosch seeks the fruit of dialogue between white and black to destroy the caricatures one group has of the other and "to drive away the phantoms we have created of one another" (20).

This is certainly a laudable aim, but it overlooked the real wrongs and injustices that were still being perpetrated against the black majority in South Africa. Because of these views, he could continue his pastoral-prophetic task among his fellow-Afrikaners, but also because of them, did he perhaps not fully understand the plight of blacks? As we discuss reconciliation below, I shall attempt to shed more light on Bosch's position on this point in the midst of the changing South African scene of the 1980s.

Church/Churches

The church occupied an important place in David Bosch's theology and life. More often than not, he spoke of "the Church" in the singular, a device that usually indicates the speaker is emphasizing the *ideal* of what the church should be. In this section I will look at Bosch's missionary ecclesiography in the South African context under three headings: unity and liberation; church-state relationships; the church and the future.

Unity and Liberation

In his article "Church Unity amidst Cultural Diversity" (1982b), Bosch discusses and rejects both an abiding connection between church and *Volk*, as propounded by German missiologists Warneck and Gutmann, as well as the more pragmatic approach of the American Church Growth Movement, which propagates the formation of culturally homogeneous churches. The Dutch Reformed Church, in its policy of establishing separate churches for different groups, went clearly against the basic biblical call to unity as expressed in such texts as Ephesians 2:14–16. Bosch shows that the policy of separateness is the result of a fateful resolution of the Synod of 1857 in which the DRC confessed that it was "desirable and in accordance with Scripture for all to worship together" but that, at the same time, made concessions to separateness "not because of theological arguments, but 'because of the weakness of some'" (24).

To the question "Why unity?" Bosch's answer is simple: "The breaking down of barriers that separate people is an intrinsic part of the gospel" (27). Bosch, therefore, considers the insensitiveness of the Afrikaans Reformed Church to the imperative of unity as a particular form of blindness that is not, however, intrinsic to the Reformed tradition. By returning to their roots they would discover that what they cherish is "nothing but a heresy that strikes at the very foundation of the Church" (28).

Church-State Relationships

Church-state relationships have been, and still are, of special importance in South Africa because of the close link of the DRC with the long-ruling National Party. On several occasions David Bosch dealt explicitly with this issue.

At the South African Christian Leadership Assembly (SACLA), held in Pretoria in July 1979 and attended by over 5,500 people, Bosch presented a paper entitled "The Kingdom of God and the Kingdoms of This World" (1979d). In it he deals with the church in general, distinguishing three types of relationship between church and social order: withdrawal, cooperation, and a third way, that of resisting and opposing the state. Bosch for a moment becomes contextual by pointing out that cooperation "is a very real temptation to the church in our country" (5). In the preceding paragraph he says of this type of relationship practiced by the church: "She actively identifies herself with the social order and the powers-that-be. She does not merely *endure* whatever the state is doing; she actually *applauds and endorses* the state's policies." It is interesting to note that Bosch avoids being more precise by not indicating to which church he refers. While almost all churches endured what the state was doing, it was the white DRC that actually applauded and endorsed the state's policies. Nürnberger, in reaction to a paper of Bosch, observed the latter's careful avoidance of "any application of his insights to the concrete dilemmas we face in this country" (Nürnberger 1977:43).

More puzzling is Bosch's evaluation of the "third way": "She [the church] may come to the conviction that she has to resist and oppose the state, even to the point of sanctioning a violent revolution to overthrow the existing regime and introduce a political system of her own choice" (1979d:6). To Bosch, though, endorsing the present establishment or a hoped-for future establishment amounts to one and the same: "In both cases the Christian faith is degraded," because "it has to provide supernatural sanction for the state's policy or for its alternative" (6). Cannot church support for a new government be *conditional*? Bosch appears to see support for any political system as an unconditioned act. Other alternatives are not explored.

In his concluding remarks Bosch puts the question whether "the church has no message for those in power, for the privileged minority?" His answer is that "She surely has. By simply preaching the whole counsel of God without rancor she imperceptibly creates an atmosphere of inner freedom" (12). This is, of course, a very idealistic but at the same time a very long-term process which does not tackle immediate short-term issues of life and death. Allan Boesak, in his "Mission to Those in Authority" (1980), showed that a message to those in power must be concrete in order to be relevant.

Bosch's SACLA paper contains also quite a number of stimulating ideas such as "when biblical statements concerning people's bodily needs are spiritualized, when structural and institutionalized sins are not exposed, we are involved with an unbiblical onesidedness and a spurious Christianity" (1979d:8). But since these statements are phrased in general terms and are not made specific, they lose much of their convincing power.

A point I want to make is that Bosch, when in rare cases he becomes concrete, refers to sick and degrading symptoms of the apartheid system, but never clearly challenges the validity of the existing South African political system itself. Had he done so, he would not have so easily attributed to the South African state the right to order civil life and he would have taken note of and protested the fact that a black majority did not have the same channels to express themselves politically as the white minority had.

The Church and the Future

At the National Conference of the South African Council of Churches, held at Hammanskraal in July 1975, Bosch presented a paper entitled "The Church in South Africa — Tomorrow" (1975c). An editorial note in *Pro Veritate*, the journal in which it was published, mentions that this paper was appreciated by the delegates and also that Professor Bosch "tackles the problem of the task of the Church in the modern world in such a way that both the 'evangelicals' and the 'ecumenicals' will appreciate his analysis." Indeed, the paper contains interesting and clarifying insights on the nature of tensions within the church of the future being not between different denominations but between two different ways of understanding what the church is. He sees these as a choice between an "aggressive church [that] must conquer the world," and a church that "must identify completely with the world."

Bosch certainly makes valid points when he says, "It is extremely important that the Church should speak to the structures of society, but is equally important not to forget the individual and his needs" (6). Bosch is especially concerned about several fallacies contained in the "complete identification with the world" model. One of them is the danger "that all the guilt for the wrongs of society can so easily be located solely outside the church" (6).

With real democracy dawning in South Africa the churches organized the National Conference of Church Leaders in Rustenburg, Transvaal, in November 1990 and looked forward to a New South Africa. Present were 230 representatives of 97 denominations which enrolled more than 90 percent of the Christian community, and more than 70 percent of the total population of the country. The interesting thing is that this conference had been set in motion by State President F. W. de Klerk when, in his 1989 Christmas address, he appealed to the church in South Africa to formulate a strategy conducive to negotiation, reconciliation and change. In the Introduction to the Conference report *The Road to Rustenburg: The Church Looking Forward to a New South Africa* (Alberts and Chikane 1991), it is mentioned that some ascribed de Klerk's initiative as emanating from sincere Christian conviction. Others viewed it as merely an astute political move. Since to many black South Africans, Christianity is synonymous with the philosophy of apartheid, the president's invitation aroused animosities. The South African Council of Churches made its participation dependent on the president's withdrawal, which he accepted.

Bosch's brief was to help to show "how the Reformed tradition has historically treated social and political issues and also to indicate how this tradition may help shape the future of our country" (in Alberts and Chikane 1991:129). In fact Bosch presents "the profile of the Calvinist view of life and the world" by speaking about the features, the failures, and the future of Calvinism in South Africa. I can quote only a few of Bosch's statements.

Under "features" of Calvinism, Bosch reacts to the viewpoint of some that on the basis of Calvinism there is an absolute antithesis between reform and revolution with a reference to history: "Scottish and English Calvinists...have argued that it is not only permitted, but on occasion even obligatory, to actively resist a tyrannical government" (134). This seems to imply recognition by Bosch, who always was opposed to revolution, that active resistance or revolution can be accommodated positively within Calvinism.

Under "failures" of Calvinism, Bosch explains that "Calvinism's penchant for advocating a *total* strategy of reform has often degenerated into a form of totalitarianism" (134). And he goes on to say, "I would like to suggest that the introduction and imposition of the policy of apartheid in South Africa is an example of such totalitarianism" (134). He further points out that Calvinists, particularly when they belonged to the privileged section of the population, had adopted a strategy of sounding progressive and relevant, while salvaging only something of social justice:

> They saw their task as being limited to formulating "principles" of justice, not to work them out in society. In a sense this was an escape mechanism, a form of self-justification, an approach that enabled them to speak about justice in theory without getting involved, to make only general statements about justice, without taking upon themselves the risk of identifying particular policies and actions as evil and others as commendable. (135)

Part of this description of Calvinists seems to apply to many of Bosch's own earlier statements. He has often been criticized for remaining general instead of becoming specific. I do not want to suggest that Bosch used theology for self-justification. Nevertheless, one suspects that part of his not becoming concrete may be explained by a wish to spare embarrassment to his fellow Afrikaners and DRC members in public, while hoping, or even expecting, that the implications of his messages would come through to them. This, in a way, is confirmed even by his Rustenburg presentation, because Bosch nowhere identifies the Calvinists he criticizes as being in fact the leaders and members of his DRC Church.

As regards the "future" of Calvinism, Bosch looks at it from an idealistic perspective, as the following shows:

A pluralist and secular South Africa will remain dependent upon the existence of believers, that is, of persons whose integrity and good conduct can be relied upon. It is only a shared moral vision that can hold society together. If Calvinists can continue to contribute to this vision, their ministry will be a blessing to all citizens.... Calvinism can call people to true conversion, a conversion that includes social responsibility and a moral vision for society. (138)

Calvinism, however, is an abstract entity, which in South Africa finds expression and incarnation in the historical reality of the Dutch Reformed Church. Since in recent South African history the position and choices of this Calvinist church have been far from being "a blessing to *all* citizens," these visions of Calvinism's contribution to the future sound somewhat premature and perhaps unwarranted. The story told by P. G. J. Meiring in *Stormkompas* (1981) sounds a more realistic note. Bishop Newbigin, when asked what, in his view, the contribution of the Dutch Reformed Church to the spread of the Gospel in Africa could be, was at first reticent to answer. Finally he said: "I don't see any role...because of the role it played and still plays as the church of apartheid...people simply will not listen to you" (Meiring 1981: 8, 11–12). Before moving beyond the past, those who identified with and even promoted apartheid have to confess their guilt and express readiness for restitution as essential aspects of any true steps toward a new South Africa. The Rustenburg Conference set an example in this respect. The Introduction of its report states:

This Conference will be remembered in Church history for the many confessions made by various denominations — most notably, by the Dutch Reformed Church — of complicity with apartheid and the need for repentance. (Alberts and Chikane 1991: 13)

Reconciliation

Bosch did not start theologizing about reconciliation only when it had become clear that the change from minority rule to democracy was imminent in South Africa. This is made clear in a 1974 article, when the apartheid system was still very much entrenched in the South African socio-political setup. Bosch expressed as his deep conviction that "Christian discipleship in South Africa —

or wherever — has to do with reconciliation. The church on earth is God's in-strument of reconciliation. Reconciliation is the message that the church has to proclaim" (1974c:13).

1974

At the Swakopmund Conference of the Christian Academy, held in South-West Africa (Namibia nowadays) in 1974, David Bosch presented a paper entitled *Navolging van Christus in Suid-en Suid-Wes-Afrika Vandag* ("Following Christ in South- and South-West Africa Today," 1974c). Reconciliation in Bosch's view encompasses both the vertical level with God, and the horizontal level among human beings. On the latter level "no genuine reconciliation is possi-ble if people do not accept each other as equals" (13). He recognizes clearly that there is therefore a problem in South Africa because many whites do not accept blacks as equals, as well as vice-versa. Bosch ascribes a very important role to changing black consciousness in the process of reconciliation, liberating them from a slave mentality and in doing so offering the possibility of liberation to whites from their impoverished consciousness. Together, the two liberations are a precondition for reconciliation.

As regards his interpretation of liberation, Bosch follows John Howard Yoder (1974), who presents two models: *exodus* and *exile*. In the exodus-model "the confrontation with the existing order has led to physical liberation of the re-ligious group"; in the exile-model "the religious group of disciples continues to live in a situation of oppression . . . without hope in any immediate physical liber-ation" (Bosch 1974a:16). Bosch then asks what could be done in a case where no exodus is foreseeable; as was, of course, the situation of blacks in South Africa in 1974. It is interesting to note that Bosch — in this phase of his theologiz-ing — seeks an answer not in political action but in the religious power of the Christian community. As an application of Jeremiah 29:5–7, Bosch says:

> People who live out their faith . . . living according to alternative inter-nal laws, must one day come into confrontation with the structures. But they do not intend to confront the structures, they do not launch self-styled programs of action. No, they merely hold to their new community, which challenges the power-structure by nothing else than loyalty to a new orientation of life. (17)

To which he adds that it "is important that in the models used nowhere is there a program of action. Our task is to build up the people of God, and in this way prepare our people for the future" (17). This model can scarcely be called a new version of the exodus-model, if one recalls Moses using political and even violent actions to achieve the physical liberation of his people.

As he advances his argument, Bosch adds warnings to praise of the emerging black consciousness to the extent that it contains elements that are unable to see the white as brother. Bosch goes on to note that this is a mirror image of white consciousness, "And because I myself am White, I am not in a position to chal-lenge Blacks on this point" (21). He refers to the way in which various black scholars handle this issue, James Cone in particular, who is quoted as saying

"Black theology will accept only a love of God which participates in the destruction of the White enemy" (Cone 1986: 136). He then quotes two black South
African theologians, whom he sees as realistic about problems, yet not cutting
off the possibility of reconciliation (21f). Bosch's spirituality of reconciliation is
authentic, costly, and challenging, but it is odd that the names of the two black
South African theologians are not mentioned, nor are references to their works
given. I cannot help seeing in this lacuna a kind of scholarly discrimination.

1986

Twelve years later much had happened in South Africa to exacerbate the relationship between whites and blacks. One recalls the Soweto uprisings, the
banning of sixteen anti-apartheid organizations, the murder of Steve Biko, and
the growing brutality of the security forces. In this turbulent period a Festschrift
in honor of Archbishop Desmond Tutu was published under the prophetic title:
Hammering Swords into Ploughshares (Tlhagale and Mosala 1986). Bosch's essay
in that volume is in great part a plea for understanding of the history and actual
predicament of the Afrikaners. Making that plea is an ambiguous enterprise in
the best of times, but especially then, since from whatever angle blacks looked
at Afrikaners, they experienced the system they maintained as their oppressor.
Bosch knows this, and, therefore, asks rhetorically "How could I — both an
Afrikaner and a Christian — dare to write on this theme. Perhaps the answer
to this question is that I should do it precisely because *I am an Afrikaner* (159,
italics added).

It is moving to see David Bosch identify himself with the glory and misery
of Afrikanerdom by talking not about "the Afrikaners" but about "we Afrikaners." He saw them as a people with a "Masada complex," a complex that had
intensified in recent years because of a loss of self-confidence, to the point that
despondency was their dominant emotion.

Bosch discerns two stages in Afrikaner history: the first in which they could
only think of themselves. During the second stage, he says, "we" were convinced
that it was our divine calling to uphold and safeguard the separate identities
of other groups as well. In order to implement this, "we" thought ourselves
appointed to restructure the entire fabric of South African society (160).

Bosch further openly admits these "fine sounding designs" had only negative
results, which "have hurt millions of people, hurt them deeply" and brought
about a situation where the "gulf of misapprehensions, fear and hatred between
White and Black has reached alarming dimensions" (160). In such a situation
talk about reconciliation seems a classic exercise in futility. Still he goes on to
talk about reconciliation, in twelve theses, a few of which I mention below.

Thesis 1: *Cheap reconciliation is the deadly enemy of the church.* "Cheap reconciliation means tearing faith and justice asunder, driving a wedge between the
vertical and the horizontal. It suggests that we can have peace with God without
having justice in our mutual relationships" (161).

Thesis 2: *All of us are prisoners of history and are, as such, challenged to become
prisoners of hope.* Here Bosch refers to "a terrible legacy of faction fighting (in our
country): Black against White, Afrikaner against English, Black against Black,

Afrikaner against Afrikaner," and so forth, but "through the grace of God some of us then discover that we are in prisons, and we begin wishing those prisons away" (162). Which makes one wonder if Bosch overlooks the distinction between prison-guards and the real prisoners.

Thesis 4: *In ordinary interhuman communication people are usually more aware of the sins of others than of their own sins.* While we must admit that all human beings are sinners, in the concrete context of South Africa, Bosch could fruitfully have used the distinction made by Raymond Fung that, while all human beings are sinners, some, in addition, are sinned-against.

Thesis 7: *Repentance and conversion always affect those elements in our lives that touch us most deeply, which we are most attached or devoted to, without which — so we believe — we simply cannot exist.* Both repentance and conversion are seen as preparatory steps for reconciliation. Bosch states that he cannot speak for black fellow Christians, not even for whites in general and Afrikaners in particular. But he clearly states the "Gospel challenges us to be willing to give up our privileges" and to say that "Only if this is the road we walk . . . shall we be free to live in a country in which we no longer have any say" (167).

With this and that which follows, Bosch indeed envisages a possible dark scenario for the future, one in which Afrikaners not only would "have no longer any say," but also could become "the underdogs," and in which a future South Africa could be ruled "by a corrupt and oppressive Marxist regime." Notwithstanding this possibility, Bosch says, "we should be able to continue being Christians" (167). He then refers to Russia, China, Vietnam, and Iran as examples of negative situations in which the church survives today. For him, it may be an advantage to live this way, "liberated from the guilt of privilege and from . . . bad conscience."

1991

David Bosch's last major article, entitled "The Changing South African Scene and the Calling of the Church" (1991e), appeared a few months before his death. Bosch starts by saying "The curse of more than forty years of the ruthless imposition of an inflexible policy of apartheid is that it left South Africans with a legacy of mutual estrangement. . . . In many respects the real trauma caused by apartheid is only now coming to the surface, particularly in the areas of education, housing, unemployment, and violence" (147–48). As regards the violence then taking place in the black townships, Bosch reacts against the many whites who find this indicative that blacks are not fit to run the country, noting that "the blame for what is happening in the Black community has at least partly to be laid at the door of the Whites" (149), which he explains by analyzing a poem written by the black poet J. J. R. Jolobe in 1936 entitled *Ukwenziwa komkhonzi* ("The Making of a Slave"):

> The anger against the oppressor and the feeling of utter impotence in the face of overwhelming odds frequently turned the oppressed against each other. Indeed, we have sown the wind and are today reaping the whirlwind. (149)

The explanation of violence given by Bosch is a psycho-social one. But another important aspect of the problem is not mentioned by Bosch — expressed by Albert Nolan and many others as the conviction that "the military and the police make use of the tensions to destabilize the country" as had been done in such places as Mozambique and Angola (Nolan, in Lascaris 1993:16).

In a separate section, Bosch deals with "our inherited anthropologies," which he identifies as: (1) an anthropology of apartheid, with stress on one's own group and consequently on racial separateness; (2) the liberal anthropology of the Anglo-Saxon world, in which the individual stands in the center; and (3) the anthropology of traditional Africa, with stress on relationships of a restricted solidarity, limited mainly to family and clan. Bosch's analysis of these three anthropologies shows that each of them has to be overcome. As he moves toward envisioning a new future for South Africa, Bosch observes:

> Our traditional anthropologies have all failed. We need an anthropology in which people count, both as individuals and as communities, in which the fears and joys of people are taken seriously, in which we will not allow traditions, systems or laws to close our eyes to people's needs and dreams. (Bosch 1991e:156–57)

It is Bosch's conviction that the Christian faith offers such an anthropology, though not "automatically." The church "may be privileged to become a community in which confrontations are *de-ideologized*" (157; here Bosch refers to Nürnberger 1991). Bosch spells out the consequences of instilling a new anthropology into South African society:

1. *For White Afrikaner Christians:* The consequences can be distinguished for persons in three categories: those who connived in the apartheid system, those who implicitly condoned it; and those who, even if they had realized that it was utterly despicable, did not oppose it courageously and consistently. For them all, "the discovery of a truly Christian anthropology will evoke repentance, a confession of guilt, and a willingness to embark on the road toward restitution" (158). In a sensitive-pastoral attitude Bosch sees a number of challenges for a penitent element in the Dutch Reformed Church in following through on the confession of guilt made publicly and also endorsed by the Dutch Reformed Church and in spelling out its consequences, offering pastoral guidance to those who haltingly confess their guilt; and in accepting responsibility for those who defiantly refuse to confess their guilt, not least since they reveal the culpability of the church, which for decades proclaimed as the will of God what they still hold (159).

2. *For White English-Speaking Christians:* Particularly those who stand in the liberal tradition, Bosch feels, have guilt to confess, since most of them acquiesced in apartheid, often guilty of the worst form of duplicity: uttering fiery denunciations of government policies, but hesitating to act boldly on behalf of the oppressed; denouncing apartheid as government policy, but practicing apartheid in their own ecclesial structures.

3. *For Black South African Christians:* Here Bosch is hesitant to become overly explicit. Still he states his view that Christian faith has widened the horizon of

Africans infinitely. Traditionally, positive relations extended only to those who belonged to the ingroup, all others were potential enemies. Bosch then hails Archbishop Desmond Tutu as a representative of African Christianity who had positively responded to the Dutch Reformed Church's confession of guilt at the Rustenburg Conference when he said: "I cannot, when someone says: 'Forgive me!!' say, 'I do not.' For then I cannot pray, 'forgive as we forgive'" (160).

Bosch, however, notes that Desmond Tutu's offer of forgiveness following the DRC's confession of guilt and complicity in apartheid was not welcomed by all. One reason, he suspects, is that some black people adhere to what he calls the *ideology of entitlement:*

> They maintained, perhaps unconsciously, that since they were victims they only had to sit back and wait until the guilty ones, in this case the whites, had cleared up the mess...and brought whites and blacks on a par. Until this happened, blacks would occupy themselves with criticism and refuse to dirty their own hands. After all, in the light of everything whites have done to them they are entitled to refuse co-responsibility in healing South Africa. (161)

In Bosch's opinion, an important contribution of the church will be that of opposing the ideology of entitlement. Yet, it is not at all clear to what and whom he refers. He reacts, in my opinion, like an Afrikaner who feels burdened bearing the blame for what went wrong.

In the last section "Journeying in Hope," Bosch expresses a wisdom that may be very appropriate to all who are striving for a new South Africa. He looks back at a 1989 event when he was one of the 115 white South Africans meeting with the leadership of the exiled African National Congress in Lusaka, Zambia, one year before the release of Nelson Mandela and the unbanning of liberation movements. Bosch remembers the atmosphere of euphoria during these four days among both black and white South Africans about the future of South Africa and about the imminence of comprehensive liberation and a fool-proof democratic system. But, it is characteristic of Bosch's courage and integrity that, at a point when the euphoria was almost tangible, he felt compelled to intervene and say:

> We should beware of facile optimism. Even if we get a negotiated settlement, our troubles will be far from over. Because of the history of our country and because of the incredibly heterogeneous composition of its population, such a settlement will remain a very fragile thing for many years to come. (162)

In the endeavor to build a better future, Bosch sees a mission for the church: "The Christian church, if it really understands its calling, will help us to remain sober about what is attainable. It will, above all, do everything in its power to create and disseminate among all South Africans a *culture of tolerance*" (162–63). Although he already sees signs of this culture emerging, his overall evaluation is that:

At the moment, and in spite of dramatic changes since February 1990, this culture of dialogue and tolerance still eludes us.... The ideal of a democratic society...is, it seems, still little more than a faint shimmer of light on a distant horizon. And yet, this is the ideal the churches should be holding up to the people of South Africa. (Bosch 1991e:163)

"Journeying in hope" is a precious heritage left by David Bosch to all Christians and to persons of good will who dream about and work toward a new South Africa.

Concluding Remarks: David Bosch's Missiology and Africa

I have analyzed and evaluated above how Africa features in the missiology of David Bosch. I now concentrate on two central issues — contextuality and relevance — which will help us establish whether and how Bosch's missiology has significance for mission in Africa.

Contextuality

We have already observed that the African context is virtually absent in Bosch's major systematic works. However, we have also found significant links to Africa in a large number of essays and articles addressing themes and theologies in Africa outside South Africa. In sum, Bosch's involvement in the South African scene produced publications which deal with Africa in ways that may surprise readers who know him only from *Witness to the World* and *Transforming Mission*. Bosch was more contextual than many were aware of. Yet, it should be noted that Bosch was so in a very peculiar way. If we limit ourselves to Bosch's missiological involvement in the South African scene, we will see that Bosch more often than not evades being concrete and specific.

Bosch, aware of criticism levelled against him in this respect, responded in the same vein. In his address "Following Christ in South- and South-West Africa Today" (1974c), he parries anticipated criticism by saying: "You do perhaps feel that I was very very vague and general. In fact, I did this on purpose....I wished to draw some general guidelines and then leave it to you and the community in which you live to apply those Biblical models" (20). A similar reply was given to his colleague Adrio König who had criticized *Witness to the World* (1980a).

There is, in my view, a twofold ensemble of reasons that explains why Bosch chose to be general rather than specific. The first is provided by Bosch himself, who — when reflecting on his theological roots — professed to be a Westerner whose formative years were in the 1960s, when theology solidly followed the classical Western intellectual styles (1982c). The Copernican revolution that many underwent in the 1970s under the influence of third world and liberation theologies did not escape the inquisitive mind of David Bosch. Still he did not adapt it into his mode of theologizing.

There are, however, early statements made by Bosch on the importance of third world theologies. For instance:

Increasingly theologians of the Third World are making contributions which church and theology in the West can ignore only to their own detriment . . . it may soon be vitally important to export Third World theologies to the West. It may help the West not only to understand the Third World but also to understand itself. (1976)

The reason for Bosch's comparative disregard for third world theologies in his major works is not a superiority complex but his assessment of the role of context in relation to the tasks of theology. Third world theologians, including African theologians, usually start from the context and bring it in intimate relationship with the Gospel message, even to the extent that the context throws new light on the understanding of the message itself. Bosch, on the other hand, remains firmly rooted in the classical methodology of clarifying and formulating ideas and guidelines that he brings to a concrete context, as it were, "from above." Third world theologians start "from below."

The second set of reasons why Bosch in most cases remained general in regard to South African issues and challenges is connected with his being a conscious and loyal Afrikaner. There is, however, no direct statement from Bosch on this, but we can safely derive it from a number of essays on the history of the Afrikaners, their close link with the Dutch Reformed Church, and on their relationship with other groups and races in South Africa.

Bosch's identification with the Afrikaner nation does not mean that he identified himself with the wrongs perpetrated by his fellow people. But Bosch refused to give to blacks and more particularly British South Africans an occasion to malign the Afrikaner position and choices without showing concern for the predicament and plight of the Afrikaners. My theory, at any rate, explains why he rejected interference from others in bringing about a conversion of Afrikaners. Their conversion, he believed, had to come from God and from within the Afrikaner community itself (1986c). It is clear that Bosch considered himself as a catalyst used by God to enlighten his fellow Afrikaners about the need for conversion, including a readiness to end apartheid.

Having offered at least a possible explanation why Bosch's missiology generally remained highly generalized, the question can now appropriately be put whether this type of missiology has relevance for mission in the African, and more particularly in the South African, context.

Relevance

One way of measuring the relevance of David Bosch's missiology for Africa is to ask whether he had an impact on African theologians. A quick survey shows that Bosch's impact in Africa outside South Africa seems to be almost nil, while in South Africa there are at least some African theologians who refer to Bosch's writings. There are, however, other ways of measuring the relevance of theology and missiology for a given context. I refer, in the case of Bosch, to the methodology, the content, and spirituality of his missiology. Since I myself, though living and working in Africa, remain a European-born Caucasian, what I have to offer are only indications why I think certain aspects of David Bosch's missiology are relevant for reflection on mission in Africa, and in South Africa in particular.

Methodology. We have noted that Bosch's missiology can hardly be called contextual since the context does not form an integral part of his theologizing. But context is not the only fact taken into account by theology. As Arthur Mc-Govern observes, "All theology involves reflection on scripture and formulating its message in a more systematic way, using unifying concepts such as salvation and redemption" (McGovern 1989:31). As regards the use of Scripture, a systematic approach to a theological problem and putting theological reflection in an historical perspective, Bosch's talent and contribution are unmistakable. His skills in this cannot be responsibly ignored by contextual theologians, even though their approaches give their theologies quite different orientations.

Content. I have already indicated that Bosch's writings on certain African realities are still of significance today. His "God in Africa" (1973c) remains a lucid essay on the relationship of the traditional concepts of God and the God of Christian Scripture. His "The Problem of Evil in Africa" (1987a) is an illuminating analysis, providing pastoral-missionary guidance for a problem that still vexes many Africans, Christian Africans included.

Regarding South African themes and issues we have already presented the view that Bosch sometimes failed to give an adequate analysis of the position of blacks. This is not in any way due to disregard or disrespect, but to the fact that Bosch looked at the black condition primarily from an Afrikaner perspective. Yet, in all his contributions addressing South African issues and challenges, one finds a deep concern not to underestimate the inherent weaknesses of all human endeavors to create a just and humane society (1972a:7). Stating this in 1972, when the apartheid system was still strongly entrenched in South African society, could easily be interpreted as acquiescing in the status quo which was keeping blacks in their subordinate place. But Bosch showed the courage of a prophet when he expressed the same concern during an euphoric meeting of white South Africans with ANC leaders in Lusaka in 1989 (1991e:162).

In a new South Africa, this prophetic viewpoint may help us look at new opportunities in a sober way, the more so, because Bosch, even in 1972, did not in any way counsel against pursuing a just and humane society, since "Faith does not imply quietism" (1972a:7). In particular, Bosch's plea to the churches for remaining consistent in their prophetic ministry after independence and by implication in the post-apartheid era, should be well heeded. Bosch also gives insight into the historical background and the contemporary angst of the Afrikaner people, which helps explain (though it does not justify) their efforts to maintain apartheid for forty years. This insight could facilitate reconciliation, provided, of course, that its basic elements such as appropriate restitution are forthcoming. In addition, Bosch's identification of the three inherited anthropologies that caused dehumanizing rifts in the old South Africa may help heal their respective weaknesses in the new nation.

Spirituality. Perhaps the most significant dimension of Bosch's missiology is its spiritual character. This should not be understood in the sense of "spiritualizing away" real problems, but as a vision and conviction deeply rooted in the spirit of Jesus Christ.

David Bosch's spirituality was intimately linked with his personality. He was unquestionably a bridge-crosser, who demonstrated in his person what mission is, namely "crossing frontiers." We see him invited to speak in circles that were politically and theologically polar opposites in South Africa — the worlds of Evangelicals, Ecumenicals, the Dutch Reformed circles. He was included in the white delegation meeting ANC leaders in Lusaka (1989) when it was still banned. Moving in different and opposing circles can create the impression that one has few convictions. In Bosch's case, he remained himself wherever he was. All his addresses and writings were inspired by a deep conviction that "Christian discipleship in South Africa — or elsewhere — has to do with reconciliation. The church on earth is God's instrument of reconciliation. Reconciliation is the message the church has to proclaim" (1974c:13).

Bosch's spirituality became once more manifest in 1986 when he was looking at the future of South Africa and the Afrikaners' place and fate in it. His picture of the future is dark, if not desperate: Afrikaners eventually becoming the underdogs, and possibly a Marxist-oriented regime trampling on the most basic human rights (1986c:167). Yet he refused to despair in the face of what, in his eyes, seemed to become a real tragedy: "I am an anti-tragedy person. I am in the hope business.... And, I am not alone in this. There are also Desmond Tutu, Beyers Naudé and tens of thousands of others" (1986b:215–16).

Peace is the fruit of reconciliation, and reconciliation in all its dimensions and ramifications was the message conveyed in the work of David Bosch. Though his missiology is not beyond criticism, its missionary message continues to be relevant to the world, including Africa.

A SOUTH AFRICAN PERSPECTIVE ON
TRANSFORMING MISSION

Willem Saayman

If the term *magnum opus* still has any currency, David Bosch's *Transforming Mission* deserves that description. It is truly magisterial in its grasp of the history of the church and of theology, original and creative in its use of biblical material, and perceptive in its analysis of the theology of mission. My more detailed comments below must be read in this broad context of general appreciation for the book. This is my first introductory comment. A second introductory comment is that my review of *Transforming Mission* is written consciously from a South African perspective. Although David Bosch shares this context, he did not set himself the task of writing a specifically contextual book on the theology of mission. His context obviously deeply influences his own theology of mission; still, his aim was to write a more "universal" book, generally with the worldwide, and specifically with the First World Western theological community as his main interlocutors. Because my response is specifically contextual, I may therefore be asking here and there for a kind of detailed discussion and analysis which Bosch did not feel necessary in the light of the more "universal" audience he was writing for. I am convinced, though, that if an important and magisterial book such as this is to become really useful, it needs specifically contextual responses from theologians in general and missiologists in particular, especially from those in the Third World. This viewpoint also obviously determines which aspects and dimensions of *Transforming Mission* I question and affirm; in other words, it is the thread which binds together what may otherwise seem to be a fragmentary review. This article is therefore not meant to be a general theological review of the book, but rather a response by a specific South African missiologist from within a specific context.

The Paradigm Theory in Church History

Obviously one cannot write a review article of this book without giving attention to the question of the usefulness of the theory of paradigm changes to analyze and understand developments in church history. I am not going to enter into a

Willem Saayman is professor and head of the Department of Missiology at the University of South Africa and General Secretary of the Southern African Missiological Society. He has had mission experience in Zambia, Namibia, and South Africa. This contribution was originally published in *Theologia Evangelica*, 1992.

serious critique of this subject, as I am not qualified to do that. Bosch's use of this theory in *Transforming Mission* has, however, already been extensively and most competently analyzed by Pillay (1990), and I refer readers to that analysis.[1] I do wish to comment, however, on one particular statement Bosch makes about paradigm change. In his description of the first paradigm change (from the paradigm of the early church to the paradigm of the Eastern church), Bosch (1991a:190–91) argues that the Christian faith is intrinsically incarnational and, therefore, "unless the church chooses to remain a foreign entity, it will always enter into the context in which it happens to find itself." This incarnation Bosch understands, in the words of Knitter, whom he quotes approvingly (190), not simply as an expression in Greek thought of what the early Christians already knew, but rather as a discovery "through Greek religious and philosophical insights, [of] what had been revealed to them." If that is indeed what incarnation in a new context means (and I agree that this is what it should mean), then church/mission history gives evidence of a third possibility next to the two alternatives of incarnation and remaining a foreign entity. That possibility, intrinsically related to the Constantinian dispensation, is for the powerful church to colonize a new context. In such a situation, the church does not discover the meaning of its message in terms of religious insights inherent in its new context by way of incarnation; neither, however, does it remain a totally foreign entity. It adapts or indigenizes its message in terms of the new context to communicate more effectively, mostly in order to consolidate its power base. Because it is in such a powerful position, though (mainly because of its alliance with a colonizing power), it can survive without genuine incarnation (which implies vulnerability and a willingness to be changed fundamentally). By conforming outwardly to religious and philosophical insights of the new paradigm, it gains a place for itself in the new context, while maintaining intact central (power) dimensions of the original ("sending") paradigm. The first paradigm shift might indeed have placed the church before the clear choice between incarnation (and survival) or foreignness (and extinction). Once the Greek and Roman Catholic paradigm shifts had taken place, though, and the church had become part of the imperial power structure, genuine incarnation became very difficult and the colonizing option correspondingly more attractive.

New Testament Models of Mission

In this section Bosch deals with the New Testament writings of Matthew, Luke and Paul.[2] He makes use of the large number of articles and books which have

---

1. A number of David Bosch's South African colleagues entered into a dialogue with his missionary thinking, as expressed especially in *Transforming Mission*, at the Congress of the Southern African Missiological Society (SAMS) in January 1990. The proceedings of this congress have been published as Kritzinger and Saayman 1990.
2. The question will undoubtedly arise as to why Bosch does not include any Old Testament material. To me it seems that he is dealing with paradigm shifts in theology of mission, which really only came into being after Pentecost. The Old Testament is not totally absent, though. Bosch does make use throughout the book of some Old Testament material, especially material from Deutero Isaiah.

appeared in the last few years on the biblical foundation of mission. This thorough overview of the material is in itself enough reason to read these chapters. But Bosch does much more than simply review the material. He puts the material together in a very creative and stimulating way, causing at least this reviewer to become quite enthusiastic again about this topic.

There is only one point on which I would take issue with Bosch here. On page 103 he quotes with approval Schottroff and Stegemann's conclusion that Luke should be called "The evangelist of the rich" rather than "the evangelist of the poor." He also approves (albeit in a qualified manner) of Albertz's conclusion that Luke is calling upon the wealthy to alleviate the plight of the poor. In the light of the preferential option which I believe the church should make for the poor, I am afraid that these conclusions can be misunderstood (indeed, have already been misunderstood) in at least two ways (I am not saying Bosch has misunderstood them thus; it is rather that I am afraid his use of these statements may be misunderstood).

(i) Because Luke's message is primarily aimed at the rich (and powerful), it is up to them to improve the plight of the poor and oppressed by means of almsgiving and other measures.

(ii) The fact that Luke's Gospel is good news equally for the rich and the poor implies that Christians should therefore feel equal concern for both groups. In fact, in the light of (i), Christians should in the first place be concerned for the rich, for it is in their power to alleviate the plight of the poor.

Let me explain briefly why I consider these to be misunderstandings, and in fact serious misunderstandings.

Throughout human history, but especially during the last few centuries, the rich and powerful have always been the subjects of history; the poor and the oppressed were merely the objects. This means that the rich and powerful monopolized both the making and the writing of history, often taking life-and-death decisions about the voiceless and powerless. Because the rich and powerful had this monopoly, they often interpreted historical events which benefitted them and disadvantaged the poor and oppressed as "divine providence," thus implying that the misfortune, poverty and suffering of the poor and oppressed could somehow be ascribed to God. It is mainly the various liberation theologies which have arisen during the past three decades that have made us aware of this. They inform us that there is another history, a history "written from the underside" — the history of the poor and oppressed. It is very important to be the subject of one's own history, because this affirms one's right to exist and generates pride in one's own existence. It destroys the subtly poisonous perception that somehow God intended one to be inferior, less than human. The Christian gospel should therefore be a subversive gospel, subverting the monopoly of the rich and powerful on the writing and making of history. At the same time it should be an empowering gospel, enabling the poor and powerless to take control of their own history. When this happens, "the witness of a poor Church can evangelize the rich whose hearts are attached to wealth, thus converting and freeing them from this bondage and their own egotism" (Puebla Conference of Latin American Bishops, quoted in Gutiérrez 1983:129).

To many Christians it is, however, unacceptable to say that God is on the side of the poor (and the oppressed), and that therefore the Christian church should exercise a preferential option for the poor. One reason why they find it unacceptable may be that they understand a preferential option for the poor to be a preferential option against the rich; in other words, that good news for the poor is by definition bad news for the rich. Having analyzed exhaustively and in great detail the biblical material generally quoted in this debate, Dirkie Smit comments as follows on article 4 of the Belhar Confession of the Dutch Reformed Mission Church, which states that God "is in a special way the God of the destitute, the poor, and the wronged, and that he calls his church to follow him in this."

> On the issue there can and must be no difference of opinion. God revealed himself as the one who wants to bring justice and true peace among people, and he calls his Church to follow him in this. There must also be no difference of opinion concerning the fact that it is a serious question which ought to help determine the actions and lifestyle, associations and loyalties, even the structure and priorities of the Church. God's justice does not in the least mean that he is neutral, unconcerned and uninvolved with regard to human misery, distress and suffering or with regard to relationships and structures of injustice, exploitation and oppression. He is the God of justice precisely because he defends and protects those without any rights or those to whom justice is not being done. His righteousness is an active, helping righteousness which saves and liberates and restores justice. (Smit 1984:59)

I think another important reason for the difficulty that many Christians have in accepting the statement that God is on the side of the poor and oppressed is the widely held assumption that God is neutral — above the fray, so to speak, calling both parties to a conflict to repentance and reconciliation from this neutral position. In refutation of this assumption Smit states clearly that God "is not neutral, unconcerned and uninvolved" (this is a synopsis of a mass of biblical evidence; cf. Smit 1984:58–59, 127–50). In other words, in situations where there is human misery because of exploitation, injustice and oppression, God is on the side of the poor, the exploited, the oppressed, the marginalized — not merely on the side of Christians who are poor and so forth, but on the side of all people who find themselves in such a situation. God is therefore not neutral. He is partisan, in solidarity with those who are denied justice — not on behalf of any political or economic system, but on behalf of his justice-righteousness (cf. Bosch 1991a:70–73) as revealed in Jesus of Nazareth. This does not simply mean that God is therefore against the rich and powerful. Precisely because of his solidarity with the poor and oppressed, God brings the liberating message of his good news to the rich and powerful also. This is so because it is an illusion for them to imagine that they can be free and enjoy peace while they are oppressing and exploiting others, whether directly or indirectly, whether by commission or omission. Only the liberation of the poor and the oppressed can set free the rich and powerful as well, because without justice there is no salvation. And in this liberation the poor and the oppressed are not merely powerless objects whose plight is being alleviated by the rich and the powerful. They are subjects of their own liberation, empowered by the good news of Jesus of Nazareth and his liberating Spirit.

The Missionary Paradigm of the Eastern Church

In his discussion of the paradigm of the Eastern church, Bosch follows Young in a mostly positive conclusion about the influence of Greek philosophy:

> Greek philosophy provided the church with the tools (and more than just the tools) to analyze all kinds of aberrations, to pursue awkward critical questions, to distinguish truth from fantasy, to repudiate magic, superstition, fatalism, astrology, and idolatry, to grapple seriously with epistemological questions which produced a fundamentally rational account of how human beings attain appropriate knowledge of God, and to do all this with a combination of intellectual rigor and a deep faith commitment; in short, to be both "critical" and "visionary" (cf. the title of Young's essay). (Bosch 1991a:200)

It is necessary to take a closer look at this conclusion, especially because this paradigm was in so many instances foundational for the Christian faith in later centuries. It seems to me this positive conclusion rests very much on an Enlightenment understanding of faith. Looking at the history of Christian mission in Africa, for example, I am not convinced that the repudiation by the Western missionaries of what they considered to be "magic, superstition and idolatry" had such positive results. "Critical" this process certainly was, but I have doubts whether it was accompanied by a "visionary" faith commitment; in other words, I agree that the critical tools provided by Greek philosophy would prove very important in the (necessary) demythologizing dimension of Christian mission in centuries to come. That this would be accompanied by a visionary faith dimension also inherited from Greek philosophy, I doubt very much. In Africa at least, it seems to me, the "magic," "superstition" and "idolatry" were often attacked without any realization of the essential role they played in traditional religion, and therefore without a realization of the requirements and necessity for an alternative vision — with sometimes disastrous results. With relation to the attack on the (thoroughly religious) traditional African view of sickness and health, an attack motivated by the fact that Christian missionaries generally regarded the traditional view as "magic," "superstition" and "idolatry," Schoeman (1990:12) states, "Where belief in supernatural causes, administered by a community of ancestral spirits linked to the living by ties of kinship, has given way without recourse to alternative philosophies (such as those of cause and effect based on scientific evidence), socially dislodged individuals are reduced to dangerous levels of personal irresponsibility."

In other words, Western missionaries could only replace the thoroughly religious traditional view on healing with rationalism, which was not compatible with the African view on sickness and well-being, and therefore did not take root. It was therefore exactly a visionary faith commitment which was lacking. I would therefore argue that the tools provided by Greek philosophy and deeply influenced by the Enlightenment proved so one-sidedly critical, and emphasized the rational so exclusively, that visionary faith could very easily come to be regarded as irrational nonsense. Perhaps this happened largely (to use Bosch's own words in a different context, 1991a:213) because "Platonic categories of thought all but destroyed primitive Christian eschatology." Whatever the reason, there seems to be enough evidence to cast serious doubt on such a positive evaluation of the effects of Greek philosophy.

A final brief comment about Bosch's discussion of the paradigm of the Eastern Church: I find it disappointing that he does not analyze in more detail the context of "the Constantinian Reversal." He provides fascinating glimpses, for example, about early examples of the intertwinement of mission and colonialism in the Eastern church — that phenomenon which would become so tremendously important centuries later in the modern Western missionary movement. Yet he leaves it at that, also in his interim balance sheet of the first paradigm shift.

The Medieval Roman Catholic Missionary Paradigm

Bosch (1991a:216–17) convincingly indicates Augustine's foundational significance for the growth of a dualistic view of reality according to which salvation of the "soul" out of the world became the most important concern. For Augustine, the question: On what basis does a person find salvation? was settled mainly in terms of an individual's wrestling with his or her conscience. That is why he could write, "I desire only to know God and my soul, nothing else." Indeed, it was a blessing to know only God and the soul, as the world was irredeemably bad, and there was nothing really which the Christian could do about it (Bosch 1991a:401). The transaction of salvation could therefore be consummated by an individual "soul" in total isolation from other human beings and from the world. This is, in my opinion, a very important observation for church and theology in South Africa, especially because Augustine's theology was (is) an important source for South African (Dutch) Reformed neo-Calvinism (cf. Groenewald 1952:508). One effect of this can be illustrated with reference to the fundamental difference between the theological reaction of the Confessing Church in Germany to Nazism and the (lack of) theological reaction of the DRC in South Africa to the growth of apartheid (cf. Durand 1985:39–41). This fundamental difference, says Durand (40), as epitomized in Dietrich Bonhoeffer, was that the Confessing Church's theological concern was both Christ-centered and world-centered, which gave rise to "implacable resistance to the German Christian version of civil religion." In my opinion, it is precisely the neo-Calvinist dualistic view of reality, rooted in Augustine's theology, which negated the importance of a world-centered Christology, and which is an important cause of the lack of theological resistance from within the mainstream of the DRC to the growth of apartheid. This dualistic view of reality is, however, not confined to the DRC. A large number of South African churches, especially, but not exclusively, the evangelical churches, maintain this view. If the South African churches are to fulfill their mission in such a way that the fatal link which grew between establishment politics and establishment religion will not be allowed to grow again in any future dispensation, they will have to take careful note of this fatal theological weakness in much Protestant and Reformed theology.

The Missionary Paradigm of the Protestant Reformation

In a very perceptive way, Bosch (1991a:241) indicates that the two leading "articles" of a "Protestant theology of mission" were the justification by faith of people regarded primarily from the perspective of the Fall. I wish to emphasize a practical consequence of the development of these two articles: when read in conjunction, they gave rise (perhaps even more so in Calvinism than in Lutheranism) to a pervasive pessimism regarding human beings, their potential and their actual achievements (Bosch briefly refers to this later on pages 288–89). As Bosch himself puts it so aptly (250), Lutheran orthodoxy "almost . . . feared that the world might improve"! This fundamentally pessimistic anthropology expressed itself in an overwhelmingly negative evaluation of other religions and the cultures of "non-Christian" people when Protestant missionaries started coming into regular contact with them some two centuries later. In this encounter, Western culture was, however, not regarded with the same degree of skepticism, mainly because Western Protestant theologians, and especially missiologists, were of the opinion that the gospel had been fully indigenized in Western culture, to such an extent that many negative effects of the Fall (walking around naked or seminaked, worshiping idols, being superstitious, etc.) had been tempered. Western civilization thus became "Christian Western civilization," and many missionaries (with exceptions such as Keysser, Gutmann, and others) assumed that it should therefore form the basis of a "universal" Christian culture. One can see how these two "articles" were therefore to become partly responsible in Protestant mission for the (near fatal) identification of Christianity with the Western cultural expressions thereof.

As Bosch points out, the Reformation also brought about a fundamental change in ecclesiology which was to have tremendous influence on the subsequent understanding of Christian mission. This was the fact that once "the Reformation shattered the ancient unity of the Western church, each of the fragments into which it was now divided was obliged to define itself over against all other fragments. . . . In all these instances the church was defined in terms of what happens inside its four walls, not in terms of its calling in the world" (Bosch 1991a:248–49). This remark must be read in conjunction with my remark above about Augustine's theological influence, an influence which is, as I have argued, at least partly responsible for an introverted Christology. When read together, it seems to me that this ecclesiological development undoubtedly contributed to the introverted inertia reigning in the institutional church which early Protestant mission pioneers such as Carey and others had to overcome. In my opinion, this continual concern with self-justification, especially in terms of correct preaching (249), is furthermore to a large extent responsible for the perennial missionary problem of the relationship between evangelization and social service. Where purity of doctrine is so important in order to justify the separate existence of a church, verbal evangelization is bound to take precedence over social service.

A short concluding remark about the question which evokes perennial debate among many Protestant missionaries and missiologists: Were the Reformers indifferent to mission? Bosch provides an excellent review of the debate, pointing out both the unfairness of judging the Reformers against a twentieth-century concept of mission, as well as the undoubted apologetic nature of the attempt to prove that the Reformers were indeed not indifferent to mission. One would hope that this issue can now be laid to rest. In the end this debate actually proves or disproves nothing of value. The true test for the missionary paradigm of the Protestant Reformation is not whether the Reformers themselves were mission enthusiasts, and what they achieved in mission, but whether Protestant praxis in its very essence serves to erect contemporary signs of the reign of God among rich and poor, powerful and powerless, oppressors and oppressed, believers and nonbelievers alike.

Mission in the Wake of the Enlightenment

I think Bosch is quite correct in treating the influence of the Enlightenment on the Protestant missionary paradigm in a separate chapter; the tremendous influence of the Enlightenment on Western society as a whole, and on church and mission specifically, certainly warrants this decision. His concise and perceptive analysis of the principles underlying the Enlightenment world-view and approach to science is very valuable in understanding mission history in South Africa. In my opinion, this will prove even more valuable, though, in the halting interdisciplinary conversation getting under way with the social and natural sciences, and which will become enormously important very soon in the light of the threat to human community posed by the spread of AIDS in Africa (cf. Saayman 1991b; Saayman and Kriel 1991).

I have reservations, though, about Bosch's evaluation of the intertwinement between mission and colonialism respectively in early and in later Protestantism in the wake of the Enlightenment. "Secular" and "religious" interests in Britain and America in early Protestant mission, he states (1991a:276), were clearly going their own ways; there was no longer "a comprehensive religiocultural-political program." Indeed, evangelical missionaries, moved to compassion by the plight of black people, and especially slaves, in the colonies, became involved in the campaign against colonial abuses. As a result, the chartered companies administering the colonies "did everything in their power to keep the missionaries out" (281). As far as South Africa specifically is concerned, the Dutch East India Company (DEIC) paid no more than "lip service" to "the Calvinist notion that this territory [the Cape Colony] was also to be evangelized" (303). Bosch concludes therefore that "the colonial expansion of the Western Protestant nations was thoroughly secular" (ibid.). A "comprehensive religio-cultural-political program" of missionary and colonial collusion indeed did not exist. Yet I doubt whether there was actually such a clear demarcation between "secular" and "religious" interests as to make possible a clear distinction of the relationship between mission and colonialism in earlier and later Protestantism. The very place of missionaries at that time in an expanding political economy created a complementary relationship with colonialists (cf. Cochrane 1987:37). As Guy (1983:183) points out with regard to Britain, for example, "the clergy was an integral part of the English ruling class, and the ideas that they propagated were part of the ideology through which that class defended, and attempted to maintain, its position within the upper reaches of the social hierarchy." This seems to indicate rather a convergence of "secular" and "religious" interests. And as Boer (1979:81) further indicates, colonialism was the economic and political expression of the restlessness of especially the upcoming middle classes in Europe, a restlessness which found parallel expression in the missionary enterprise. The DEIC indeed paid little more than lip service to the evangelization of the Cape Colony, but through their (direct or indirect) control over the only established church in the Colony at that time, namely the Dutch Reformed Church, they firmly controlled efforts by others to evangelize the indigenous inhabitants of the Cape, as the Moravian missionary Georg Schmidt was to find out when he tried to baptize his own converts. The resistance of missionaries such as Wilberforce, Carey, Blumhardt and others (to which Bosch refers) was, therefore, in my opinion (like that of de las Casas in the Roman Catholic church!) not a fundamental resistance to the intertwinement of mission and colonialism as it explicitly existed in Roman Catholicism and in later Protestantism. Freund's explanation (1984:157) seems to me more acceptable:

> It was not unusual for missionaries to fight the settler interest where this was a factor, which enormously increased respect for them among Africans. Even then, with rare exceptions, they did not oppose the essence of the colonial system: segregation, land alienation and migrant labor. Few if any missionaries challenged the political and economic imperatives of colonial domination, as opposed to specific policies, and they usually accepted the racist aspect of it fairly easily.

Early Protestant mission, especially when viewed from the vantage point of the "objects" of that mission (cf. Saayman 1991a:22–35), was therefore in my opinion in a different way as firmly intertwined with colonialism as Roman Catholic and later Protestant mission — a development of which Bosch provides an excellent analysis. Although the Enlightenment obviously played a very important role in giving form and content to the relationship between mission and colonialism, I would therefore argue that the roots of the relationship in Protestantism lay in the Protestant missionary paradigm itself and was not largely ascribable to the influence of the Enlightenment.

I wish to single out specifically Bosch's excellent discussion of the rise of Protestant missionary societies (1991a:327–34), which he considers "one of the most remarkable phenomena of the Enlightenment era" (327). Voluntarism was the guiding principle for the rise of these societies, and this voluntarism rested on two convictions: the right of private judgment in interpreting Scripture, and the right of like-minded individuals to band together in order to promote a common cause (328). This development was made possible by the social and political egalitarianism of the emerging Western democracies, with their free enterprise economic systems, and in which state churches increasingly lost influence (329). All of this was possible mainly because of the Enlightenment. In our time many missionaries and missiologists are once again promoting the founding of ever more missionary societies "to get the job done." Bosch's analysis of the rise of missionary societies in history, especially his excellent exposure of their contextual roots, should play a very important part in any discussion of the formation of missionary societies in our time, and should indicate the necessity of proper social analysis before such societies are formed.

This entire chapter should be compulsory reading, at least for theologians and theological students. The Enlightenment presuppositions about "science," "knowledge," "facts" and "beliefs" have been internalized so successfully also in Western theology that we are hardly aware anymore that they are very specific, contextual, cultural presuppositions which are not necessarily "true" everywhere and at all times.

An Emerging Ecumenical Missionary Paradigm

It is impossible to do justice to this excellent, but extensive, chapter (122 pages) in a review article; it actually needs an article of its own. Every one of the themes Bosch discusses here actually forms an excellent missiological article on its own. As I am admittedly attempting to do the impossible, then, I will have to be highly selective. My choices will again be determined by my specific contextual viewpoint.

Bosch starts his analysis of the emerging new paradigm of mission with a section on the missionary church. I wholeheartedly agree with his choice of starting point. For at least the past three decades, the main missiological problem has been ecclesiological in nature. It has been an abiding legacy of the modern Western missionary movement, both Protestant and Catholic alike, that mission was seen as a consequence of faith, an appendix to the church. The church could therefore be church without mission — a misperception which Bosch conclusively destroys. Indeed, "[the church's] mission (its 'being sent') is not secondary to its being; the church exists in being sent and in building itself up for the sake of its mission" (Bosch 1991a:372). Would that all churches and theologians would write those words in scarlet letters as the first article of faith! Such an ecclesiology, I would argue, will advance the Christian community a long way toward the comprehensive understanding of salvation that we so desperately need, an understanding "beyond every schizophrenic position," taking account of people "in their total need," involving "individual as well as society, soul and body, present and future" (Bosch 1991a:399). It is my contention that many of these schizophrenic misunderstandings came about exactly because Christians thought and acted as though the church could be church without mission.

I have perhaps my greatest difficulties with Bosch's point of view in his section on mission as contextualization (1991a:420–32). Although he considers contextualization an essentially legitimate process (425) and is quite positive about some of the gains Christian theology owes to contextualization, he eventually gives more space to what he terms the inherent "ambiguities" of contextualization. The most serious danger he sees is the process of contextualism, which means "universalizing one's own theological position, making it applicable to everybody and demanding that others submit to it." This process, he says, is simply the mirror image of the imposition of Western mission theology on the Third World in earlier centuries (428). He mentions especially two sources to validate his fear of contextualism: an inclination among some Latin American Liberation Theologians to "promulgate their peculiar brand of contextual theology as having universal validity" (ibid.), and South African Liberation Theologian Albert Nolan's claims about the popular struggle against the oppressive apartheid system in South Africa (428–29).

Most certainly there was a tendency toward universalizing Latin American Liberation Theology, but this tendency was resisted fairly early on in the development of Liberation Theologies elsewhere precisely by other contextual theologians — as, for example, by contextual theologians from Asia in the example Bosch quotes (428), as well as by African theologians. As far as Bosch's difficulties with Nolan is concerned, Nicol (1990) provided a perceptive analysis of Bosch and Nolan by way of a comparison of their major writings to date (e.g., Bosch 1980a, 1991a, Nolan 1988). This analysis, in my opinion, opens avenues to put Bosch's problems with Nolan and the attendant fear of contextualism in context. Nicol states the central difference between them, as he perceives it, thus (1990:86): "Nolan's aim is to engage the church actively in social change, while that is precisely the area where Bosch's theology runs into problems. There is a basic tension in Bosch between the distinctiveness, uniqueness, weakness of the church and his desire that she should stimulate real social change."

Because his main concern is the social engagement of the church in its specific context on behalf of the poor and oppressed, Nolan emphasizes God's providential activity in that context (Nicol 1990:87) with a degree of certainty which comes across as arrogant sweeping statements to Bosch. The way to counter these generalizations, though, is in my opinion not by reminding Nolan of a more universal approach, but by confronting him with very specific contextual theologies from other contexts which gainsay his generalizations. Bosch's primary concern, on the other hand, is salvation, so that he emphasizes the saved, alternative community, a community which is bound through shared faith and salvation history primarily to the universal Christian community (Nicol 1990:87–90). Bosch (1991a:428–30) therefore "reads the signs of the times" in a way that is quite different from the way Nolan reads them, because they read them from quite different perspectives. In order to attain the goal of liberation, Nolan emphasizes especially the power of God acting through human beings, while Bosch emphasizes especially God acting through human weakness (Nicol 1990:87). In this respect Bosch's point of view approximates Third Way theologies, which Balcomb (1990:41) characterizes as follows vis-a-vis liberation theologies:

> Third way theologies consistently advocate that the alternative way of the church is to eschew power, while liberation theologies consistently maintain that the power issue cannot be avoided, that it is essential to a hermeneutic of both church and society, and that a negation of this idea is a negation of the role of ideology in the church and a mask for the continued maintenance of power in the hands of those who already have it. It seems to be a truism that those who are especially concerned about avoiding the subject of power are those who have it and those who are especially concerned about not avoiding the subject of power are those who do not have it.

Bosch's viewpoint undoubtedly has validity — power and success have never been exclusive criteria for authentic Christian faith. Yet, as Balcomb points out, it cannot be denied that it is easier to propagate weakness and failure as authentic marks of the Christian faith if one identifies primarily with a relatively powerful community (as, e.g., the universal Christian community). If one speaks, though, as Nolan does, from a perspective of primary identification with the disenfranchised, poor and oppressed, it is much more difficult to advocate weakness in an attempt to avoid the troublesome reality of ideological power alignments in society (cf. Balcomb 1990:36–37). Seen from this perspective, I cannot share Bosch's fear for imminent contextualism in the process of contextualization in South African theology, a process which, in my view, has scarcely reached the end of its beginning.

Conclusion

Obviously *Transforming Mission* is not a mission encyclopedia or an exhaustive mission history; certain omissions are therefore to be expected. Yet some exceptions have to be pointed out as strange. One is the near total silence about the Pentecostal contribution to mission. Pentecostalism has been described (correctly, in my opinion) as the third main force in Christian mission (next to Roman Catholicism and Protestantism — cf. Pomerville 1985; Newbigin 1954). Any Christian group who can grow to a total of 200 million members worldwide in the relatively short space of eighty years must be considered a dynamic missionary force, and leaving it out of a review of mission theology is, in my view, hardly justifiable. A second conspicuous omission is a specific analysis of women's contribution to mission and the missionary dimension of the liberation of women (it is curious, for example, that Bosch does not include either North American feminist or womanist theology in his list of United States liberation theologies on page 432).

I conclude with the statement with which I started: this is a magisterial book. As a textbook, it will be around and will be appreciated in many seminaries and theological faculties for a long time. I am very much aware of the fact that I have not done justice to it in this review article (mainly because of considerations of time and space). Still, my attempt has, I think, some value, for if this book is to be truly useful, it will have to be "contextualized," grounded in our various contexts. David Bosch has done us a great service. Let us take him seriously exactly by entering into various critical, contextual dialogues with him.

– 4 –

A Passover of Language

An African's Perspective

John S. Pobee

A Man of Sorrows and a Man of Courage

In my then capacity as the President of the International Association for Mission Studies, I wrote an *In Memoriam* for the journal *Mission Studies* on the occasion of David Bosch's death (Pobee 1992a). Among other things, I said:

> Some beat the system from within; realism is as important in resistance as revolutionary rhetoric. Because he adopted the approach of fighting quietly and creatively from within the *status quo*, his integrity was sometimes impugned. But I am persuaded he was genuine. For precisely the foregoing reasons, he was a man of courage.

That life of his was in a way the exposition of mission in bold humanity. His life was not some quixotic act or the operation of someone who had a saviour complex; he led that life because of his acute sense of the urgency of mission of God in his time and place, a sense which was undergirded by a deep spirituality. That spirituality was at once obedience to the Will of God as he discerned it and humble boldness, pain and loneliness.

Perspective of African Instituted Churches and African Theology

I seek to write this piece as a kind of response to the description laid out above, from the perspective of African theology. African theology represents a variety in a genre. At one end is the fabrication of Christian faith in the form of African Instituted Churches, a kind of indigenizing movement in Christianity, a "place to feel at home" (Welbourn and Ogot 1968; Barrett 1968; Assimeng 1986; Makhubu 1988). These have a constituency who are largely "mere mortals, the poor," though not exclusively so. At the other end is the theology represented in the so-called historic churches, which inevitably were at first "extensions of 'home churches' abroad" (Nketia 1962:112). In between there is a whole range

---

John S. Pobee of Ghana is coordinator of Ecumenical and Theological Education at the World Council of Churches and former President of the International Association of Mission Studies.

of theological expressions. Whatever the range, they represent the dissatisfaction with the theology minted in Europe and appropriated by churches founded from the North. That dissatisfaction is expressed as African theology, or more accurately theologies, which are not just a protest against the North Atlantic captivity of churches and theology but also are an attempt to culture the mystery of God, especially through Jesus Christ, in the African soil and water it with African hands.

Permit me to quote two statements of the spirit and intention of African theology — one from the last century, the other from our times, if for no reason than to hint that the search for African theology has been in the offing since the 19th century.

The first I take from Mojola Agbebi, also known as David Brown Vincent (1860–1917), a Nigerian and English-speaking African who wrote: "To render Christianity Indigenous to Africa it must be watered by native hands, turned by native hatchet and tended with native earth. . . . It is a curse if we intend for ever to hold at the apron strings of foreign teachers doing the baby for aye" (Vincent, in Ayandele 1989:200). That is an eloquent plea for attempts at harmonizing African ethos, institutions, natural and national habitudes with the biblical faith. This was a need felt already in 1889.

The other one is the contemporary call from Jean-Marc Éla, a Roman Catholic priest from Cameroun, a French-speaking African. He too writes:

> In Africa, the confrontation between the message of the Gospel and the African universe must bring forth a meaning with the poor to transform the lives of African Christians. Today the faith of the Church in Africa is in danger of death because the Church tends to forget that its cultural dimensions are marked by its Greco heritage. If the faith of the Africans is not to die, it must become a vision of the world that they can feel is theirs; European cultural orientations must be stripped away. There is an urgent need to reject present foreign models of expression if we are to breathe new life into the spoken Word. Our church must express a Passover of Language, or the meaning of the Christian message will not be understood. One of the primary tasks of Christian reflection in Black Africa is to totally reformulate our basic faith through the mediation of African culture. In place of the cultural presuppositions of Western Christianity, namely *logos* and *ratio*, we must now substitute African symbolism. Beginning with the ecclesial furrow where the language of faith germinates, we must restore the Gospel's power to speak to Africans through the primordial symbol of their existence. (Éla 1988:44)

This is an expression of the spirit and intention of African theology and African Instituted Churches: it is about the search for a Passover of Language.

Passover of Language

Needless to say, the title of my piece I owe to Éla. But I choose that language to signal a number of things which must not be lost sight of in mission.

First, the word "language" describes more than syntax and morphology. It is the vehicle and weight of a worldview. Therefore, in mission there should be the engagement of the African worldview and the biblical worldview. And it is in that engagement that life is released. Second, the Passover, as a spring festival, signals that mission should be renewal that brings deliverance. Third, in the tradition of Judaism, a practice evolved on the basis of Malachi 4:5–6 that at the Passover a cup of wine was set aside for Elijah, the prophet of the endtime, and at a certain point in the proceedings a door was opened to see whether Elijah was standing outside.

The imagery of Passover signals that mission is also about the opening of doors for divine intervention. Fourth, against the background of Jewish worship being punctuated by the feasts of Passover, Weeks and Tabernacles at which all males were required to appear before Yahweh with offerings as well as for feasting and enjoyment, the imagery of the Passover as applied to mission is a call for mission to be a happy social experience to which the poor are invited.

I wish now to illustrate some of the foregoing from the African story. But before I do that, let me also indicate some of the characteristics of African theology.

What are the characteristics of this African theology? First, it is characteristically concerned for theology to have intellectual rigor. To that extent it shares the character of theology minted in the North. But this is secondly, combined with the missiological vocation of theology. Identifying and scientifically and critically addressing the cutting edges of mission in Africa then is the vocation of African theology. It is here that the reality of the poor becomes significant. This explains the emphases in African theology and also indicates that theology is essentially a second step. Thirdly, the missionary vocation of theology is inextricably linked with the ecumenical vocation of theology in Africa, not only because ecumenism is a gospel imperative but also because of the context of pluralism in which theology is done in Africa. Fourth, the style of theology is not only propositional nor has to be propositional but is done also in art, music, poems, etc. We are becoming more and more conscious that African theology also takes the form of oral theology (Mbiti 1978; Pobee 1989).

Practice of *Tabula Rasa* a Denial of Mission in Bold Humility

That the practice of *tabula rasa* was characteristic of missions hardly needs arguing here. That practice said in not so many words that non-Christian culture could never be a *preparatio evangelica* and, therefore, had to be destroyed before Christianity could be built up. Whatever the rationale for that position, it is also true that proponents of that view had bought also the ideologies of Christendom, of the anthropological racists of the 19th century, of the Eurocentrism of the time, and of social Darwinism. The Christian mission was dyed in the wool of those ideologies which were at once ideologies of power and fear: power that sought the assimilation of other to itself; fear of mixing and engagement.

What was at stake in the practice of *tabula rasa* in Africa? It amounted to a denial of the incarnation. The model of the incarnation reminds us of the humility and boldness required to have the soul of the eternal and non-negotiable gospel of Christ translated in a real, specific cultural situation, however imperfect that context may be. It demands the bold faith that God's Spirit can never be trapped forever in any culture. Further, the spirit of the incarnation points us to the transitoriness of any theological construct.

The exaltation of contextual theologies of Europe as the norm of theology in that sense is not sensitive enough to the contextual nature of every incarnation of the Word of God. For that reason African theologians have emphasized indigenization, inculturation, etc. To hold together the need to translate into the specific context and the essential transitories of each construct, I have proposed the word *skenosis* as the apt description of what African theology should be about (Pobee 1992b). It is an attempt to capture the spirit of humility and boldness that should attend the essential and necessary task of mission being a tabernacling of that Word of God. David Bosch was one of those who supported the process of *kenosis*.

Talk of African theology has often worried some people, including Africans who stigmatize it as the heathenization of Christianity. For example, Solomon M. Muthukya, onetime General Secretary of East African Christian Alliance, wrote: "the secret behind the Africanization of Christianity is the work of Satan himself, the spirit of the Anti-Christ. He aims at the heathenisicism of the African Church" (Muthukya:7). "This is what they mean by African Christianity. No mention of the one and only saving Gospel of Our Lord Jesus Christ. No mention of sin. No place for the authority of an inspired Bible. Instead their arguments are based on the traditional background of the African people, their culture, customs and belief. If natural culture and religious customs are acceptable to God, why did Christ send his disciples to preach the Gospel to every creature in the uttermost parts of the earth?" (Pobee 1992b).

In the light of what we have said earlier, one hardly needs to argue that Muthukya's description is a caricature of African theology. His critique represents the fear of living the spirit of incarnation in its humility and boldness. Mission in bold humility is incarnational.

Sensitivity to the Political Reality

For some other people, African theology is racism donning religion and theology. That is in part the legacy of the Enlightenment culture of which David Bosch wrote eloquently (1991a:262–348). The particular element of that culture concerning us here is the privatization of religion. The writings and the life of Bosch signal some of the issues at stake in this complex. First is the nature of evangelism. He argued forcefully that the purpose of evangelism is not so much some temporary gain or eternal salvation; it is essentially a call to service and discipleship. Indeed, in mission and evangelism, the church begins to discover its true nature and authentic calling (Bosch 1986d). That nature and authentic calling is about the church being the sign and vehicle of the gospel of hope which is denied those who are marginalized and oppressed and dehumanized.

The quotation from Jean-Marc Éla goes in the direction of the spirit of David Bosch's argument.

Thus when one raises the issue of mission in bold humility, the real issue is the nature and authentic calling of the people of God as sign and instrument of hope embedded in the gospel.

Bosch's clarity on the missiological vocation of theology was evident in other ways. He wrote, "the curse of more than forty years of the ruthless imposition of an inflexible policy of apartheid is that it left South Africans with a legacy of mutual estrangement. Black and White lived in two worlds and most whites knew more about Europe and North America than about life in Black ghettos of their own country" (1991e:147). For him education, housing, unemployment and violence, all of which were marks of the apartheid system, were missiological issues and spiritual matters. That analysis of the missiological vocation of theology is and should be on the agenda of African theology, for it can be good news only if it addresses the hopes and fears of *homo africanus* in boldness and humility.

This consideration has been seen as the point of difference between African and black theologies in Africa. James Cone and Gayraud Wilmore have written as follows: "African theology is concerned with Africanization. Black Theology is concerned with liberation. But Africanization must also involve liberation from centuries of poverty, humiliation and exploitation. A truly African theology cannot escape the requirement of helping the indigenous churches to become relevant to the social and political ills of Africa which are not unrelated to Euro-American imperialism and racism" (1972:21). And so, African theology has been criticized for not being sufficiently, if ever, sensitive to the issue of liberation. I myself consider the comment a simplistic reading of the goal of African theology. The inherited theologies have made no place for the identity and ethos of *homo africanus* and put them in a North Atlantic captivity. African theology seeks to undermine that captivity by working at the identity of *homo africanus*, and that itself is a quest for liberation. It is a protest against the fear which aggressively tries to cow others into submission.

Bosch was not content with just an analysis; he struggled to find a way forward. That is evident not only from his publication "The Roots and Fruits of Afrikaner Civil Religion" (1984b:14–36) but also in his ruminations on mission in Jesus' way. He argued that that mission is about empowering the weak and the lowly, the kind of pass-over from captivity of Egypt to liberation in the promised land. He further argued that mission is about healing that is more than a cure of bodies but a proleptic manifestation of the presence of God's reign — God visiting humankind. He stressed that healing is linked with faith, salvation and forgiveness, i.e., unconditional acceptance and forgiveness of sinners, for the transgressions are so great that only grace could make up for it (1989a). Unconditional acceptance requires humility and boldness. It is not only apartheid South Africa that needs this gospel of healing but also the African societies riddled with tribalism, poverty, dictatorship, each of which results in polarization and violence. With this emphasis, Bosch was articulating what African theology should be saying.

As he once put it, Africa was ripe for nationalistic revolution and spiritual revival, a very holistic perception of reality which is characteristic of African culture and a mark of ecumenical vision.

Martyrdom as the Way of the Passover of Language

In the *In Memoriam* mentioned above, I mentioned Bosch's loneliness, the attacks on his integrity, sometimes from the very people he tried to help, and his being a man of sorrows. Those who will live the Passover must suffer. It is a truism that the word *martus* has two senses: that of the witness and that of the one who makes the ultimate confession of faith with his or her life. If I may use the language of late Judaism, martyrdom is "sanctification of the Holy Name" (Pobee 1985). That is what mission is all about. The experience of suffering in any form in pursuit of the vision of God's reign is itself a missionary activity. Mission in bold humility often goes through the valley of persecution and martyrdom, and that is a Passover of language from the forces of death to liberation in God's kingdom. The willingness to suffer in the interests of new life in Christ is rooted in the sense of concern, responsibility and gratitude for the invitation to join the eschatological community.

Let me attempt to draw the threads together. It has been suggested that bold humility is a characteristic of mission described as a Passover of language. It is to eschew all language of exclusion — cultural, political and social — to a new life of inclusion which sanctifies the Holy Name. David Bosch's life story is a glimmer of that vision, a costly one which carried with it loneliness, pain and suffering and sorrow. It is my conviction that African theology should be informed by that vision and this leads me to my last point.

In contributing to this book, we are celebrating the memory of a great man who died tragically in a car crash. But as an African it is my concern to have both celebration and cerebration. It is not just an intellectual and cerebral activity; it is a celebration of the experience of glimpses of God's rule. That is what mission should do: celebrate the faith so that it can be experienced as a vehicle of good news of hope in the African context. That is the path of the Passover from the language of death to the language of life.

– 5 –

LIBERATING MISSION
A LATIN AMERICAN PERSPECTIVE

Curt Cadorette

Reading a text as substantial as David J. Bosch's *Transforming Mission* is a demanding but worthwhile task. The reader is forced to reflect on the past, present, and future of mission as something integral to the life of the Christian community. Perhaps one of Bosch's most gripping descriptions of mission, of which there are several, occurs when he links the *missio ecclesiae* with the *missio Dei*. In Bosch's words, the task of the Christian community is to represent "God in and over against the world, pointing to God, holding up the God-child before the eyes of the world in a ceaseless celebration of the Feast of the Epiphany" (Bosch 1991a: 391). How could mission possibly be described in a more provocative and inviting way?

Following Bosch's argument in *Transforming Mission*, this celebration of the God-child's epiphany must be celebrated contextually, lest it be an imposition or abstraction. We are forced to ask, then, how the incarnational event, the central datum of Christianity, can be understood and celebrated in Latin America at the end of the twentieth century. To answer such a question adequately we must grapple with several complex issues. The first is the history of Christian mission in this vast and multicultural continent. Mission in Latin America was part of a violent colonial enterprise. The Catholic missioners who evangelized Spain and Portugal's colonies did so in the name of an imperial Christ remarkably like the monarchs who sent them. They witnessed and sometimes turned a blind eye to horrific, sinful behavior. They also helped create new societies that, despite their hierarchical and unjust features, allowed the victims of the conquest to survive, albeit in great pain. Knowing the general contours of mission history in Latin America is crucial for discussing mission's present and future. Since the 1950s Latin American countries have undergone profound social, political, and economic transformation. This is the second issue we must analyze in some depth. Pre-capitalist economies have been industrialized and agrarian societies urbanized. Modernization has generated wealth for a few and unprecedented levels of poverty for the majority. Mission in Latin America today means

Maryknoll missioner Curt Cadorette has worked in Peru and taught theology at the Maryknoll School of Theology, Maryknoll, New York. He currently teaches in the Religious Studies Department of the University of Rochester.

grappling with severe social pathology that will not disappear in the near future. The rise of liberation theology, base communities, evangelical Christianity, and neo-conservative Catholicism are, in many ways, reactions to the social and cultural changes that recently have convulsed this continent. The churches' response to modernization is the third issue we will examine. Finally, as a postscript, we can grapple with the future of mission in this oppressed but believing continent.

Colonial Catholicism: The Contextualization of Christendom

For nearly four centuries the primary instrument of mission and evangelization in Latin America has been the Roman Catholic church. Protestant missionaries did not arrive until the nineteenth century and had little impact until the 1950s. Even today Catholicism commands the nominal allegiance of most Latin Americans. It is something taken for granted, a religious tradition most people tap for rites of passage, but rarely take seriously. Intense religious conviction is the stuff of priests, nuns, and growing numbers of evangelical Christians — a population seen as somewhat atypical but benign. Catholic Christianity, however, is still a force to be reckoned with. The institutional church plays a public role in societies where church and state, although now legally separated in most Latin American countries, tend to interact with regularity. Secularization has occurred, but less intensely than in the so-called developed world. Crosses dot most hills, and images of saints are enshrined in most homes.

In no part of the world were Christian mission and colonialism more intertwined than in Latin America, a fact Bosch alludes to in his discussion of the medieval Roman Catholic mission paradigm. Perhaps wary of offending Catholic sensibilities, however, Bosch is not as critical of Catholic colonial mission as he might be. Because of the *patronato,* the church and state were inextricably bound together, the former ultimately subservient to the latter. Mission was subsidized as well as supervised by the crown. At times the church used its power and privilege to good purpose. On occasion it defended indigenous peoples from the rapacious greed and savagery of European colonists. At the same time, the church regularly betrayed the gospel it preached. Too often it acquiesced before injustice for the sake of institutional well-being and a false peace with brutal colonizers. Despite the fact that the church was instrumental in passing the Law of Burgos in 1512 and the New Laws of 1542 which set apart protected territories for Indian peoples and prohibited their enslavement, cathedrals were adorned with gold and silver extracted from Mexican and Peruvian mines where millions of indigenous people were worked to death.

Bosch, quoting Hoekendijk, correctly points out that the Spanish and Portuguese missionaries who arrived with Cortés and Pizarro were, in fact, involved in a "...continuation of the Crusades" (Bosch 1991a:226). A few missionaries, Montesinos, de las Casas, and Sahagún being the most notable, recognized the pathological nature of the conquest. Before the word genocide existed, they used its equivalent as they described the trauma and death taking place before them. Their pleas for justice, however, were largely ignored. The church had too much to gain by turning a blind eye and the Crown too much to lose if the gospel were taken seriously. The integrity of mission in Latin America was compromised from the outset, but not fatally. Some missioners, an important few, knew the differences between the *missio ecclesiae* and the *missio Dei*. They planted seeds that came to life as a contextualized Latin American church capable of producing prophets and martyrs, especially in the twentieth century.

Even the most open-minded missioner in colonial Latin America, however, worked with the assumption that there was no salvation outside of the Roman Catholic church. Las Casas may have hinted at an inchoate theology of religions and Sahagún entertained the possibility of God's grace inspiring indigenous, non-Christian peoples, but neither questioned the soteriological necessity of the Catholic church or the superiority of European culture. The few examples of contextualized mission, mostly undertaken by the Jesuits in Peru and Paraguay, were seen as protective and temporary phases in the eventual integration of native peoples into European culture. Having learned much from the subjugation of Jews and Moslems in the Iberian peninsula, missionaries were well equipped to attack and disassemble the religious and cultural worlds of the people they were sent to save. By the middle of the seventeenth century they began mopping up the remains of shattered indigenous cultures or, in their terminology, extirpating the last traces of idolatry (see Dussel 1992). Although Christendom was breaking apart in Europe, it survived in Latin America. Independence from Spain and Portugal in the nineteenth century had little effect on the religiosocial system then in place. In fact, it was so cohesive and efficient that the Reformation and even the Enlightenment were kept at bay almost to the 1950s.

Roman Catholicism gained millions of new members by virtue of the conquest of Latin America. The institutional church, however, was enmeshed in a Constantinian arrangement that made its proclamations of the gospel sound hollow. In societies suffused in a Catholic ethos, criticizing the church was tantamount to criticizing society's most cherished assumptions. Intellectually the church was a self-certifying institution that fended off criticism by declaring it heresy. Latin Americans, like the Spanish and Portuguese, saw the church as their primary source of cohesion. Few questioned the *patronato* or even the Inquisition. Transplanted to the Americas, the church acted exactly as it had in Spain and Portugal. It taught immutable truths and inculcated a ferocious sense of Catholic identity in the faithful. It did not succeed, however, in turning America's new Catholics into Europeans. Somewhat like varnish, Iberian Catholicism only covered the surface of Latin America. It was the religion of the elite, but not of the masses.

Indigenous Americans and African slaves began to re-appropriate Catholicism and make it their own. The first instance of re-appropriation took place in 1531 when a woman known as Guadalupe appeared to a Nahuatl-speaking Mexican named Juan Diego. The apparition of the Virgin of Guadalupe can be understood in many ways, but it is undeniable that it had a powerful and positive impact on the self-understanding of native Americans. From that point on, they could use their oppressor's religious system to defend themselves and survive — and it was one of the few survival tools at their disposal. Through apparitions, processions, and pilgrimages they appealed to the Catholic sensibilities of their conquerors. They also began to assimilate the utopic and eschatological dimension of Christianity itself. The Beatitudes and Matthew 25 did not escape their attention, despite the church's efforts to spiritualize their meaning.

Through the medium of an imposed religion, a conquered people continued to articulate their own self-understanding and cultural values. Popular religion, denigrated by Europeans and ignored by the church, helped the victims of the conquest resist their oppressors, although always in *sotto voce*. To use James C. Scott's (1990) terminology, they challenged the public transcript with a hidden transcript that was theologically orthodox but politically heretical. In effect, they began to use the gospel for their own liberation. Popular Catholicism, of course, is a complex, ambiguous phenomenon. It can be fatalistic and magical as well as affirming and liberating. The salient point is that as Latin America was Christianized, Catholicism assumed various theological and socio-political modalities — from the "pure" Catholicism of elites to the so-called syncretistic and subversive Catholicism of indigenous Americans and African slaves who arrived in the sixteenth century. Institutionally speaking, Catholicism in Latin America was monolithic. Functionally, however, it was made up of disparate parts that reflected, and still reflect, the social, cultural and racial divisions of its people. This may help explain why a form of Christianity, imported and imposed, managed to take such deep root. The institutional church never had total control over its own mission. Missioners served a hierarchical, Eurocentric institution, but the people they evangelized soon began to read and exegete the gospels on their own. They created a Latin American, popular Catholicism less Roman than most assume. Luckily, the *missio ecclesiae* has never been synonymous with the *missio Dei*, a fact that explains the vitality and diversity of the Christian community here today.

The Late and Chaotic Arrival of Modernity

In the first quarter of the nineteenth century, the children of Iberian colonists assumed power in Latin America. An inept Bourbon monarchy and the Napoleonic Wars allowed one province after another to gain independence. The church adapted by swearing allegiance to the new republics, using the *patronato* as a paradigm for church-state relations. Despite political autonomy, the compasses of the new oligarchs continued to point to Europe. They were not Latin Americans but Europeans born in Latin America. Their aristocratic lifestyle was maintained through the extraction of natural resources marketed in Europe and North America. Colonial social and economic patterns remained intact. A *mestizo* majority worked at the behest of their Euroamerican retainers, supervising the labor of indigenous peoples and slaves in haciendas and mines. Race and class fixed a person's fate for life. As a concession to the new order, the church allowed more *mestizos* to be ordained to the priesthood, a rarity in the colonial period. Bishops, however, were still drawn from Creole families throughout the nineteenth century. The church's task was to sanction this static system and ameliorate its worst effects through charity. Popular Catholicism allowed a bit of free space in the form of fiestas and pilgrimages in which people could take some pleasure in their lives, free from the gaze of their *patron* and even the parish priest.

Well into the twentieth century, the church provided more social services than the state. Schools, hospitals, and orphanages were run by religious orders, following colonial tradition. The state in Latin America was a precarious proposition. Vast and harsh territories made communication difficult. Government was often synonymous with the nation's capital. It had little impact on provincial hinterlands which were still managed like feudal domains. Spain and Portugal were interested in capital extraction, not the internal development of their colonies. The new oligarchs were just as disinclined to develop their nations' infrastructures as their ancestors. Most lived in colonial capitals enjoying wealth produced by serfs and slaves in the provinces. Indians and enslaved Africans were seen as an underclass, people so primitive that most could not speak Spanish or Portuguese. The state existed for the convenience of the powerful, not the powerless. It regulated capital extraction, not the well-being of its citizens. Political debate took place only in oligarchic circles, but it was largely a fight about the division of spoils. By virtue of their race, class, or gender, most Latin Americans were economically and politically disenfranchised well into the twentieth century — a situation that struck social elites as perfectly reasonable. The Catholic church was a staunch defender of the status quo. Thomistic to the core, it believed in hierarchy. Conscious of the criticism of Enlightenment thinkers and the chaos of the French Revolution, it saw modernity and democracy as heretical errors that threatened the common good.

The arrival of modernity in Latin America was largely the result of external events in the first half of the twentieth century. In the 1940s the market for raw materials dried up because of the Second World War. Even after hostilities ceased, synthetics replaced natural products like nitrate and rubber, the mainstays of the old export economy. Clearly, modernization and industrialization were necessary to redress Latin America's sinking fortunes in the new world order. Peasants were encouraged to migrate to urban areas and work in newly built factories, lured by the prospects of modest comfort and a real future for their children. The development process, overseen by the state, was construed as a type of salvation. Participating in it became everyone's patriotic duty. The oligarchy was asked to invest its capital and workers their labor in a common enterprise that would recreate nations. Middle-class Europe and America became paradigms for the future and W. W. Rostow's *The Stages of Economic Growth: A Non-Communist Manifesto*, the definitive map. In fact, in the 50s and 60s a real middle class began to emerge and per capita income began to rise. The International Monetary Fund and World Bank provided Latin American countries with the funds they needed to transform themselves into industrial nations. The United States, which saw Latin America as "its" continent, vital in the global struggle against Marxism, offered additional assistance and supervision through the Alliance for Progress and Peace Corps. With the exception of Cuba, it managed to keep Latin America under its control.

The sanguine projections of the 50s and 60s, however, turned sour in the

70s and 80s, not only in Latin America but throughout the developing world. Enormous loans came due, precipitating a global monetary crisis. Third world industrial products generated little income in markets that were not really free. The middle class began to shrink, and poverty began to grow as inflation exceeded 10,000% per year in countries like Peru and Bolivia. With the safety net of feudal paternalism long gone because of urbanization and the breakdown of extended families, poverty became misery. Recently established socio-political arrangements broke down as the left, right, and center of the political spectrum offered one failed solution after another. The almost universal answer to the imminent collapse of both state and society in Latin America in the 1970s was the imposition of military rule, sometimes referred to as the national security state. A type of evil pestilence was unleashed whose stench is still in the air today. It has all been documented in gruesome detail (Lernoux 1980). Right-wing repression led to left-wing extremism — or vice versa in some countries. Over 100,000 people died in Guatemala, 75,000 in El Salvador, 30,000 in Peru, and tens of thousands in Chile, Argentina, Uruguay, Paraguay, and Brazil. Mass graves are still being uncovered in the world's most Christian continent. Many of the victims of this recent horror were committed Christians, Catholic and Protestant, martyred by members of the military acting, as they saw it, in the defense of Christendom. The role of the church during the past decades of repression is complex and checkered. In some instances it was courageous and prophetic. In others it was cowardly and complicit (Mignone 1986). Of course, the cowardice of certain bishops in Argentina must be measured against the courage of others, something that is true of the entire institutional church. The experience of martyrdom, however, has forever altered the church's social role and self-understanding. Because of its martyrs, it has a newfound credibility in Latin America.

The Christian Churches: Modernization and the Postmodern Crisis

The Poor and the Christian Community

The watershed event for the Catholic church in Latin America was surely the Medellín Conference of 1968, whose insights were critiqued and carried forward in both Puebla and Santo Domingo in 1979 and 1992. To use one of Bosch's favorite concepts, Medellín was a paradigm shift. Like the other paradigm shifts he examines, it had its social and theological reasons. Medellín was neither magic nor a vagary of history. As early as the 1950s members of the Catholic episcopacy in Latin America were aware of the social changes taking place around them. They knew that traditional Catholicism was becoming an anachronism in societies undergoing rapid industrialization and urbanization. Accustomed to poverty, they were seeing a new and more deadly type. They recognized that the church could no longer serve as the religious legitimator of the status quo that was becoming a synonym for injustice and death. Although they accepted many of the ideas associated with developmentalism, they were hardly naïve about its limitations. They knew they lived in societies whose social structures were sinful. They pointed out that progress was more than a question of projects and the modernization of economies.

The bishops assembled at Medellín used the upbeat language of the 1960s to describe the hopes and aspirations of the day, somewhat like the authors of *Gaudium et Spes*, written just a few years before. In many ways, however, the bishops at Medellín were far more realistic than the proponents of developmentalism. The Medellín Document has its utopic qualities, but it is likewise eschatological. Precisely for this reason, most of the Medellín Document still rings true today. Medellín led to two momentous shifts in the Latin American church — the preferential option for the poor and the growth of base Christian communities. Both phenomena require elaboration in view of the fact that Bosch's treatment of them in *Transforming Mission* is condensed and decontextualized.

The preferential option for the poor is often construed as a socio-political statement or decision. It is neither. It is really a christological and soteriological assertion whose foundation lies in the God revealed in both Hebrew and Christian scripture. What Medellín claimed, and Puebla and Santo Domingo reiterated in 1979 and 1992, is that to understand Jesus and the reign of God he proclaimed, Christians must live as he did — among and committed to the poor. They must opt for the least important members of society, the insignificant and redundant, whose lives count for nothing in the eyes of the powerful. Discipleship in Latin America means commitment to people whose lives are threatened by unjust poverty, a sign of sin and refusal to believe in the God of life. The disciple does not opt for the poor and oppressed out of a sense of *noblesse oblige* or some romantic assumption about their intrinsic goodness, but because in their midst the Christian encounters the God Jesus proclaimed. This encounter frees us from sin and the power of deadly idols. A preferential option for the poor has nothing to do with class warfare or party politics, but it does have profound social and political implications. Christians are called to challenge and remake their world so it reflects the God they believe in. They are called to unmask the social and political idols that immolate the poor.

The bishops' plea for Christians to opt for the poor had to be translated into structural change in the church itself. They threw their support behind a new model of the Christian community whose name is now almost synonymous with progressive Latin American Christianity, the base community. Because of Vatican II and its redefinition of the church as the People of God, rather than a perfect society or mystical body as in previous ecclesiological metaphors, it was possible to understand and restructure the believing community in an innovative, nonhierarchical way. The believing community was redefined as a living body of brothers and sisters that evangelized its own members and society. In the post-Medellín period, base communities grew dramatically in many Latin American countries. Most were made up of poor men and women who gradually gained confidence in themselves and their vocation as disciples. Medellín thus unleashed an ecclesiological revolution. One of the world's most hierarchical religious institutions began to work in a nonhierarchical way, evangelizing

from the bottom up rather than from the top down. The socio-political implications of this shift were not lost on ecclesiastical and political conservatives who
branded base communities as focal points of subversion, which, in some ways,
they were.

Base communities also solved the demographic and sociological challenge of
evangelizing burgeoning populations in Latin American countries. The traditional parish that had served the Catholic church for centuries was no longer
effective. With base communities, far more people could have contact with the
church and laypeople could play an actual role in its mission as local evange-
lizers. In effect, base communities helped create a church of the poor rather
than a church for the poor. The ecclesiological and political implications of
base communities are self-evident. As contextualized expressions of faith, base
communities quickly demystify the institutional church as commitment replaces
ordination as the measure of authenticity. As an informed, critical body of believing people concerned with changing society and denouncing injustice, the
base community also generates critical political consciousness. In the 70s and
80s military governments openly persecuted base communities. In Guatemala,
membership was tantamount to death.

Liberation Theology and the Mission of the Christian Community

In *Transforming Mission,* David Bosch offers erudite and useful information
about the intellectual currents that have shaped the Christian community's
understanding of mission in the twentieth century. One has to ask, however,
just how causal such intellectual and theological currents' systems are. Did the
theology behind Medellín "cause" anything, or did the bishops assemble in 1968
because of social and theological changes in Latin America? The question can
be answered in many ways. Medellín clearly had a major impact on the Latin
American church, but it was also caused by events taking place in society and
the Christian community. Surely one of the most significant "causes" or forces
behind Medellín was the rise of liberation theology in Latin America in the
mid-60s. In a conference of committed Latin American Christian students, a
then unknown Peruvian priest-theologian, Gustavo Gutiérrez, spoke about the
need for a new theology that would be more responsive to the needs of the
poor. He spoke of this theology as part of a liberating movement that could
help reshape the continents. In 1971 he published *A Theology of Liberation,* thus
giving a name to a movement already underway. Gutiérrez and other liberation
theologians shared a common passion — making discipleship a source of life in
a world of deadly oppression and poverty. As Bosch points out in *Transforming Mission,* most liberation theologians were influenced by the Enlightenment
and European theological discourse. Almost all had studied in Europe. When
theologians like Gutiérrez, Segundo, and Boff returned to Latin America in the
50s and 60s, however, they began to contextualize their ideas. They drew on a
rich tradition of critical social theory already well established in Latin America.
More important, however, was their use of the human experience and faith of
the poor themselves in theological discourse.

Liberation theology in Latin America has evolved since its inception thirty years ago. The upbeat and rather abstract theology of the 60s and early 70s became more balanced and concrete in the 70s and 80s. The experience of continent-wide repression sobered many progressive Christians' expectations. Systematic torture and savage massacres were never foreseen, but they happened with frequency well into the 90s. Neo-conservatives in the church, Catholic and Protestant, were few in numbers in the 60s; by the 80s they were a significant force in the Christian community. The marginalization of indigenous peoples and the oppression of women, both pervasive vices in Latin America, as well as the liberating potential of popular religiosity, were not dealt with in the first years of the liberation theology movement in Latin America. These topics, however, would be addressed in the 1980s. Since Bosch's treatment of liberation theology in Latin America is succinct and somewhat dated, it is necessary to fill in details missing from *Transforming Mission*.

While the proponents of developmentalism were trying to jump start Latin America, liberation theologians were elaborating a new approach to theology and the mission of the church. As Gutiérrez pointed out in his earliest writings, the primary social datum and theological challenge for Latin American Christians was the reality of the "non-person," a synonym for the millions of men and women whose humanity had been overlooked in the past and whose existence did not really figure in the plans of development theorists (Gutiérrez 1973:13–25). Gutiérrez insisted that development was a cultural and spiritual challenge, as well as a question of transforming socio-economic structures. In *A Theology of Liberation* he insisted that all people, regardless of their social class, had to take stock of the power of sin that shaped their self-understanding and social lives. Gutiérrez perceived two powerful forces in the history of the poor, among whom he was born and continued to live: a utopic aspiration embodied in hope and an eschatological awareness visible in their struggle for justice (Gutiérrez 1983). These powerful, subterranean forces explained the meaning of history whose entelechy is the revelation of God's own self. Using the historical and theological vision of Hebrew and Christian scripture, he attempted to neutralize a long tradition of dualistic Augustinianism in Latin American Catholicism that had led to pessimism and passivity toward history and social injustice (Gutiérrez 1973:34). In the name of the God who preferentially opts for the poor, Gutiérrez called on Christians to struggle against the personal and social sin killing Latin Americans.

Juan Luis Segundo, writing in Uruguay, one of Latin America's most secular and European countries, criticized Gutiérrez's idealism, as Bosch points out. Segundo was less sanguine about the role of the poor in the transformation of history. Wary of both populism and left-wing Hegelianism, he called for a more incisive analysis of historical events, a wise perspective, given the hyperbole of the developmentalist era and the occasional romanticism of some liberation theologians. His great methodological contribution, drawn from Ricoeur, his mentor in Paris, was the notion of the hermeneutic circle which entailed an ongoing revision of theological insights (Segundo 1976). Segundo, noted for the incisiveness of his thought, became a liberation theologian critical of liberation theology. He and Gutiérrez, friends since the 50s, looked at the liberation

project differently. One was sober and precise, the other idealistic and expan-
sive. As Bosch mentions in his critique of liberation theology, this first phase
of liberationist writing was influenced by the Enlightenment project, although
not as naïvely as he seems to assume (Bosch 1991a:358). Liberation theologians
used the ideas of Enlightenment thinkers, including Marx and Freud, but they
did so critically. They were aware from the outset of the historical and cultural
specificity of Latin America. They realized that the Enlightenment project was
a class-based illusion whose promised freedoms were denied in practice, at least
to the poor and oppressed. In fact, the Enlightenment had contributed mightily
to their oppression by offering hopes that were crushed by the socio-economic
system it created (Bosch 1991a:499).

With a working methodology in hand, liberation theologians were ready to
wrestle with the question of Jesus, as well as his socio-historical embodiment
in the Christian community. Two individuals stand out in this effort, Jon Sobrino in El Salvador and Leonardo Boff in Brazil. Sobrino was cognizant of
the damage done by the semi-docetic christology of colonial Catholicism that
turned Jesus into a hieratic, Spanish-speaking judge. He stressed the need for a
new awareness of the historical Jesus, although conscious of the limitations of
what we can know about him. At the same time, he recognized that knowledge
about Jesus was no substitute for action in Jesus' name. In Sobrino's theology
the Christian uses knowledge about Jesus to be a better disciple. Knowledge
and action are dialectically related. Jesus is constantly incarnated in the believing community by disciples who follow him, and they gain progressively deeper
insight into who Jesus is. When christology shapes ecclesiology, as it should
and does in Sobrino's writing, the *missio ecclesiae* can truly partake in the *missio Dei*. Sobrino also insists that it is impossible to be a disciple without the
support and challenge of a believing community, but the community is not the
purpose of discipleship. Christians follow Jesus in community for the sake of
their salvation and the world Jesus loved. Committed to making God's reign
real, they reach out to the victims of sin and injustice as Jesus did. By doing so
they also make the church a christological force in the world — its only reason
for existence. Sobrino's christology is grounded in personal experience. His as-
sertions have been validated by people like Oscar Romero, his brother Jesuits in
El Salvador, and thousands of committed Christians in Latin America. Their
willingness to give themselves up to death in the name of their brothers and
sisters has helped revitalize the Christian community by making it truly christological. Their christological sacrifice has also played a role in ending one of
Latin America's most bloody civil wars, thus demonstrating the intimate link
between the paschal mystery and the world. Death and resurrection, that of
Jesus and his disciples, thus have an impact on society and history. They point
to the soteriological foundation of the struggle for liberation.

Likewise convinced of Jesus' ongoing embodiment in the Christian community, Leonardo Boff tried to put forward a more liberating ecclesiology. In books
that won him little affection in the Vatican, he criticized Christendom and its
defenders, pointing to the ongoing abuse of power by people in the institutional
church. He proposed a "bottom up" ecclesiology that incorporated the poor

and oppressed in the church, not as a token group, but as leaders. Boff asked why committed men and women could not celebrate the eucharist in priest-less communities, the norm in Brazil and most of Latin America. He bluntly asserted that the church's refusal to ordain married men and women was a vi-olation of their baptismal rights, echoing Galatians 3:28. Boff was, and is, the most outspoken of all Latin American liberation theologians. He does not hes-itate to question non-liberating church structures, asking aloud if they are not a manifestation of sin, a sentiment that Bosch also entertains (1991a:378). Boff's passion was often misconstrued as an attack on the church by those vested in the preservation of the traditional system. What he called for, however, was the reform of anachronistic and dysfunctional aspects of institutional Catholicism. Given the Catholic church's history of ecclesiocentrism and tendency to equate ecclesiastical structures with revealed truth, Boff's ecclesiology was bound to be seen as threatening. His motive in writing, however, was to facilitate the reform of the church so it might better carry out its liberating mission.

In the last two decades liberation theology has taken deep root in Latin America, although it has many vocal critics, in and out of the church. None-theless, many of its insights into the nature and mission of the Christian community are now accepted as self-evident. Even John Paul II uses concepts and vocabulary drawn from the works of liberation theologians who otherwise have few supporters in Rome. The abstraction of the first phase of liberation theology diminished in the 80s and 90s as its proponents became more confi-dent of their project and Christian communities lived the gospel in a liberating way. Liberation theology was becoming more inclusive and rooted. Responding to well-founded criticism, the first generation of theologians paid greater at-tention to the experience of indigenous peoples, blacks, and women. Through grassroots organizations and study centers indigenous peoples began to articu-late their experience as the most marginalized sector of Latin American society. Theologians like Elsa Tamez and Ivone Gebara began to produce texts that reflected women's experience of sexism and gave voice to their aspirations for liberation, in the Christian community and civil society. References to European theology decreased, while references to the daily experience of the poor and op-pressed increased. Their specific language, culture, and religiosity became part of theological discourse. Liberation theology was becoming what it was really intended to be, a liberating way for the Christian community to do theology.

Simultaneously, an effort was underway in the 80s to create a deeper, more durable spirituality capable of sustaining Christians subjected to criticism from conservative elements of the church and violence at the hands of military gov-ernments. Gustavo Gutiérrez and Jon Sobrino, among others, wrote about the need for a vision of liberation rooted in scripture, liturgy, and the life of the be-lieving community. They pointed to Jesus' passion and death as a prelude to his resurrection and a paradigm that could help Latin American Christians under-stand the martyrdom they were experiencing. By the 80s no one could be naïve about the power of evil. The challenge was not to fall victim to despair in the face of routine torture, rape, and death inflicted on those committed to justice. A spirituality emerged that served the believing community well. Few left it, and many continued to play significant roles in the life of the church and society. It is unfortunate that Bosch's premature death cheated him of the chance to savor the maturation of liberation theology and its impact on the Christian community.

Postmodernity and the Mission of Latin American Christianity

Throughout *Transforming Mission*, Bosch is faithful to an incarnational definition of mission. He tries to balance the immanent and transcendent dimensions of the God-child symbol that informs his entire work. He sees the Christian community as a participant in an epiphanic process that takes place in history. If the Christian community is to know and proclaim God, it must likewise know and be committed to the world. It is a dialectical community called to ask hard questions about society and history, about where we are going and why. As Bosch points out repeatedly, when the church looks inward, at least for too long, it can lose a sense of itself and the world it is called to help redeem. It becomes sectarian and toxic, obsessed with orthodoxy rather than orthopraxis. On the last page of *Transforming Mission*, Bosch makes a powerfully critical statement about the history of Christian mission: "We may have been fairly good at orthodoxy, at 'faith,' but we have been poor in respect of orthopraxis, of love." Those are sobering words that the Christian community in Latin America must keep in mind. They explain many of its past failures, as well as some of its present problems.

The cost of mission well done, of liberating discipleship, is always high, as recent historical events have shown in Latin America. When the Christian community knows itself, its environment, and what the gospel asks of it, hostility from those with a vested interest in injustice is inevitable. To the extent that Christians embody redemptive love in a world of despair, they can expect to be persecuted. Love is subversive. Understandably, some Christians long for a return to Christendom, that idyllic moment when there was little ambiguity and no persecution. No longer uniform, theological discourse is seen as enervating. No longer controlled from the top down, the Christian community seems fractious. This is particularly true among Catholic conservatives, a small but powerful minority in Latin America. To counteract what it perceives to be chaos, Rome has appointed conservative, authoritarian bishops who, in some cases, are overtly hostile to liberation theology and base communities. They are controlled by a hierarchical ecclesiology and a reactionary set of socio-political assumptions. Ecclesiocentric in the extreme, they conflate the *missio ecclesiae* with the *missio Dei*. Polarization is a serious threat to the internal life and external mission of the church today. Finite energy is wasted on internal issues that should be used in external evangelization. Were Bosch alive today, his assessment of Latin American Christianity, particularly that of the Catholic church, might well be harsh.

Mission in Latin America today, however, is still promising and challenging. By committing itself to a more integral, liberating form of evangelization, the Christian community can literally save lives. In the last ten years one Latin

American country after another has come under the sway of neo-liberalism. Elite technocrats, psychologically and physically removed from the people they govern, now exercise near total control. A new type of authoritarianism has emerged. Repression, torture, and even extrajudicial executions are still common, but they are effected with sophistication. Although neo-liberalism has brought some measure of fiscal stability to countries afflicted by destructive inflation, economic stability has been purchased at the price of greater poverty. Latin American stock markets are booming while per capita income is falling. Free market capitalism has turned savage, with little concern for the common good. Safety nets no longer exist, with deadly consequences for the most vulnerable members of society. More and more people are economically and socially redundant, truly non-persons whose existence counts for nothing. Street children in Brazil, Colombia, El Salvador, and Peru are routinely "liquidated" as hopeless misfits. In the minds of neo-liberal theorists, compassion is not a virtue but a vice. Human beings are simply mechanisms. Those that work well are maintained while those that malfunction are discarded. Efficiency is the only issue in a post-modern, post-ethical world devoid of transcendence. The ideas of Adam Smith and Friedrich Nietzsche, melded together and distorted, reign as self-evident truths only fools contest. Of course, there is still the question of controlling the unruly masses. They can be mollified with occasional elections, provided they have no real effect. Neoauthoritarian leaders pay lip service to democracy, although they hold it in contempt. So too with religion. It is a useful distraction for the poor and oppressed, but ultimately an illusion that has nothing to do with an efficient economy or modern political system.

The fact that some conservative members of the Catholic hierarchy are obsessed with the memory of Christendom demonstrates how fixated they are with the past and ecclesiastical power (Walsh 1992). Either they are suffering from induced naïveté or they have never read the New Testament seriously. Conservative evangelicals are likewise uncritical of neo-liberalism, driven by anti-socialist zeal and a desire to ingratiate themselves with people in power. Fortunately, most Christians see just how anti-Christian neo-liberalism is. In their 1992 meeting held in Santo Domingo, the Catholic bishops of Latin America pointed to neo-liberalism as one of the believing community's most significant challenges (Conferencia General 1992:paragraphs 181, 199). Such a position is an ethical necessity and welcome sign of common purpose. The Latin American bishops have also been helped by the social encyclicals of John Paul II. As he has pointed out, contemporary capitalism, often predicated on an absolute materialism, is ultimately a source of despair. Utterly Darwinian, neo-liberalism is predicated on a cynical, anti-human elitism that has led to the "culture of death" John Paul II condemns in *Evangelium Vitae*.

On the local level of poor neighborhoods, where the majority of Latin America lives, poverty is more deadly than ever. Malnutrition and disease stalk the innocent, while alcoholism and drug addiction consume those who have despaired. Violence is rampant and, in some countries, now the leading cause of death among young males. The mission of the Christian community is as obvious as it is difficult. It is called to be a source of life and hope liberating people from murderous destruction. The church of the poor that has emerged in the last few decades is well placed for this mission and is carrying it out. Although micro-level phenomena like soup kitchens, health centers, mothers' clubs, and religious services might seem insignificant, they are enormously important in impoverished environments. They are even more important when the poor themselves create and run such services. As such they are liberating and saving. On a theological level, these instances of Christian mission are a powerful proof that death is not the final word. They are also eschatological countersigns that refute the idolatry of a cynical, post-modern world by proving that the incarnation is an ongoing event. The God-child is still with us. If David Bosch were alive today, he would also be optimistic about mission in Latin America. Despite its ups and down, it has not failed. It is truly a liberating sign of God's liberation, a celebration of the Epiphany that will sustain the people of this continent in the next millennium.

- 6 -

ESCHATOLOGY AND MISSION IN CREATIVE TENSION
AN INDIAN PERSPECTIVE

Jacob Kavunkal

Until about Vatican II, the mission with which the church in India was busy and the missiology that underpinned it were mostly the product of a colonialistic background. In fact, the Indian church was seen more as a "mission" of the western Churches. The Church in India depended on the western "mother" churches for its theology, spirituality, personnel and funds. True, there was an ancient church predating colonialism. But the spirit of the times made it impossible for that church to escape the woes of colonialism.

This situation began to change by the middle of the present century. As early as 1910 at Edinburgh, Indian theologian V. S. Azariah gave expression to the Indian aspiration for a new approach to mission (Kane 1983:348). In modern times, as far as the Catholic Church is concerned, it was the Plenary Council of India held at Bangalore in 1950 that for the first time declared explicitly the positive value of other religions and for the need for a new missiology in the light of other religions (Neuner and Dupuis 1973:271). In this it was echoing the theological spirit of J. N. Farquhar, who spoke of Christ as the Crown of Hinduism (1913). In fact Farquhar could be considered as the initiator of the modern theories of "fulfillment" put forward by several western theologians (Race 1982:52). India became the focal point of a worldwide theological discussion again when the International Theological Seminar held at Bombay in 1964 described other religions as the ordinary ways of salvation and Christianity as the extraordinary way of salvation (Neuner 1967).

Those who are open to the Indian context and the background of the Indian church will not be surprised by the creative way Indian Christians are trying to proclaim what they have experienced in Jesus Christ without denying the authentic religious experience of their neighbors. An equal concern for the Indian church is that the vast majority of the Indian masses are denied the fruit of their labor and participation in determining their future. Has the mission of the church anything to do with those condemned to a dehumanized existence but going through an awakening today?

Jacob Kavunkal, an Indian member of the Divine Word Missionary Society, is Director of the Isvani Kendra Missiological Institute run by the Society in Pune, India. He is active in research on issues related to inculturation and interreligious dialogue.

Another aspect of Indian reality is the growing degradation of basic human values. Values such as family ties, respect for the elders, search for the transcendent, well-being of those under one's rule or care, honesty, peace and harmony are becoming rare. No doubt, this moral degradation is assuming global dimensions and this situation could be described as the result of the economic and technological globalization process. But then it only indicates the new urgency of an "enreligionization" process where all religions must collaborate to nurture these basic human values.

Eschatology and Mission in Creative Tension

From this Indian scenario, I found Bosch's concept of eschatology and the mission of the church of particular interest and extremely refreshing. Bosch concludes the section, Elements of an Emerging Ecumenical Missionary Paradigm, the most important section of the book, as far as the present mission is concerned, with the subsection, Eschatology and Mission in Creative Tension.

Bosch inherited his interest in eschatology from Oscar Cullmann, his doctoral guide. However, here Bosch has overcome his initial negative attitude to eschatology and places it in the right perspective. We cannot be fixated either on the parousia or on history. An exclusive emphasis on the parousia neglects the problems of this world, while a sheer historical approach robs us of the teleological dimension of mission (Bosch 1991a:508). Christian hope comes from what we have already experienced. Salvation history unfolds itself in secular history. We have to see the hand of God in secular history. The world is no longer a hindrance but a challenge. Christ's death is a victory over all sorts of evil and gives us hope for the wholesale transformation of the status quo. We can no longer neglect our responsibility for involvement in a world en route to its fulfillment. Christians are to become a ferment of God's new world. On the other hand, we must always bear in mind that our blueprint for societal and political order can never match the will and rule of God. The ultimate triumph remains uniquely God's gift. It is God who makes all things new (Rv 21:5). Hence Bosch describes mission as "action in hope" (510).

Eschatology Experienced in the Historical

Bosch's firm conviction of the indissoluble unity of world history and salvation history makes him approach other cultures and religions with a positive view and take history seriously. The God of the Bible does not act on a purely "spiritual" plane, nor is eschatology a totally new creative irruption, but both are intimately related to history. Incarnation is God's "yes" to history. True, it is also God's "no" to history, in so far as history has veered off from the divine will.

What has taken place in the ministry of Jesus is the motive for mission in the church. It is not a blind looking ahead for the sudden irruption of a blessed heaven as a "deus ex machina," but something that already took place in Jesus Christ, which the community of the disciples is sent to continue. "In Christ the forces of the coming age have flowed into the present," stresses Bosch

(1980a:236). Christianity is to proclaim not a metaphysical and noetical Christ, but the Christ who, through his death and resurrection, won victory over death and all sorts of evil, who through his ministry restored human dignity to all those who were dehumanized in any way by the society of his time.

Mission today is God's involvement in world history. God, out of his love, brings God's shalom, peace, well-being, justice, reconciliation and communion in his son Jesus Christ. Jesus is God's involvement with the world. Quoting Cullmann, Bosch stresses that the "already outweighs the not yet" (1991a:509).

As Kevin Livingston has pointed out, this relation between eschatology and mission is an important dimension of Bosch's missiology (Livingston 1990:3–19). I believe this is the key to mission in India today. We have to reflect in humility God's dealings with the world as manifested in his Christ and we have to situate our Christian call within this mission. In Christ we see how God is concerned about the whole of humankind and every dimension of human existence. With the ecclesiasticization and spiritualization of salvation, mission in the past was heavily eschatological (Bosch 1991a:394–95). The missionary labored for a vertical salvation totally coming from outside, from God. The missionary's involvement with history was external to the missionary agenda proper.

Other Religions on the Eschatological Horizon

India is the home of many religions, either giving birth to them or giving place to them in the Indian soil. All these religions are very much alive and active here. They offer spiritual solace to the vast multitude of the people in the subcontinent. Most of these religions existed here even before the birth of Christianity. On the other hand, even after the coming of Christianity and after 2,000 years of missionizing, the religious map of India has not changed substantially. Less than 3 percent of Indians find their salvation through the Christian faith alone.

This invites us to ask what the role of Christianity is in Asia. Obviously this is different from asking what the role of other religions is in the world, which would be a Christianity-centered approach. In other words, we are not trying to find a justification for awarding some sort of legitimacy to other religions. Our living experience itself is the legitimacy for them. In the religious experience (i.e., the God-experience) normally speaking we do not come across any substantial difference between Christians and the followers of other religions. The difference lies in the fact that for Christianity the God-experience is to flow into the experience of the neighbor. For Christianity, service to the neighbor is as important as worshiping God (Mt 22:36ff). In fact the very criterion for the eschaton is this service to the neighbor (Mt 25:31ff). Even with regard to service, some would say that under the influence of the Christian West, Hinduism and other major religions are going through a change. Today one comes across numerous mission hospitals, charitable homes, orphanages, etc., managed by other religious organizations.

Hence we have to ask what it means to be a Christian among followers of other religions. Naturally we have to return to the Bible, to the gospels in particular, to find an answer.

In the gospels we see Jesus manifesting God's love to the whole world. The very fact of his coming is described in terms of God's love for the world (Jn 3:16). Everything he did and said had to do with this love. He feeds the hungry, heals the sick, restores the handicapped to wholeness, as the manifestation of divine compassion. At times he does these despite the sacrosanct Sabbath laws. Human beings are more important than the Sabbath restrictions because humans are the beloved of God. In fact a major reason for Jesus being put to death was his breaking the Sabbath restrictions (Mk 3:6). It could be said that he was the manifestation of the face of God. God is Christlike: this is what we learn from the life and ministry of Jesus. "He who has seen me has seen the Father" (Jn 14:9).

On the other hand, Jesus never degraded religion or spoke against it as such, though he did degrade the hypocritical religious leaders and their hollow religious practices (Mt 23:1ff). Jesus, in fact, was a perfect Jew: he lived as a Jew and died as a Jew.

Similarly, we do not come across anything in the ministry of Jesus that is contrary to the realism that prevails in the Old Testament. In the Old Testament, God is the Creator of all who has entered into a covenant with all humanity (Gn 6:18; 9:11–17). God is the Lord of all human history, not only of one particular people or one particular aspect of human history (Am 9:4ff; Eccl 1:10; Ps 32:5). The Wisdom literature celebrates the presence of the Lord in human beings as Wisdom, leading and guiding them (Wis 2:23; Sir 17:3,8,19). In the New Testament, Wisdom is identified as the Logos that creates and enlightens every human being coming into the world (Jn 1:1ff).

Hence Christianity cannot be seen as a cause of depreciation of other religions or meant to swallow other religions. Rather we should be more alert to God's plan of salvation, a plan operative in all nations since creation. We have to fall in line with this plan without diluting the Christian mission of witnessing to God's love manifested in Jesus Christ.

It could be said that every religion has a core experience. The core experience of Christianity is the God-experience of Jesus Christ as the "Abba." All Christian practice must be an expression of this experience of God as the intimate "abba" of all. Jesus' mission was nothing but a making explicit of this God-experience.

The vertical relationship with God as the "abba" has its parallel horizontal implication in the radical love extended to the neighbor, to the extent of forgiving one's enemies, praying for those who persecute, and laying down one's life for one's neighbor (Mt 5:43ff; Jn 10:15). The major contribution that Christianity can and must make is to manifest the experience of this twofold relationship: of God as the intimate "abba" and others as brothers and sisters. This is to be expressed through service. Hence Jesus presents his whole life as a service and left service as the distinguishing characteristic of his disciples (Jn 13:14). Interestingly, Christianity is welcomed and accepted in India precisely for its spirit of service.

This spirit of service has nothing to do with unilateral claims of superiority and uniqueness. In the midst of religious pluralism, Christian uniqueness is not a question of metaphysical claims but a matter of the quality of life that Christianity engenders in the followers of Jesus Christ through his Spirit. This in turn must attract more to join the community of the disciples of Jesus.

As David Bosch has written in another context, Christian uniqueness is not a beauty contest (1992:577–96). We are the followers of the one who could not (did not) prove his power by saving himself from the cross. Christian uniqueness is this weakness and this vulnerability. "The cross confronts us not with the power of God, but with God's weakness. A cross-symbol, above all, of shame and humiliation — cannot feature in a divine beauty contest: who would ever think of suggesting a cross as sign of beauty and strength?" (1992:583).

Instead of brandishing the cross as a sign of might and superiority, it has to become the true sign of the Christian today: a sign of weakness and helplessness of unarmed truth. St. Paul expressed this with the phrase, "self-emptying" (Phil 2:7). If Christ did not save himself, nor are we Christians called upon to save him. We are called to be his faithful disciples. That is the mission that the church can render to India.

In the face of communalism and inter-religious violence rocking the nation, Christianity must become an agent of healing and reconciliation through its characteristic spirit of love and service. Christianity is basically not a confessional communion, but a community of relationship based on the "abba" experience. This relationship is foundational to the community of the disciples, the church, not credal formulas and ritual practices.

This tendency to relationship invites the church in India to enter into dialogue with the followers of other religions, taking them as equals. This dialogue is not aimed at convincing anyone of Christianity's superiority or saving Jesus Christ, but for building up communion with those in whom the Spirit of God is present. Thus we work for the realization of that communion. In this dialogue we naturally make Christ known, since we are entering into dialogue as the disciples of the one who built communion and prayed for it (Jn 17:21).

Right from the beginning of human history, humanity has searched for God. But what is new in the Bible and in the life and ministry of Jesus is the divine search for humans. Jesus went to the extent of relativizing God to the realization of the full humanity of humans. This is especially seen in Jesus' interpretation of the Sabbath laws. For Jesus, faith has more to do with life with one's neighbor than with worshiping God with elaborate rites or developing refined doctrines.

Naturally we will try to ensure that this communion we seek to achieve through interreligious dialogue reflects the qualities of the eschatological communion that has been inaugurated in Jesus Christ. Thus it is rooted in the faith in the One God, the Father/Mother of all, and it will try to get rid of all discrimination, exploitation and injustice.

It is not within our mission to make a neat theological accounting or explanation for other religions, placing them in what we think is the hierarchy of God's priorities. We are not called to canonize all religions or condemn any. That is God's own work, which we will experience only on the last day. If we could explain everything about other religions and their salvific possibilities, then the divine role becomes superfluous. The God of the Bible is a God of surprises. Though God is the Creator of all and the Lord of History, he sends his Christ to manifest his compassion and draw all to himself, even by laying down his life for others. The church is called to continue that service.

The Socio-Economic Context and Eschatology

There has been a feeling in some quarters that the church in India has failed in its mission, since it has not made much headway among the Indians. I would say that if we speak of the "failure" of Christianity in India, it should not be because of the small percentage of Christians in India but because the church has often failed to make the love of God manifested in Jesus Christ present through the life of the community. For instance, in so far as the church in India is a victim of the pernicious caste practice, it is failing to manifest God as the "Abba" of all and failing to project that communion to which we journey together.

The vast majority of Indians continue to eke out a life that is inconsistent with human dignity. Asian bishops have described the poor as "the people who have been robbed of the opportunity of sharing in materials and resources by unjust social, political and economic structures" (Resales and Arevalo 1992:15).

Today we see a strong awakening of the little ones in India. They are becoming conscious of their God-given possibilities and of the powers and forces blocking the way to the realization of these possibilities. This awareness of the poor has given rise to many forms of theologies, the most important of which is Dalit theology, to which Bosch understandably has not made a reference.

Dalit is the name adopted by the so-called outcasts of caste-ridden Indian society. The term "dalit" is derived from the Sanskrit root "dal" which means to crack, to split, to destroy. Thus Dalit, used as an adjective or noun, means the oppressed or broken ones. Their situation is one of being "no-people." The term Dalit is also an expression of their hope of recovering their past identity. Dalit refers to the state of a section of people, to which they have been reduced. And now they are living in that predicament.

Dalit theology is born out of the suffering of the oppressed. It expresses the shared longing and efforts of the Dalits to abolish their existing unjust situation caused by caste hegemony, the most detestable form of dehumanization inflicted in the name of falsely assumed ritual purity and pollution. It divided the society into the powerful — the elite and the privileged — and the powerless — who are reduced to slavery. Dalit theology springs from the experience of the oppressed peoples' struggle for recovering human dignity and self-expression. There is a growing awareness among the Dalits of their "disinheritedness" and uprootedness and of the domination of the brahminical (priestly) caste. Dalit theology operates through the process of conscientization for organization of the voiceless.

Almost 16 percent of the Indian population are Dalits, and they constitute 60–70 percent of all Indian Christians. Yet they do not share even 10 percent of the ministerial role in the church. That alone can show how they are discriminated against, even within the church. In the church as well as in society at large, their situation is marked by alienation inflicted upon them on the grounds of the religious tenets of Hinduism. They experience various forms of economic exploitation as a result of this social marginalization. The feeling of shame resulting from the age-old treatment they have gone through hampers their feelings of personal dignity and honor.

General Christian theology is not very relevant for the Dalits; it has little impact on their living condition. In this sense, Dalit theology is a counter theology and theology of struggle. It is praxis oriented, seeking to alter the existing state of affairs. It is directed not so much to conversion to the church but to a conversion that effects a change in the human condition of society as well as that of the church. The Dalits are a third world in the Third World, and hence a Dalit theology will make a significant contribution to the theology of the Third World. From the reality of the hierarchical structure of Indian society and the woes suffered by the Dalits, it is to be admitted that the development of a praxis-centered Dalit theology can ring in the divine reign more than any other aspect of the mission of the church. Only a radical transformation in their socio-economic reality can enable the Dalits to believe that God "has seen their affliction and heard their cry" (Ex 3:7).

From what has been said, it should not be construed that the poor of India are constituted only of Dalits. Another section of the Indian population whose lot is similar to that of the Dalits is the tribal people. While the Dalits are part of the Hindu social hierarchy, the tribal people are not, since they are not Hindus. Yet their social fate is that of the Dalits, and in fact sometimes the term Dalit includes the tribal people, who form nearly 8 percent of the population of India.

There are many more belonging to other social groups who are also poor. If the psalmist asked the Lord, "How can I sing your praises in the foreign land?" (Ps 137:4), today the poor of India ask: "How can we sing your praises in a state of oppression and alienation?" Our mission must enable them to experience the arrival of the Kingdom in Jesus, even as the poor of Jesus' time experienced it through his ministry (Mt 11:4ff). Only then can they look forward to the New Heaven and the New Earth (Rv 21:1ff).

As a consequence, the church will be more preoccupied with the problems of the world — particularly of the little ones of this world, including women, who are socially marginalized, and children denied their right to childhood — than with its own institutional setup. It will rise to all occasions where it is called to raise its voice against injustice and dehumanization, even if by doing that its own institutional setup is threatened. It will not shy away from political pressure in so far as such political pressure can bring about social transformation. The church can become an unrest-creating and disturbing presence where social evils such as self-seeking, exploitation, oppression, discrimination, marginalization, child labor, and bounded labor abound.

Certainly the church's mission is not confined to an earth-bound salvation. Rather the salvation it witnesses to through the transformation of this world is the New Creation (Rv 21:1ff). This type of eschatology-oriented mission is a demand on the entire Christian community, not the business of a few select members categorized as missionaries. Mission becomes the very life-style of the community rather than the charism of a few.

Indian Cultures in the Light of Eschatology

The whole point of this renewed emphasis on the anticipation of eschatology in mission is that such a mission takes this world and its cultures seriously. Such a mission will not identify itself with any particular culture. Until recently, we went wrong in identifying Christianity with the Western cultures. Coinciding with colonial expansion, mission naturally paid scant attention to the local culture or local religions. True, in India and China farsighted missionaries like De Nobili and Ricci tried some sort of accommodation, but the spirit of the times overpowered their vision.

To begin with, we have to emphasize that the word "culture" can mean different things to different people. It is no longer understood as the refined behavior patterns of society. Today it includes the worldview of any particular group, with its expression in lifestyle, language, and ways of relating to others. It is the way of life of a people, including the way they die! That is to say, culture comprises the hopes, aspirations, problems and agonies of a people.

Accordingly, the understanding of inculturation has widened. It is no longer a process of the articulation of the faith in and through the forms and categories of a people, but also the way that people understand and interpret faith from their context. It refers to the gospel's entry into "every sector of the life of the people of a given era as well as its ability to receive all that is of genuine human value in a particular context" (John 1993:261).

Hence inculturation has to do not only with religion and expressions of religious symbols but also with the social process and the concerns and struggles of a people. This becomes ever more vital when mission is perceived as anticipating the "new creation." Over the past 2,000 years in India, how far has the Christian presence changed the quality of life of people, especially of the poor? It has been admitted by leaders like Gandhi that Christianity has been instrumental in reforming Hinduism from within (Shourie 1994: 4–5). But has Christianity improved the standard of living for the poor? Inculturation is a process of humanizing the life of all people in the light of the new heaven and the new earth.

In this respect, not much has happened. The caste system and other evils of Indian society thrive among the Christians, too. The class system goes unchallenged among the community of the disciples. The Christian community often leads a life unaffected by the concerns of the social mainstream. We have little to say on national issues. We are more concerned with the safety of our own minority institutions and our survival as a privileged minority. In one sense, an urgent demand of inculturation would be getting rid of an exaggerated "minority" complex. We are called to be salt, leaven and light. These are expendable symbols to permeate the rest.

Accustomed to the colonialistic period, the church in India, even after independence, prefers to keep an alienated identity. The tradition of keeping aloof from the mainstream culture with a falsely assumed superiority complex makes it difficult for the Christian community to enter the national mainstream and the culture. Many see inculturation as a step backward in the sense of returning to the "pagan" cultural practices they had given up long ago. On the other hand, the same Christian community zealously guards the dehumanizing elements of the same "pagan" culture, such as the caste system.

The Christian community must go through the paschal mystery. We have to die to the death-inflicting and dehumanizing practices of our culture and at the same time rise to a new life by accepting all the genuine human values of our culture. Further, we must respond to the Indian reality creatively and responsibly. The Indian church has to decipher the mystery of Christ in the poor. This conversion to the poor and this option for the poor are integral parts of inculturation in India, just as interreligious dialogue is integral to inculturation.

The Church and the Not Yet

What has been said may give the impression that the mission of anticipating eschatology into history has no concern for church expansion. This cannot be, for two reasons. First, there has to be a community. The divine plan manifested in Jesus (Eph 3:3) demands the existence of a specific community. Immediately after announcing the arrival of the Kingdom, Jesus constitutes a community to which he entrusts his mission (Mk 1:14ff). The calling and the sending of the twelve are luminous signs that the reign of God presumes an actual people, in and through whom the Kingdom can be realized. The coming of the Kingdom in Jesus Christ and the eschatological new creation are proleptically presented in the community.

This community is to continue his ministry after the Easter experience. Through his death and resurrection, Jesus is established the Lord of all creation (Mt 28:18) and the source of the Spirit (Jn 20:22). Hence the post-Easter apparitions are accompanied by the mission mandate.

This community is called to render visibility to the Kingdom, even as Jesus himself was the Kingdom. In Jesus, people could experience the presence of the Kingdom (Mt 11:4ff). Similarly, today the community of the disciples must make present now that which will be perfectly realized at the end, "when all things are subjected to the Son, then the Son himself will also be subjected to him who put all things under him, that God may be everything to every one" (1 Cor 15:28).

In this the church's identity is not primarily that of possessing something like salvation or revelation, but one of service, i.e., making present the reality of the divine reign, divine compassion. By rendering visibility to this love, the church invites all to take note of this love and respond to it. This the church does as the first fruit of the things to come (Rom 8:23; 11:16). Hence the church's mission is not so much proclaiming, "come to us" as "let us follow him!" (Bosch 1991a:376). People can be part of the divine reign without becoming part of the church. Yet in so far as Jesus Christ instituted the church and bequeathed his mission to it, it is the efficacious sign willed by God of the presence in the world and in history of the reality of the reign of God. Hence the church has to be there as the servant of the Kingdom. This implies that mission must give rise to local communities of faith to serve as the servants of the divine reign to the particular context.

Conclusion

The church's mission has its origin in what God did in Jesus Christ, which will be fully realized at the parousia. The church, through its ministry, makes present in history (though imperfectly) what happened in Jesus Christ and anticipates the end times. In the Indian context of the dehumanizing poverty of the masses of people who at the same time are also religious with a culture of their own, mission is the actualization of the creative tension between eschatology and history. Eschatology determines the horizon of Christian mission, even if we are groping to it in hope. Hence neither the eschatologization nor the historization of mission can alone be valid. It is both future-directed and oriented to the here and now.

In this understanding of mission, "a Christian is not simply somebody who stands a better chance of being saved, but a person who accepts the responsibility to serve God in this life and promotes God's reign in all its forms" (Bosch 1991a:488), following the basic paradigm of God's love and mercy revealed in Jesus Christ. This a Christian does by maintaining good conduct among all peoples so that they may see the good deeds of the Christian and thereby God may be glorified on the "day of visitation" (1 Pt 2:12).

7

THE MISSION DYNAMIC

Wilbert R. Shenk

The New Testament defines the *raison d'être* of the church to be missionary witness to the world, thus at one stroke sharply focusing its purpose while subsuming other functions under mission.[1] Accordingly, both Christian witness and discipleship are worked out in scripture in light of that primal tension which marks the relationship between the people of God and the world which does not acknowledge God's sovereignty, with a view to elucidating the church's calling to be the agent of reconciliation between the world and its Creator (2 Cor 5:16–20).

This is not, of course, the impression one gets from a perusal of a vast array of works which fill theological libraries. Ecclesiology, for example, rarely engages the question of mission, and theologians typically conceive of their task as essentially an exercise in responding to intellectual questions that the culture addresses to the Christian faith or as engaging in intramural debate.[2] This shift from the kind of theology found in the New Testament to that produced out of the Western intellectual and ecclesiastical tradition has resulted in theology devoid of mission.

David J. Bosch, in whose honor this essay is offered, was greatly concerned about theology sans mission. Bosch (1980a:21–27; 1982d; 1983a:490f; 1991a) argued repeatedly and persuasively that the church's approach to theology, especially after the fourth century, had lost sight of the fact that "mission is the

---

Wilbert R. Shenk is professor of missiology at Fuller Seminary School of World Mission and active in the International Missiology of Western Culture Project, as well as past president of the American Society of Missiology.

1. Minear (1960) demonstrated the rich imagery New Testament writers use to describe the nature and mission of the church. Certain key texts do establish the purpose of the church. Matthew 10 sets the basic paradigm for the disciple community (cf. Ridderbos 1962:37). The mandate given by the Messiah following the resurrection (Mt 28:18–20) connects the purpose of the disciple community to the pattern already established and makes it normative (cf. Bosch 1991a:73–83). Ephesians 3:10 emphasizes the *public* and *proclamatory* role the church is to play. First Peter 2:9 casts the purpose of the church in terms of its responsibility to "proclaim the mighty acts of him who called you out of darkness into his marvelous light," in support of which the church should be a set-apart, holy people.

2. F. D. E. Schleiermacher is usually credited with introducing mission to the modern theological curriculum, including it under practical theology, a precedent that continued until well into the twentieth century. Conceptually, that mode of thinking, the legacy of fifteen centuries of Christendom, remains influential to this day.

mother of theology."[3] When theology becomes disconnected from its origin, it is no longer nurtured by its true source. Such theology either will succumb to traditionalism and self-preservation or drift on cultural and historical currents. The evangelical vitality of theology will be in direct proportion to the degree to which it engages the life-purpose of the church.

This essay interprets mission in terms of its constitutive dynamic in order to demonstrate that the *missio Dei* is essential to the integrity of theology. This mission dynamic will be described as consisting of five interacting elements: reign of God, Jesus the Messiah, Holy Spirit, church, and eschaton. For our purposes here we will consider each in turn; but, in fact, they are interdependent.

The Reign of God

Missio Dei

The reign of God, thrust into the center of history in the Christ-event, is the horizon of salvation within which the *missio Dei* is being fulfilled.[4] *Basileia* originates with God and expresses God's will and purpose. The redemptive power of God is now being guided by a particular strategy in order to bring the divine purpose to completion by delivering the creation from the powers of decay and death.

Something extraordinary has been set in motion: instead of *futurum,* a prolongation of the old, it is *adventus,* a new beginning. The reign of God will be realized through the inauguration of a new order — characterized by justice/righteousness, peace and life — which ultimately will supplant the old order, the reign of death. God wills that life, not death, have the last word.

Interpretations

In view of the fundamental importance of the reign of God for Christian faith and existence, it might be assumed that the church has kept it at the center of its life and teaching from the beginning. But following Jesus' earthly ministry various interpretations of the rule of God emerged. There were four main views: a) the eschatological, which emphasized the futurist aspect; b) the spiritual-mystical, which focused on the immortality of the soul and the immaterial; c) the political, in which an earthly empire is identified with the

---

3. See Bosch (1972b) for a study of the German systematic theologian, Martin Kähler, who regarded mission as indispensable to proper theological thinking.

4. Here we assume as background such studies as Bright (1953), Küng (1967), Ladd (1964), Moltmann (1967), Perrin (1963), Ridderbos (1962), and Schnackenburg (1963). More recent surveys include Viviano (1988) and Willis (1987). These studies divide into two groups: those which closely link or interpret the meaning of *basileia* in relation to the *missio Dei* and those which do not. For example, Bright, Ridderbos, Moltmann, and Küng do this effectively. In Viviano's survey of scholarship over the past two millennia, the basileia-mission nexus hardly figures. For a Christocentric and missionary interpretation of the meaning of history, see Berkhof (1964). For an innovative approach to systematic theology that starts with the rule of God, see McClendon (1994, part 1).

kingdom of God; and d) the ecclesial, which merges church and kingdom (Viviano 1988:Chapt. 2; cf. Driver 1993:83–85). Each has exerted great influence in the life of the church, but all are reductionisms that have contributed to the obscuring of the full meaning of the reign of God.

In the face of this partial eclipse of the messianic reality and against a background of hopelessness, oppression and suffering throughout history, there have been periodic resurgences which have reawakened hope by pointing to the promise of the reign of God (Oosterwal 1973; Desroche 1979). One may mention, for example, the Blumhardts in nineteenth-century Germany and their remarkably creative and multi-dimensional influence which was grounded in a renewed emphasis on *basileia*. A full-orbed understanding of mission can only be secured by embracing this "basileic" vision of the mission of God.

Impact

Because the coming of God's reign disturbs the status quo, it sets off two reactions. First, by exposing the basic egocentric structure of human nature and behavior, it is perceived to be a *skandalon*. This, in turn, produces *krisis*, the moment of truth which calls for decision in light of the new possibility: "*Repent!* Turn toward God and be incorporated into the new order." This is both invitation and warning. Those who refuse God's gracious offer will remain in the grips of the old order and its destiny. *Basileia* challenges human motivation and character at the deepest levels by unmasking the nature of power that is unsubmitted to the will of God.

The reign of God is a mystery which we never fully grasp. Although the whole of Jesus' words and acts were a running commentary on the reign of God, at no point did he offer a considered definition. Instead he spoke in parables and performed deeds that brought God's saving power into the lives of people. Nonetheless, few caught its larger meaning. Even the disciples who formed Jesus' inner circle did not discern what it was about until after his resurrection and ascension (e.g., Lk 24:25–27, 44–49; Acts 1:3). In the end, the kingdom could be apprehended only through eyes of faith. It is not subject to human control, nor can it be manipulated for selfish ends.

Basileia, the reign of God, is the essence of the *missio Dei*. The gospel is rightly termed the good news of the kingdom. This is the animating center of mission and theology: God as *agape* coming to the world for the world's salvation through the reign of righteousness.[5] Its meaning must be further elaborated in terms of Jesus the Messiah who, as servant of the *basileia*, pioneered the way and demonstrated its meaning (Heb 12:2), the Holy Spirit that guarantees the realization of the *basileia* (Eph 1:13f), and the church which in this interim age lives out God's rule and bears witness to it in light of the eschaton.

---

5. The one substantial attempt to develop a theology of mission from this viewpoint is that of Georg F. Vicedom (1965), which grew out of the discussions in the International Missionary Council in the early 1950s. Those discussions were upstaged and derailed by "secular" and "death of God" theologies in the 1960s.

Jesus the Messiah

"Messiah" becomes the root metaphor for the new order because it is actualized through Messiah (see Shank 1993). The new is signaled in various ways. Most importantly, God is disclosed to be drawing near and entering redemptively into the human situation. In contrast to the traditional Hebrew reluctance even to utter the name of Yahweh, Jesus is acclaimed as "Emmanuel," God taking on human form and embracing the human situation in the incarnation.

Messiah's Mission

All three synoptic gospels link Jesus' baptism, attestation by the Holy Spirit of his messianic authority, the testing of Jesus in the wilderness, and the start of his public ministry. Jesus began his public ministry with the declaration that God's *basileia* was now breaking forth (Mt 4:17; Mk 1:15). The evident authority that marked his ministry and so impressed his audiences (Mt 7:29) arose from the fact that Jesus identified fully with *basileia* in his person, message and works (Mt 6:10, 26:39; cf. Heb 10:7,9, quoting Ps 40:6−8). Although *basileia* is scarcely mentioned in John's gospel, a motif running through the gospel — which is fully consistent with it — is Jesus' consciousness of being sent by God to carry out God's will so that the world might be redeemed (e.g., Jn 3:16f, 30; 17:3, 1, 21, 23, 25) (Comblin 1979:Chapt. 1).

The parallel passage in Luke (4:16−22) emphasizes both that Jesus stands in the great prophetic line ("there was given to him the book of the prophet Isaiah ... 'Today this Scripture has been fulfilled in your hearing'") and is doing what has not been done before ("proclaiming the acceptable year of the Lord"). This announcement is the hinge linking two aeons. It signaled that the central prophetic promise to the people of Israel (e.g., Is 61) was now being fulfilled.

Thus the lines of engagement are drawn. The reign of God being manifested in Jesus the Messiah fundamentally contradicts the kingdom of the world. The forces of Antichrist are prodded to action. The axial principle of God's rule runs counter to that of the world. The mission of Jesus the Messiah is to liberate from the kingdom of death. As we follow the public ministry of Jesus, we come upon a series of scenes in which this confrontation is played out as physical, psychological, social and spiritual forces under the sway of the old order resist and refuse to acknowledge God's reign now made manifest in the Messiah (e.g., Mt 8−10:1, 5−42). What is of particular import is the way in which Jesus met this challenge.

Two Kinds of Power

In Jesus the meaning of redemptive power is redefined. The old order is governed by the myth of redemptive violence and, in fact, is being consumed in the endless spiral of violence (Wink 1993:13−17). Every attempt to end violence with violence sows the seeds of further conflict. The power of destruction and death that controls the old order operates at both personal and collective levels (Rom 5:8−14). It is the mission of the Messiah to intervene personally in this reality and break the destructive cycle.

As David Bosch (1991a:108–13) has pointed out, at the start of his public ministry Jesus renounced vengeance as the basis of his messiahship (Lk 4:16–20). Instead, Jesus instituted the new messianic order founded on redemptive *agape* as the direct answer to the spiral of violence. Against the age-old pattern of settling accounts by vanquishing the enemy through multiple forms of "ethnic cleansing," God through Jesus the Messiah made peace by "breaking down the dividing wall of hostility" and creating "one new man in place of the two" (Eph 2:14b–15). The scope of God's saving purpose cannot be reduced to the personal only. Rather the personal and the social are intermeshed. Reconciliation between erstwhile enemies is effected only through combined personal and social transformation.

Suffering Servant

By the time of Jesus, the *ebed* (servant) spoken of in Isaiah (42, 49, 50, 52, 53) was interpreted as referring either to the coming Messiah or to Israel itself. References to *ebed*'s suffering and humiliation had been expunged from the official interpretation (Shank 1993:59f). According to the accepted line, if *ebed* were indeed the Messiah, the anointed one destined to "bring forth justice to the nations" (Is 42:1), he would be a leader who, through superior political and military power, would vanquish all Israel's enemies. Messiahship was thus cast in conventional political terms and tied to Israel's own fortunes.

Jesus confuted this traditional understanding at two fundamental points (Cullmann 1963:55). In the first place, he restored the meaning of the covenant God made with Israel. God's covenant with Abraham and his descendants was predicated on the calling out of this people that they might become the means of blessing all peoples (Gn 12:1–3). Jesus' contemporaries had turned the meaning of covenant inward. They expected the messianic age would bring blessing to Israel.

The second reversal in understanding had to do with the role of opposition and suffering (Shank 1993:60; cf. Cullmann 1963). At every step, Jesus encountered opposition from the religio-political leadership because his message seemed to undermine their power. His message included strong words that judged them and their abuse of power. The message of Jesus concerning God's new order exposed the sin, corruption, injustice/unrighteousness and false worship that characterized the religio-political institutions and, in the end, these forces combined to put him to death. He called individuals from all classes and clans to repent and submit their lives to God's rule.

From the moment of Jesus' baptism, when God's Spirit came on him in anointing power, he assumed his role as *ebed* of God chosen to bring God's shalom without resort to violence or deceit (Is 53:9). As his ministry unfolds, Jesus appeals to this servanthood as validation for what he is doing (e.g., Mk 10:45). It is a servanthood that leads to his death on behalf of the "ungodly" (Rom 5:6). Instead of the traditional Christendom interpretation of divine power as the power of the *imperium,* the Messiah of God is the crucified God whose sacrifice opens the way to life lived by resurrection power (Moltmann 1974:190f; Koyama 1984:Chapt. 20).

All three of the great Christological passages in the Pauline writings refer to the vicarious redemptive suffering of the Servant (Rom 5:12–14; 1 Cor 15:3; Phil 2:7), thereby emphasizing that God's reign is founded on *agape* that accepts and salvifically absorbs the suffering perpetrated by the powers of the present age. Violence can only be transformed by redemptive love. The death and resurrection of Jesus the Messiah is God's final reply to the power of death and the old order. The empty cross signifies the vindication of God's Suffering Servant.

The Holy Spirit

The Genesis account of creation notes that "the Spirit of God [or NRSV, wind] was moving over the face of the waters" (Gn 1:2b) as God began creating an ordered universe out of chaos. At the beginning of the mission of the Messiah, John the Baptist declared, "I saw the Spirit descending from heaven like a dove, and it remained on him" (Jn 1:32). In creation and new creation, God the Spirit is the agent.

Pentecost

The parting words of Jesus to his disciples was the promise that the Spirit would come to them and that coming was linked directly to the continuation of the messianic mission (Lk 24:45f; Acts 1:8). At Pentecost the disciples experienced what they believed to be the fulfillment of the prophet Joel's prophecy. The Holy Spirit was made manifest to them as wind, fire, and prophetic speech (Acts 2). Wind (Hebrew: *ruach*), or breath, signifies life. The Spirit is God's breath or life. A special dignity was conferred on humankind at creation when God breathed into Adam "the breath of life." The Hebrew scriptures described the Messiah as the one in whom God's *ruach* would be fully present, infused with God's life, anointed by the Spirit.

Scripture also speaks of the Spirit as fire which judges (Mt 3:11), purifies, and blends together disparate parts. At Pentecost the disciples were being tested and prepared for the rigors of witness. To do this they needed to be forged into a unity.

At Pentecost the Holy Spirit demonstrated the new *koinonia* God was creating. Because of their rebellion at Babel, humankind was sentenced to live out the consequences of the "confusion of languages." At Pentecost the Holy Spirit reversed Babel. A new people, drawn from the nations, whose linguistic particularity is the means for each to hear of "the mighty acts of God" (Acts 2:6, 11), is called forth. Their unity is expressed neither through culture nor ritual but in worship of the God revealed in Jesus the Messiah (Acts 2:14–36).

The Holy Spirit and Messianic Mission

As the mission of Jesus the Messiah unfolds, the Holy Spirit is shown to be the leader: at the conception (Mt 1:18; Lk 1:35), Simeon's revelation (Lk 2:25–35), Jesus' baptism (Mt 3:16; Mk 1:10; Lk 3:22) and temptation (Mt 4:1; Mk 1:12; Lk 4:1), inauguration of ministry (Lk 4:18), inspirer and guide of Jesus (Lk 10:21, 12:10; Jn 3:34), the one who enabled Jesus to bring his sacrifice

(Heb 9:14), the power by which Jesus was resurrected from the dead (Rom 1:4; 1 Tm 3:16), and the one who accompanies Jesus' disciples in the continuing mission (Lk 24:49; Jn 20:21–23; Acts 13:1–3). (See McClendon 1994:Chapt.4.) At times the Spirit precedes Jesus, while at other times the Spirit follows. Often the work of Jesus and that of the Spirit so intertwine that it is not easy to distinguish the one from the other. Always the relationship is one of mutual support in pursuit of a single purpose: realization of the *basileia*.

Although many volumes of so-called mission theology have been written with little or no attention being paid to the Holy Spirit (Kuitse 1993:106–10), the New Testament gives clear guidance (see Berkhof:Chapt. 2). The *missio Dei* cannot be understood apart from the work of the Holy Spirit. Jesus warned the disciples against attempting to engage in mission without the Holy Spirit ("but stay in the city, until..." [Lk 24:49]; "charged them not to depart from Jerusalem, but to wait..." [Acts 1:8]) for the Holy Spirit, who is the Spirit of Jesus the Messiah, is leader in mission, equipping and empowering for the arduous task of bearing witness in the world where there will assuredly be opposition and persecution (Mt 28:20; 2 Cor 4:7–10). "The Anointed One becomes the Anointing One" (Kuitse 1993:112) as the Spirit of Jesus the Messiah endows the disciple community with the spiritual gifts needed for witness in the world.

The Two Poles

In these last days the Holy Spirit holds together the two poles of God's saving action: the christological and the eschatological. During this interim the Spirit is "the expansion of the divine saving presence over the earth" (Berkhof 1964:35). The covenant made with Abraham established a pattern by which the divine blessing will be carried to the nations. From the Faithful One, the Suffering Servant, through the Faithful Community, the Spirit leads in continual witness to the world of God's salvation until the end of time.

The Church

After nearly two thousand years, people easily forget the formal order of relationship between reign of God, mission and church. We have already noted the four understandings that have shaped the way Christians have thought about the reign of God, each a reductionism that conceals and suppresses vital dimensions. It is hardly surprising that many of the faithful have had neither a vivid sense of the meaning of God's rule for their lives nor for the mission of the church. We must, therefore, reassert both the indispensable role the church was appointed to play in the continuing mission of Jesus Christ in the world and the essentiality of mission to the identity of the church.

From a biblical and theological viewpoint, the church without mission is inconceivable, and yet for Christendom the operative understanding of the nature of the church did not trade on the notion of mission (Neill 1968:71–84). At this point two extremes must be avoided. On the one hand, Christendom held to a view of the church as institution. On the other, we must reject some elements of the instrumental view of the church promoted by the parachurch movement.

Three points must be kept in focus. First, the rule of God is prior to mission. Indeed, mission is the means by which basileia is being realized in the world. In the second place, as a corollary, we note that mission is prior to church (see Berkhof 1964:30–31, 38–39). The church can only be called into being by the preaching of the gospel of the kingdom. Jesus began by proclaiming this gospel and gathering together those who responded. These he taught and then commissioned to continue doing what he was doing. In this age the task of proclaiming the gospel is never finished. Each generation must hear it for themselves. The church becomes something other than a living witness to the gospel when it seeks to preserve the faith through scholasticism or sacerdotalism. Rather, the church lives out of the gospel by proclaiming the gospel. Third, at Pentecost the Holy Spirit equipped the disciple community to continue the mission of Jesus Christ in the world (Kraus 1993:chapt. 4).

Twofold Purpose

The calling of the church is to glorify the Triune God by 1) faithfully witnessing to the reign of God and 2) by living as a sign of that reign. To state it differently, the church has a single purpose which consists of two aspects. These two dimensions cannot be sustained in isolation from each other. They must be held together and allowed to interpenetrate if this purpose is to be realized.

The legacy that Christendom bequeathed to the church was effectively to reduce it to the status of an institution for the care of the faithful (see Troeltsch 1960). When missionary witness is reserved for the few who are sent to faraway places, and when Christian existence is understood mainly as insuring one's own salvation, the ecclesial reality has been distorted and the church trivialized by reason of being disconnected from its *raison d'être*.

The Question of Relevance

When the church lives in conscious response to the reign of God, its life is governed by only one criterion. Indeed, the power of the church's witness depends on the extent to which *basileia* defines and shapes that witness. When the church attempts to make its ministry relevant by rendering *respectable* service, it has adopted another criterion and becomes merely mundane (Yinger 1957:144f). Conventional respectability operates by another calculus than *basileia*. It is geared to maintenance of the cultural status quo. What set the ministry of Jesus apart was that his every action and word pointed to God as source of life. To do this requires breaking free from the power system of the dying world order and embracing the reign of God. The modern problem of "word and deed" would have been entirely foreign to Jesus' way of thinking. His actions and his words were univocal — an integral witness to the transforming love of God.

The missionary relevance of the church to the world must be modeled on that of Jesus the Messiah. Jesus continually raised the most basic questions with his contemporaries: Whom do you serve? What is your purpose and destiny?

Do you live by the power of life or death? His contemporaries did not accuse Jesus of being irrelevant or unrealistic. It was clear that he loved the world more passionately than the self-centered religious and political leaders. His crime was exactly the opposite: he exposed the abuses of power that were destroying life and called people to follow the way of liberation.

Missionary Church

The missionary church witnesses by being a "contrast society" (Lohfink 1984: 157–63) or "microsociety" (Miller 1993:137–45) in which the life-defining features of the larger society are transformed so their destructive power is re-deemed. For example, conventional peoplehood based on blood, soil and culture is transmuted through the regenerating work of the Suffering Servant of God wherein the meaning of blood, soil and culture are restored to what God the Creator intended. Indeed, mission combines two fundamental thrusts — the universal and the particular — in one action. The universal moves to bring all under the sovereignty of God, thereby relativizing all other loyalties and claims. The thrust of particularity moves toward every people and each person, for each bears the *imago Dei;* none is excluded from the reach of God's love, each is invited to be reconciled to God.

In the Sermon on the Mount, Jesus used the metaphors of salt and light to describe the way in which the disciple community should live in the world (Driver 1983:33–36). Several points may be emphasized. First, Jesus' discourse at this point focuses on the importance of the ethical response of the community, for this is what gives concrete expression to the reign of God (cf. Blough 1993). The messianic community's life is shaped by the ethics of the Messiah. The authority of this stance for the early church is reflected in these passages from St. Paul: "When reviled, we bless; when persecuted, we endure; when slandered, we speak kindly" (1 Cor 4:12f). "We are treated as impostors, and yet are true; as unknown, and yet are well known; as dying, and...yet not killed; as sorrowful, yet always rejoicing; as poor, yet making many rich; as having nothing, and yet possessing everything" (2 Cor 6:8–10). The church as the messianic community embodies the message, proclaiming by life its meaning. Its very attitude toward the suffering perpetrated by opposition forces is the result of living in the power of the Holy Spirit in anticipation of God's final triumph at the eschaton.

Second, these metaphors speak to the matter of means and tactics in witness. Both salt and light have a permeative effect, entering into and changing the host environment. Light exposes ruthlessly; it is entirely public. Salt penetrates and acts upon. Third, salt and light become active agents only when they are released into the environment. They then become life-giving. Jesus called the disciples to live out their covenant relationship with God as a missionary community characterized by salt and light as transforming agents.

Eschaton

The New Testament opens with the announcement that in sending the Mes-siah, God's promise to Israel of liberation is being fulfilled. Yet it soon becomes clear that this is a promise in process of being fulfilled. As Jesus comes to the end of his earthly ministry, he hands on responsibility to his disciples to continue this still-incomplete mission (cf. Jn 20:20f). Jesus speaks of this mission of proclaiming the reign of God throughout the world as being directly linked to the "end" (Mt 24:14) or consummation. At the ascension of Jesus, the disciples were assured that he would return again to claim his victory and to be with them (Acts 1:11).

We are thus confronted with what is usually termed "the already/not yet" of the kingdom. From the earliest days of the church it was understood that Jesus had inaugurated the reign of God but it would be fully realized only at "the last day" (Jn 6:39–54) "when all things are subjected to him" and the Messiah himself "will also be subjected to the one who has put all things in subjection under him" (1 Cor 15:28). The reign of God has indeed become present in Jesus the Messiah, and in the power of the Holy Spirit the church has continued Messiah's mission. But this is an interim. The forces of Antichrist have not been completely subdued. The world continues to be under the sway of demonic principalities and powers. Nonetheless, confidence in the final triumph of the Messiah nerves the disciple community to remain faithful in witness.

The New Testament is pervaded by this eschatological tension (Shank 1993: 222–26), a tension linked to messianic mission with its notes of judgment, urgency, hope, deliverance, and salvation. On the one hand, the disciple community already is sustained in the Spirit by the first fruit of God's reign. On the other hand, "the sufferings" only heighten the expectation of the final deliverance of God's people from "this present time" (Rom 8:18). Indeed, there are signs everywhere that the whole creation is filled with this longing for liberation, not only because it promises release from hostile forces and death itself but because of the prospect in Jesus Christ of full knowledge (1 Cor 13:14; cf. Gn 2:16f).

The consummation of Messiah's mission thus is presented in the New Testament as bound up with the missionary mandate Jesus gave to his disciples. The *promissio* of the eschaton is correlated with *missio* and "the Christian consciousness of history is a consciousness of mission" (Moltmann 1967:225). The eschaton represents the goal toward which the reign of God is moving. Mission takes its orientation from that ultimate goal.

Jesus spoke of the consummation of the reign of God in terms of a great messianic banquet — the event which the Jewish people believed would inaugurate Messiah's reign. The metaphor of the messianic banquet is rich in meaning: a time when God's people would enjoy shalom through the direct mediation of the Messiah. Jesus reinterprets this banquet, however, by speaking in universal terms about the inclusion of the Gentiles at the banquet table. The guests at this feast will be those who confess their dependence on God while "workers of iniquity" will be excluded (Mt 8:11f; Lk 13:28f). God has graciously provided the present time so that men and women can prepare to share in that blessed banquet in the presence of Messiah.

Conclusion

The mission of the Triune God is to establish *basileia* over the whole of creation. This is being realized through the *missio Dei.* The character of the *missio Dei* is defined by the ministry of God's Messiah, Jesus the *ebed,* whose servant-hood was empowered by the Holy Spirit. It is by the Spirit that the church is endowed with spiritual gifts and empowered for ministry as the messianic community. The *missio Dei* will be consummated in the eschaton; but in the interim the eschaton infuses the messianic community with hope and power as it continues its witness amid opposition and suffering. The interaction of these elements represents the mission dynamic which, in turn, defines the vocation of the disciples of Jesus Christ in the world.

8

AMERICAN WOMEN AND THE DUTCH REFORMED
MISSIONARY MOVEMENT, 1874–1904

Dana L. Robert

Background

At the Synod of 1857, the Dutch Reformed Church launched a missionary movement from the Cape Colony. A shortage of clergy meant that the DRC at first used missionaries from Europe and then laypeople for its mission work in the Transvaal. In 1886 the first South African clergyman volunteered to become a foreign missionary to Malawi (Nyasaland), his salary paid by private subscription among the Dutch Reformed clergy. With the sending of its first clergyman as a foreign missionary, the South African mission movement came of age. The period from 1857 to 1886 was thus crucial to solidifying mission interest among a hesitant Afrikaner people and shaping the nature of the missionary effort to come. Out of that fledgling Afrikaner missionary initiative has developed a movement of tremendous intellectual and spiritual vitality. David Bosch's *Transforming Mission,* indeed, his entire life and work, epitomize that movement. I offer the essay that follows as a step in the direction of helping understand the role of women in the South African mission context and their background in shaping the context that produced David Bosch.

As Willem Saayman has pointed out, Bosch was strangely silent about the contribution of women to the mission of the church (Saayman 1992: 432). That observation must be balanced against his commitment to solid historical studies, which leads to the conclusion that he was unaware of scholarship on women in mission. Indeed, in Bosch's defense, mission history in general has failed to study women's contributions, or even to acknowledge that women have held and have practiced particular missiologies. This ignorance must be corrected before missiological inquiry can claim to be based on a full understanding of the "tens of thousands who have preceded us."

A month before David Bosch died, he and I sat in the refectory at Yale Divinity School. He had come to talk about *Transforming Mission* with a group

Dana L. Robert is associate professor of international mission in the Boston University School of Theology, where she specializes in courses on mission and the history of mission. Her research revolves around retrieving the record of the role of women in mission. She visited South Africa in 1993 to study the South African sources quoted in this paper. This contribution was originally published in *Missionalia,* 1992.

of mission leaders. I was an official respondent to his presentation. I asked him what he knew about the mission history of women in his own DRC and found that, although he knew almost nothing, he thought it needed study.

By the time I went to the University of South Africa in 1993, tragedy had intervened and David was dead. I came to trace the missiology of "woman's work for woman" across the Atlantic from its American roots to the Afrikaner community of the late nineteenth century. Although David was ignorant of the women who went before him, South African women who, in all probability, shaped the piety and commitment that marked his life, he encouraged the research that I am pleased to contribute to this volume on his work.

It may be helpful to state briefly the point at which my work on women in mission and the present piece intersect with David's work. The chief point of contact lies in the way my analysis of how American women catalyzed a missionary movement among Dutch Reformed women in the late nineteenth century joins his analysis of mission following the European Enlightenment — particularly in regard to "voluntarism" and "missionary fervor, optimism, and pragmatism" (Bosch 1991a: 327ff). The voluntarism and fervor of American women helped create an analogous movement among women in the DRC. Although the spirituality of Afrikaner women has been characterized as inward turning and submissive, even tribalistic, the beginnings of their involvement in mission shows an alternative, more active model. Self-organized, self-funded, self-appointing, and committed to evangelism and education among women and children, Dutch Reformed women pursued an educational model of mission. In every mission of the church, we shall see, they opened schools that converted and nurtured indigenous peoples in the Christian faith. Translating the Bible, teaching children, visiting women in their homes, Afrikaner missionary women formulated for the South African context what Bosch called "mission in the wake of the Enlightenment."

Women in the Dutch Reformed Mission Movement

One of the key factors that made a mature missionary movement possible in the Dutch Reformed Church was the participation of women in the enterprise. Without women's encouragement, organizational ability, fund-raising efforts, and eagerness to go as missionaries themselves, missions would never have won approval in Afrikaner society. Yet Dutch Reformed mission history says little about the role of women in mission, seeing them as wives and nameless assistants to men, rather than as full participants in their own right. A recovery of the history of women's participation in Dutch Reformed missions would not only balance the overly institutional portrait of South African mission history now available, but would help explain the dynamic behind the mission movement itself, particularly in its formative years.

The Mount Holyoke Connection

How did Afrikaner women attain a mission consciousness that was in many respects in advance of the men? I argue in this paper that the interest of Dutch

Reformed women in the mission of the church was shaped and facilitated by the presence of over forty American women who arrived in South Africa from 1873 to 1887, of whom approximately half were graduates of Mount Holyoke College, the preeminent missionary training institution for American women in the mid-nineteenth century (Stow 1887:344). Spreading across southern Africa, the American women founded girls' schools in Wellington, Stellenbosch, Worcester, Graaff-Reinet, Swellendam, and Pretoria, the most advanced of which was Huguenot Seminary, South Africa's first college for women. Both Dutch- and English-speaking students educated at these schools established daughter institutions throughout rural South Africa. Taking as their model the Mount Holyoke system, American and South African women in partnership created a missionary ethos and provided training for the first South African women missionaries and professional educators.

The first girls' school established by the Americans was Huguenot Seminary in Wellington.[1] At the beginning of the second term in 1874, the pupils at Huguenot conducted outreach among railroad workers and began a Sunday school for "coloured" children in Wellington that continued for twenty years until they turned it over to the Dutch Reformed Mission Church. By the end of the first year, student Johanna Meeuwsen had gone out from Huguenot with a friend, Miss Horak, as South Africa's first single women missionaries. In 1878, the founders of Huguenot began a woman's mission society to support Huguenot graduates. As the Huguenot Missionary Society expanded across Cape Colony through the efforts of alumnae, it became in 1889 the Vrouesendingbond (Woman's Missionary Union), the first women's organization in the Dutch Reformed Church. The goal of the Vrouesendingbond, as stated in its founding constitution, was "to link together the Christian women of the land, in order to encourage and further Gospel work for the women and children among the heathen, or among those who know not God" (Huguenot Missionary Society:72). In the meantime, the brother of Abbie Ferguson, founder of Huguenot, had become the first principal of a men's missionary training institution in Wellington. By 1897, Huguenot Seminary had sent out 600 women as teachers and 51 alumnae as missionaries, including the wives of the founders of the DRC Malawi (Nyasaland) and Zimbabwe (Mashonaland) missions, missionary wives in Lesotho (Basutoland), Kenya (British East Africa), Botswana (British Bechuanaland), the Transvaal, the Transkei, and single women in the same and other locations, including Sri Lanka (Ceylon). In addition to the Vrouesendingbond, American teachers at Huguenot introduced into South Africa the Young Woman's Christian Temperance Union, the Christian Endeavour Movement, and in 1890 the Student Volunteer Movement for Foreign Missions, American organizations that stimulated missionary commitment and piety.

American women teachers inspired and educated for missionary work virtually the entire first generation of South African Dutch Reformed missionary

---

1. The use of the term "seminary" connoted preparation for all of life. Pupils at female seminaries received not only academic instruction, but religious and domestic training as well (Woody 1966:395).

women. The purpose of this paper is to examine the precise nature of their influence. What kind of mission theory did the Mount Holyoke system assume and promote? What social portrait can be drawn of the American women and the South African women who worked with them? And finally, the most important question: what does the evidence suggest about the long-term impact of American training on the history and missiology of Dutch Reformed women missionaries?

The Mount Holyoke System

In 1872, Andrew Murray, Jr., the greatest *dominee* of the DRC in the late nineteenth century and leader of its evangelical and missionary wing, read a biography of Mary Lyon, founder of Mount Holyoke Seminary in South Hadley, Massachusetts. The details of his resultant decision to ask Mount Holyoke for missionary teachers are taken from Murray's own account published in *The Huguenot Seminary Annual* of 1898. Murray recalled that soon after he moved from Cape Town to Wellington in 1871, the only girls' school in town lost its teacher. Faced with the need to recruit a new one, Murray decided to write to the United States rather than to his ancestral home of Scotland for teachers. What was it about Mary Lyon that convinced him to write to Mount Holyoke? In Murray's words,

> The first thing that struck me was the wonderful way in which she gave the Head, the Heart, and the Hand an equal place in her training. At a time when there was not a single College or School for women, on a permanent footing with an endowment, in the States, she maintained that it was needful that the provision should be made, and women receive the best intellectual training possible, to enable them to fill their place aright. The faculties given by God ought to be fitted to do their work effectively. With this she believed the cultivation of a truly moral and religious character to be of supreme importance. While she aimed at, and succeeded in leading on to, the highest mental culture, she was never content until her pupils had learnt to seek first the kingdom of God, and devote themselves to Christ and His service. With these high aims in Head and Heart, she combined most remarkably the culture of the Hand.... She honored domestic work, not only as a duty to be willingly accepted when it was a necessity, but as a means of developing one's whole nature, as a healthful relaxation from mental fatigue, and as a fitting for true independence and power to rule or to help others. (Murray 1898:2. See also Ferguson 1898:8)

Murray was attracted to Mary Lyon's methods because they balanced high intellectual attainments with practical training in domestic work. Lyon's chief purpose in education was to bring her pupils to saving knowledge of Jesus Christ and then channel their lives into self-sacrificial Christian service. Coming from a humble background herself, Lyon sought to train the daughters of the working and middle classes; therefore, the students at Mount Holyoke did all their own cleaning and cooking. This combination of Head, Heart, and Hand, and its potential for nurturing democratic ideals, was what attracted Murray to the Mount Holyoke system. When for his seventieth birthday Murray was asked to list the dozen men who had most influenced him, he included in the list one woman, Mary Lyon (*Huguenot Seminary Journal,* 1898).

After writing to Mount Holyoke and requesting a teacher, and receiving the response that Abbie Ferguson and Anna Bliss had agreed to come, Murray prepared and printed in Dutch an abridged life of Mary Lyon. He began to preach sermons on the need to educate children for work in God's kingdom and through a circular raised over 1,500 pounds to pay for the passage of the American women and the outfitting of a suitable school building. Since Wellington had been a site of major French Protestant settlement in 1688, it was decided to name the school the Huguenot Seminary. The school opened in January 1874. The need for expansion of the facilities was immediate, and so Murray embarked on a four-month tour to raise further funds in the Dutch Reformed churches. The tour raised 2,300 pounds for the girls' school, as well as getting churches in other locations interested in soliciting money for their own Mary Lyon school. The following year, the Dutch Reformed Church in Stellenbosch raised money for an American teacher, and the year after that, the church in Worcester (ibid.:1–4; DuPlessis 1919:274–86).

Mount Holyoke Seminary became the model for all the schools founded cooperatively by American teachers and the Dutch Reformed clergy who raised the money for the teachers through their churches. For example, the constitution of the Bloemhof Seminary, founded in Stellenbosch in 1875, stated that "Furthermore as regards principles and the application thereof this Institution shall be similar as far as possible to the praiseworthy Mount Holyoke Seminary for young women in America" (Stadion 1949). Mount Holyoke had been founded in 1837 by Mary Lyon, an experienced teacher and avid supporter of foreign missions, as the first school in the United States that attempted to give girls the equivalent of a male college course, including such subjects as Latin, mathematics, theology and the physical sciences. Lyon's experiment in female education came at a time when American women were breaking into the teaching profession, the first occupation available for educated women in the United States, and 82.5 percent of Mount Holyoke's graduates between 1838 and 1850 became teachers (Horowitz 1984:27).

Mary Lyon's theology was at the heart of her educational system. A Baptist turned Congregationalist, the passion of her life was foreign missions (see Fisk 1866; Hitchcock 1852; Green 1979). She was steeped in the theology of the New Divinity, the modified Calvinism expounded by the followers of Jonathan Edwards. It was Edwards' followers who launched America's foreign mission movement with the founding of the American Board of Commissioners for Foreign Missions in 1810. She taught a weekly theology class based on Edwards' *History of the Work of Redemption.* The theology of New Divinity was evangelical, believing that without a commitment to Jesus Christ, persons would suffer eternal damnation. Her belief that a personal conversion was the starting point of Christian outreach meant that spiritual discipline was the core of the Mount Holyoke system. Through Bible study, frequent revivals, and training in self-sacrifice, most of the early graduates became active, evangelical Christians. The disciplined Mount Holyoke lifestyle, divided as it was among self-monitored spiritual, domestic, and intellectual exercises, gave the school a reputation as a kind of "Protestant nunnery" (Horowitz 1984:57–58). Critics of the school noticed that Mount Holyoke graduates often married later than other women or not at all, and they left the school with a pious zeal to change the world.

By 1887, Mount Holyoke Seminary had sent out 175 foreign missionaries to 18 countries. Many other alumnae, single and married, had become teachers on the western frontier, to southern blacks, or served in other home mission situations. The school was known as a "rib factory" where theological students with missionary appointments could count on finding a wife. The mission legacy of Mount Holyoke was no accident: it was the result of careful cultivation by Mary Lyon, who believed that one should "study and teach nothing that cannot be made to help in the great work of converting the world to Christ" (quoted in Thomas 1937:29). Her heart burdened for foreign missions, Lyon reflected that "There is not a day in which I do not ask how can I enlighten the understanding, and direct the feelings of my pupils aright on this great subject, the salvation of the world" (quoted in Fisk 1866:162).

The starting point of Lyon's program to enlist the school for the support of foreign missions was the conversion of each pupil. Mandatory church attendance with the memorization of sermon headings, twice daily worship, and one hour of daily private prayer were the basis for awakening the piety of the students. Systematic Bible study was part of the curriculum. Each term, Lyon divided the students into the "professors" and "non-professors" of Christianity, and made the unconverted the subject of prayer and special exertions throughout the year. Frequent revivals were the result of the supercharged spiritual atmosphere prevalent at Mount Holyoke. At the twenty-fifth anniversary of the school, it was estimated that of the 1,000 students who had entered the school "without hope" regarding their eternal salvation, three-fourths had found it during their time at the seminary (Green 1979:251).

Mary Lyon was no spiritual enthusiast. She did not believe in wallowing in religious emotion, but rather in harnessing conversion for changed behavior. She quickly channelled the emotions of the converted into outreach, and to Lyon, mission work was the highest form of benevolence. The first extracurricular activity permitted at Mount Holyoke was a missionary society. Every January, the school observed a fast day for missions. Twice yearly, Lyon solicited money for foreign missions, and each girl had a mite box in which to save her pennies for the cause. Returned missionaries were frequent visitors to the campus and noted with approval the school's weekly program of mission study and its multiple subscriptions to the major mission journals.[2] Lyon herself gave a large percentage of her small income to missions, as did her teachers. Setting an example to the

---

2. For a detailed description by a missionary of his visit to Mount Holyoke, see Waterbury 1870:194–202. Scudder was so impressed with the devotion of the students to missions that he told them, "I could not but add, that if the Saviour had committed the preaching of the Gospel to females — to such as were before me — they would treat him differently [than men] — they would flee in larger numbers to the heathen" (197).

students of financial commitment, she gave between 40 to 50 percent of her income to missions during the last few years of her life. Pupils and teachers together gave $7,000 for missions from 1842 to 1849 (Fisk 1866:174).

Andrew Murray's solicitation of teachers from Mount Holyoke was thus not only an attempt to raise the educational level of Afrikaner girls but a plot to plant evangelical piety and support for home and foreign missions among the women of the Dutch Reformed Church. In 1874, when Abbie Ferguson and Anna Bliss began at Huguenot, they decided to adopt the Holyoke system. Abbie Ferguson and Anna Bliss were both the daughters of Congregational clergy. They attended Mount Holyoke after the death of Mary Lyon, graduating in 1856 and 1862 respectively, yet at the time they were students, Lyon's system of education was still being followed to the letter. The founders of Huguenot remained at its head until 1920, overseeing many changes, including its growth into a woman's college, branch schools, and several missionary training institutions. In 1922, Bliss became the first woman to receive an honorary doctorate from the University of South Africa.

The success of Andrew Murray's plans was borne out in the handwritten journals of the first three years of Huguenot Seminary, recorded by the first missionary teachers. The journal of Huguenot for 1874 shows that it opened on January 19 with noon services at the Dutch Reformed Church. The first element of the Mount Holyoke system to need translation into the South African context was the elaborate system of bells that demarcated prayer and study time, as well as the rules whereby girls monitored their own conduct and reported on lapses to the community. The system of domestic work in which pupils did their own cleaning was the foundation on which Mount Holyoke based self-discipline and service to others. At Huguenot, according to the journal, domestic work "had excited much curiosity and called forth many questions before we came together, and the pupils had come to look upon it as something very formidable." In South Africa, where hard household labor was considered undesirable for white women, the teachers of Huguenot found it necessary to discuss at length with the pupils the need for them to scrub their own floors. During the second week of school, the pupils unanimously voted to do their own scrubbing (*Huguenot Seminary Journal* 1874).

Having established the domestic and academic sides of the program, as well as the monitorial system, Ferguson and Bliss turned to the spiritual. One of Mary Lyon's principles was that privacy was conducive to spiritual discipline, thus there would be only two girls per room who could share a large prayer closet. The monastic nature of the dormitory arrangement was repeated exactly at Huguenot. Ferguson and Bliss soon divided the 37 pupils into two groups for daily fifteen-minute prayer meetings. The South African girls found this strange, for those from Christian homes were accustomed only to weekly prayer. On the second Thursday after opening, Ferguson requested those students sure of their salvation to meet with her in one room, while the rest were to meet in another. Thus began a weekly attempt to move all the girls in the unsaved category to the saved, with sermons designed to awaken religious experience from their pastor, Professor Hofmeyr of Stellenbosch, and other visiting clergy.

The initial reaction of the pupils to the division between sheep and goats was not positive. According to the Ferguson-Bliss journal, "There was a good deal of talk about it among the pupils, it was something so unheard of here. Some, though they hoped they were converted, had never yet openly professed, others dreaded the consequences of such a profession before the school; others, again thought that it was wrong to draw lines and would certainly lead to deception on the part of some. To each one it was a day of solemn heart searching, and I do not think there was one, who did not feel it to be one of the most earnest days of her life." Every Thursday night, a few believers were added to the original 13 girls who had professed salvation. After four or five weeks, the pupils found themselves "a united family in Christ Jesus." The next morning at daily devotions, the consecration of the girls to Christ was sealed by Ferguson's sermon on "What shall I render unto the Lord?" (*Huguenot Seminary Journal* 1874).

And so Mary Lyon's program for the conversion of her pupils was transferred to South Africa, to become a uniform feature of the American-led female seminaries. After their conversion, the girls were guided into Christian service. At the beginning of the second term in 1874, the Huguenot pupils began a mission Sunday school for Afrikaans-speaking "colored" children, which came to have an average attendance of 150. As the children began to wonder what they could do to be saved, the Huguenot pupils began "cottage meetings" among them. Pupils also taught reading, writing, and arithmetic to needy children at an evening school. Other pupils began tract distribution among railroad workers.

By the commencement of the third term in July 1874, it was clear that so many young women from across the Cape Colony were interested in entering the seminary that more teachers needed to be acquired from the United States. The success of Huguenot was assured when, at the end of the third term, all ten of the pupils sent up for government examination to become elementary school teachers passed the battery of tests in math, geography, grammar, spelling, school management, and Dutch. Huguenot pupils represented one-third of those who passed the government examination that year. The ladies of the Dutch Reformed Church helped the pupils raise money to expand the school. Farmers often brought fruit and vegetables to feed the students. A church deacon directed the construction of a new building for the growing school. Abbie Ferguson and Anna Bliss evaluated the close of a successful first year with the words, "We hope for our pupils not only that they are saved; but with most of them, that there has been a deep-earnest work in their hearts, which, we trust, will show itself in consecrated work here after" (*Huguenot Seminary Journal* 1874).

The handwritten journals of Huguenot for 1875 and 1876 reveal that disciplined efforts to convert and channel the girls into Christian service was a central part of every school term. As at Mount Holyoke, students raised money for foreign missions, in 1875 sending money to Austria to support a mission child and also raising money for missions in Africa. As pupils became Christians, they learned to give public testimony to their faith. Daily Bible lessons and devotions guided the pupils through the complete Bible. Visiting Afrikaner clergy and American missionaries spoke to the pupils to strengthen their commitments to outreach. At the end of 1876, Abbie Ferguson held a controversial public meeting of confession and penitence and held devotions on Isaiah 61, reflecting that Christ came to proclaim liberty to the captives and bind up the broken-hearted. As word spread of the spiritual activism at Huguenot, European missionaries stationed in South Africa began to request applications for their daughters. Groups of people in isolated rural areas started to ask that Huguenot-trained teachers come out to open schools for children.

The Mount Holyoke system, combining intellectual, spiritual, and domestic discipline, successfully duplicated in South Africa the evangelical activism and voluntaristic ethos that had so motivated American women toward missionary service in the nineteenth century. By accustoming pupils to doing their own housework, it not only prepared them for any frontier situation in which they might find themselves, but it undercut the racist idea that domestic work was something suitable only for blacks. The engagement of Huguenot pupils in evangelistic and social work among the "colored" population prepared them to serve unafraid as teachers among people whom they perceived to be different from themselves. The Mount Holyoke system helped move Afrikaner women and girls from a passive, tribal view of salvation to an activistic one, where conversion walked hand in hand with outreach to peoples of diverse ethnic backgrounds.

Another important result of the Mount Holyoke system was that it moved Boer girls from an agricultural to a Western view of time. Many of the students at Huguenot came from isolated farms where time was related to the cycles of nature, just as half a century earlier the farm girls of New England went to study at Mount Holyoke. Ferguson and Bliss noted in the *Huguenot Journal* for 1875, "Promptness is not one of the virtues of the people, and we have in consequence felt that it was an important lesson to be taught." A visitor to Huguenot Seminary in 1876 noticed first of all the frequent ringing of bells. She was impressed by the system of self-monitoring that resulted in perfect order, with students quiet at certain hours, chores and studying done with regularity, and all lights out by 22:00. The visitor summarized her impression for an article in the *Christian Express*. "The results of the whole system seems to me to be that the pupils in Huguenot Seminary are taught experientially the value of time...."

For rural women in late nineteenth-century South Africa, just as for rural women in early nineteenth-century New England, the mastery of time was a prerequisite for Christian service. In the words of Helen Horowitz, a scholar of American women's colleges, Mary Lyon was important because "She broke into a woman's life — governed by tradition and natural rhythms, ruled by the heart and the demands of the flesh — to transform it into a life that could be planned" (Horowitz 1984:12). Unless a woman could control and regularize her schedule, she had neither the ability to become educated nor to engage in outreach. A result of being captive to Western time is that such captivity creates a goal-oriented lifestyle.

A major contribution of the Mount Holyoke educational system to the raising of mission consciousness among Afrikaner women was that it moved them from natural to modern concepts of time.[3] And who is the most likely to become an evangelist of the gospel of westernization? The recently converted. The visitor to Huguenot in 1876 noted, "It was a beautiful sight to see these girls, some from neighboring Dutch farms only lately beginning to study for themselves, teaching writing, arithmetic, and reading to these bright eyed, woolly headed children, some of them indeed big headed boys. On Sunday I saw assembled about 80 children of all colors taught in classes, also by volunteering young ladies." Westernization of time, evangelical piety, voluntarism, independence and self-reliance, seeing people in terms of salvation rather than of race — all of these were contributions of the Mount Holyoke system to raising the mission consciousness of South African women in the late nineteenth century.

The Teachers from Mount Holyoke

The archives at Mount Holyoke College hold files of thirty alumnae who became school teachers among whites in South Africa during the late nineteenth and early twentieth centuries. Constructing a social portrait of the missionary women helps in the evaluation of their impact on South African missionary activity and the impact of South Africa on them. Nearly all the women were from New England, the northeastern part of the United States. Of those whose religious background is known, most were Congregationalists. Thus the majority of American teachers in South Africa came from the church of the American Puritans and would have shared the foundational theology of the Dutch Reformed Church. Andrew Murray, Jr., and Abbie Ferguson participated together in the holiness movement, sharing a commitment to enabling others to reach deeper levels of spiritual consecration.[4] Their commitment to evangelical pietism spread to a number of the American teachers, two of whom in fact became members of the Salvation Army while they were in South Africa, as did one of Murray's daughters. The overall religious ethos of the American teachers was that of moderate Calvinism with strong pietistic leanings.

The American teachers generally taught several subjects each at the various schools, ranging from Latin to history to geography to English to mathematics, as well as doing religious work among and with the pupils. Some of the later teachers were quite specialized, however. In 1907 Vernette Gibbons began

---

3. As anthropologists John and Jean Comaroff and others have noticed, part of the westernizing nature of the missionary enterprise was its attempt to modernize time, to force people to live by the clock rather than by the natural rhythms of life (see Comaroff 1991). The history of mission work at Huguenot College demonstrates that missiologists must examine not only how the westernization of time was a result of missionary activity, but how it created the climate for Protestant missionary outreach. Against the Comaroffs' analysis of the Southern Tswana, however, the Huguenot experience shows that the adoption of Western time was an empowering rather than enslaving experience for Dutch Reformed women.

4. Murray's activity in creating the South African Keswick movement and his writings on spiritual consecration are well known (see Douglas 1981). Ferguson's diaries show that she shared Murray's perspective on spirituality. She was influenced by such writers as F. B. Meyer, A. J. Gordon, A. T. Pierson, and other Reformed or Keswick advocates of deeper spiritual life. The holiness movement, in both its Reformed (Keswick) and Wesleyan (Methodist) forms, was an important catalyst of mission commitment for American women in the late nineteenth century (see Robert:forthcoming).

the chemistry department at what was by then Huguenot College. Susan Leiter served as head of the physics department at Huguenot for seven years. Several teachers were educational specialists. Mount Holyoke graduate Carrie Ingraham began the first kindergarten in Stellenbosch, and Evelyn Metcalf, class of 1879, was a trained kindergartner who taught in that field in both Wellington and Stellenbosch. Martha Newton, who began a public school in Swellendam, returned to Huguenot and began a demonstration school so students could have teacher training as part of their course of study.

Some of the American teachers remained in South Africa for only a three-year term, but others spent their lives and died there. Of the thirty teachers from Mount Holyoke, at least ten, or one-third, stayed in South Africa for the rest of their lives. Susan Clary died of consumption shortly after opening Prospect Seminary in Pretoria in 1878. Three women, or one-tenth of the total for whom Mount Holyoke has records, married South Africans and pursued charitable works as members of South African society. Carrie Ingraham, for example, married Friedrich Jannasch, the son of Moravian missionaries and founder of the South African Conservatory of Music. In 1900, she opened a hostel for female music pupils and acted as substitute mother for over four hundred young women. Theresa Campbell married John Mackay of Port Elizabeth, a Scot and member of the Cape Parliament. She had begun schools in Riverdale and Bradock, and then after her marriage served as president of the Colonial Women's Christian Temperance Union. Mary Cumming married Thomas Gamble, pastor of a Congregational church in the Cape Colony. But most of the women who remained in South Africa stayed single and devoted their lives to educational and mission work. The American women who remained exercised leadership in a host of organizations of American origin, such as temperance work, the Christian Endeavour movement, Chatauqua courses, mission societies, and the like.

The most interesting evidence regarding the missiological commitments of the American women comes from the files of the seven women who, in addition to their work among white South Africans, also worked as educational missionaries among black Africans or African Americans. Approximately one-fourth of the Mount Holyoke women who taught in the white schools in South Africa also taught in educational institutions for freed slaves in the United States, for black African women, or for both. Five of the thirty women taught at schools for freed slaves or at church-sponsored schools for southern black women in the United States either before or after they worked in South Africa. Four took appointments from an American missionary board for work among Africans.

Two of the Mount Holyoke women who worked among diverse races were Caroline Frost and Juliette Gilson. Their careers strike one with how Mary Lyon's balanced emphasis on Head, Heart, and Hand was seen by American teachers as applicable to both black and white. The balance of evangelism and civilization so typical of American women's mission theory was assumed for Afrikaner and Zulu women alike. In retrospect, historians can see that an emphasis on manual labor would have different social implications for white and black girls: whites were being trained to be mistresses of their own homes, whereas blacks were de facto being trained for domestic servitude. But in theory,

Head, Heart, and Hand were believed equally necessary for Boer girls as for girls from an African kraal.

Before teaching at a branch of Huguenot seminary in Paarl, Cape Colony, Caroline Frost had taught for four years in schools for southern blacks in the United States. Talladega College, where Frost spent three years, was a black women's school sponsored in Alabama by the Congregational Church (see Jacobs 1987:155–76). After three years at Talladega and three years at Huguenot Paarl, Frost moved to Natal in 1900 and worked in the Umzumbe Home for Zulu girls. In 1899 she had decided that her calling was to work with blacks, and so she obtained a regular missionary appointment with the American Board. In applying to the board, Frost stressed that she was not an evangelist, but a teacher who wished to "teach what saving grace had to do with this life" (Emerson, n.d.). Thus, in her mission philosophy, Frost wished to educate girls in the material aspects of Christian life, or what was then called "Christian civilization."

In 1909, the South African government was willing to support a "normal school" for blacks. The two highest classes from three mission boarding schools for blacks were merged into a coeducational teachers' training institute at Amanzimtoti. Frost went as a founding missionary to the Amanzimtoti Institute and remained there until 1940. By then, the institute, renamed Adams College, was a leading place for the higher education of South African blacks. At Adams College, Frost taught botany and developed the gardens, acted as supervisor of dormitories, was in charge of the library and mission archives, and lectured on missions in pastors' courses, among other things. Her commitment to holistic training for both whites and blacks resulted in one of the finest educational institutions for South African blacks in the early twentieth century.

Juliette Gilson, class of 1868, arrived in Stellenbosch in 1874 and founded Bloemhof Seminary for girls, which by 1902 had 200 students. Upon celebrating its centenary in 1975, Bloemhof could boast that its famous graduates included such women as the wives of General J. C. Smuts, General J. B. M. Hertzog, and the wife of the first South African Governor-General of the Union of South Africa. In 1884, Gilson left Stellenbosch to take charge of a mission school for black girls, and then taught at Umzumbe Seminary in Natal. After earning a theological degree at Hartford Theological Seminary, Gilson went to Zimbabwe (Southern Rhodesia) in 1896 as a missionary with the American Board and tried unsuccessfully to integrate the Mt. Silinda School, a mission school originally for blacks. In 1902, she began a school for the children of white colonists who had trekked northward because of the Boer War and received land grants from Cecil Rhodes.

In August 1903, Gilson wrote a confidential report to the American Board comparing the white settlers whose children attended Chimanimani School to the black families represented at Mt. Silinda. At first she attempted to educate black and white together at Mt. Silinda, but racial prejudice caused the founding of separate schools. Gilson complained of the low moral and intellectual state of the Rhodesian Boers, noting that five out of eleven European marriages in the past two years had pregnant brides. She noted cases where white men seduced school girls and of the hypocrisy of a Dutch church elder who was arraigned for inhumanely beating a black who would not sell him cattle. Gilson stated that the black pupils at Mt. Silinda were superior to the whites at Chimanimani and that the Boers were not only bad farmers but that they were illiterate and had to turn to the blacks to read documents for them. She appealed for money for the white school because since the whites owned the land, unless their moral life could be improved, they would continue to drag down the blacks.

The tentative conclusion one reaches from looking at the careers of Frost and Gilson is that an important segment of the American teachers in South Africa believed that poor whites and blacks were both in need of training that would convert, educate, and teach them the value of work. From the American women's perspective, the difference between races was more a matter of the degree of "Christian civilization" than of inherent racial characteristics. Although the South African context resulted in racially separate schools and racially segmented patterns of employment, the Mount Holyoke missiology of Head, Heart, and Hand was at a theoretical level color blind. Huguenot and Bloemhof for whites, Umzumbe and Inanda for blacks — all four schools were staffed by graduates of Mount Holyoke College during the late nineteenth century. Abbie Ferguson and other teachers from Mount Holyoke made frequent visits to their fellow alumnae at Inanda, and women missionaries to the Zulus often came to speak about their work to the Huguenot pupils. Could it be that the purpose of each school was originally the same: to train Christian wives, mothers, teachers, and missionaries?

The Missionary Movement from Huguenot

By 1875, the Mount Holyoke system of intellectual, spiritual, and domestic training was beginning to see results, as pupils began to leave Huguenot to become missionaries and teachers. Abbie Ferguson inculcated missions interest by speaking on missions every Monday morning. On Monday evening, as had the Mount Holyoke students before them, Huguenot pupils brought in their missionary offerings, remarking, "We never knew anything about missionary work before, and felt no interest because we didn't know, but now we see there is something for us to do." At the beginning of 1875, one student who had been expected to return did not. As was recorded in the journal of Huguenot, "A Macedonian call had come to her during the vacation. She had heard the Lord's voice in the call, and when we came together, was on her way to a distant mission station in the Transvaal, having devoted herself to work among the Kaffirs; and so in Miss Johanna Meeuwsen, we send out our first missionary..." (*Huguenot Seminary Journal* 1875). Meeuwsen had been an avid participant in the Monday morning missionary meetings. Bliss and Ferguson felt she needed another year of training before she went to Saulspoort, 50 miles north of Rustenburg in the Transvaal. But Meeuwsen felt the Lord was calling her immediately, and so she became the Dutch Reformed Church's first single woman missionary. The Huguenot pupils began to collect money for Meeuwsen's work with children, even receiving thank-you letters from them.

By the end of 1875, the first Dutch Reformed woman was prepared to open a school on the Mount Holyoke model. Miss Helen "Ella" Murray, Andrew Murray's sister, who had spent two years at Huguenot, went to Graaff-Reinet to open Midland Seminary and wait for the arrival of American teachers. She began immediately to apply American techniques to awaken religious interest and conducted her first prayer meeting held in Graaff-Reinet, during which a number of girls came to Christ. Miss Murray held the fort until Sarah Thayer arrived from the United States in 1876. Murray continued in a leading role at Midland Seminary, and in 1884, as Principal, she spoke at the Huguenot tenth anniversary exercises on "Bringing Our Pupils to Christ." The partnership between Helen Murray and the American women illustrates that along with girls straight off the farm, Huguenot attracted many daughters of clergy and missionaries, who needed only a few years of training to take their place in ministry. When one looks at the names of the early Huguenot graduates who became missionaries and missionary teachers, one sees the same surnames as those of male mission leaders.

As students began to respond to the needs of rural whites and blacks for missionary teachers in southern Africa, their classmates became a major source of financial support for them. The support was institutionalized when in 1878 Ferguson and Bliss read the ten-year report of the Woman's Board of Missions of the American Board, the first denominational women's missionary agency in the United States. This board had raised money to send out single women to work with women and girls, its first missionary being Mary K. Edwards, founder of Inanda Seminary for Zulu girls in South Africa and visitor to Huguenot in 1876. Huguenot pupils and alumnae decided to form a woman's missionary society in South Africa, modelled on the Woman's Board of Missions. Unable to find other South African women interested in mission, the Huguenot pupils decided to found their own Huguenot Missionary Society. The missionary society idea quickly spread to seminaries in Worcester, Stellenbosch, and Graaff-Reinet. As students graduated, they founded mission circles for women and children wherever they went to teach.

Fortunately for South African mission history, the minutes of the Huguenot Missionary Society are deposited in the Cape Archives. From these minutes, one could construct a history of Dutch Reformed women's initial involvement in missions. The minutes of the Huguenot Missionary Society contain reports of letters from the earliest missionary women describing their mission work, record the visits of nearly every pioneer DRC male missionary candidate on his way to the field, and record the spread of mission circles from Wellington to the rest of the Cape. The importance of these minutes as an historical source is enhanced by the fact that no collections of Dutch Reformed women's missionary papers are on deposit in the Dutch Reformed Archives held in the Cape Archives. The lack of women's missionary letters means that the secondhand reports of correspondence in Huguenot Missionary Society minutes are the best source available at this time.

From the minutes of the Huguenot Missionary Society, one can conclude that just as the first American missionary women considered their primary role to be teachers, so did South African women missionaries. The picture one gets of early South African missionary women is that they shared the American women's commitment to "woman's work for woman," that the primary *raison d'être* for women missionaries was to reach women and children through schools. According to a circular letter sent by Abbie Ferguson at the founding of the Vrouesendingbond, the main work of the Huguenot society "has been caring for the missionary teachers who are laboring at the mission stations of the Dutch Reformed Church." The missiological commitment to education and to "women's work" was carried over from the Woman's Board of Missions to the Huguenot Missionary Society to the Vrouesendingbond. The earliest missionaries supported by the Huguenot Society worked to master African languages, taught children to read and know the Bible, and ultimately opened more formal schools, including boarding schools.

The first missionary adopted by the Huguenot Missionary Society was Cato Greeff, but on her way to the Transvaal she married the missionary Reverend J. P. Roux. Deciding to adhere to the principle that they would support single women who needed their help more than did married women, the Huguenot Missionary Society adopted Johanna Meeuwsen (already in the field) and built her a boarding home for girls at Saulspoort. They continued to correspond with Cato Greeff Roux and sent supplies for the girls in her school. One of the most important aspects of the Huguenot Missionary Society's work was that although it was proud of Huguenot's missionary wives, it took its central task to be the support of single women who could be full-time teachers. Its affirmation and financial support of singleness placed strong-minded single women missionaries in all the mission fields of the Dutch Reformed Church. The example of the single missionary women in providing an alternative role model to motherhood for Afrikaner women should not be underestimated.

In 1881, two Huguenot graduates married missionaries. Ottelie Marx, the daughter of Moravian missionaries, married the Rev. A. du Toit, and Martha le Riche married the Rev. P. Maré. Mrs. du Toit wrote to the missionary society describing the lack of support she and her husband received from the church. Unfortunately, both Mrs. Maré and Mrs. du Toit died after a short time in the field.

Early single missionaries from Huguenot included Florence and Aline Mabille of Basutoland (daughters of French missionaries to Lesotho); Maria Truter of Saulspoort, Transvaal; and Mary Murray and Deborah Retief of British Bechuanaland. After serving for a number of years as a single missionary, Maria Neethling married the widower Reverend Henry Gonin, who, though Swiss, had been the Dutch Reformed Church's first missionary in the Transvaal. Gonin's daughters by his first marriage also attended Huguenot, and in 1883 Fanny Gonin joined her father's work in Saulspoort. In a letter to the Huguenot Missionary Society, Gonin reported that she was busy studying Setswana and that the pupils in her school knew more Bible "than many a white child."

By 1884, Huguenot graduate Hester le Roux was teaching in her father's mission school. Engela Hofmeyr had grown up in the Transvaal as the daughter of the pioneer DRC missionary there, layman Stephanus Hofmeyr. After attending Huguenot, she married missionary J. W. Daneel and succeeded her parents at Zoutpansberg. Although standard mission histories note that Daneel succeeded Stephanus Hofmeyr as the leading missionary in Zoutpansberg, the missionary succession was actually through Engela Hofmeyr Daneel. Clearly, Huguenot was the place for missionaries to send their daughters, in hopes that they would succeed them in their work.

In 1886, the Huguenot Missionary Society decided to print a Dutch version of the mission newsletter it sent to its related mission circles. The newsletter was called the *Zendingbond* and was sent to pastors' wives across southern Africa. By 1889, the leaven of the Huguenot Missionary Society had succeeded in raising enough mission interest among women of the Dutch Reformed Church that the Vrouesendingbond (Woman's Missionary Union) was founded at Huguenot with Mrs. Emma Murray as the first president and Huguenot graduates, friends, or teachers as the rest of the officers. The Huguenot Missionary Society became a branch of the larger Vrouesendingbond. The historic significance of the Vrouesendingbond for Afrikaner women was underscored in 1953, when M. E. Rothmann recalled at the conference of the Afrikaanse Christelike Vrouevereniging:

> When I was a child 70 years ago, the women did hardly any public work as yet. In our town [Swellendam] the only thing somewhat related to this was a small ladies committee who called themselves the "Wardladies..." where they collected funds for poor children's school fees.... The first country-wide organization run by women was the Vrouesendingbond.... I would like to point out two things about the V.S.B. The first is that it did not originate with us. Although it took root very quickly and strongly, it was an American initiative. It was founded in Wellington, under the leadership of Miss Ferguson and Miss Bliss.... The Americans came with the conviction that a woman is of the greatest worth, and that only the best teaching was good enough for her. And this quiet conviction of theirs had, quietly, far-reaching results. After some years the schools for girls were no longer behind those of the boys — were in many ways ahead of them. All this was an inspiration to the women. And the result of this was the founding of a country-wide women's organization, the Vrouesendingbond.[5]

As the first national organization for Afrikaner women, the Vrouesendingbond is of great historical importance.

Upon meeting with the Missionary Committee of the Dutch Reformed Church, the Vrouesendingbond received permission to appoint and to pay all the salaries of single woman missionaries. The close relationship between Andrew Murray and Abbie Ferguson, as well as Huguenot's distinguished record in supporting women as missionaries, was probably responsible for the revolutionary step of permitting DRC women to appoint officially their own missionaries.

---

5. I am indebted for this reference and translation from Afrikaans to Marijke du Toit, who found it in the M. E. Rothmann collection at the University of Stellenbosch Document Center.

Even in the United States, where women had been involved in foreign missions since the 1810s, many denominational women's missionary organizations lacked the power of appointment. By 1898, the Vrouesendingbond united 48 local societies across South Africa.

Under the umbrella of the larger women's society, even more Huguenot women served as missionaries. In 1890, three single women were sent to work among the thousands of blacks and whites in the diamond fields of Kimberley, and a single woman went to teach women and children in Bechuanaland. Single women from Huguenot established missions among gold miners, as well. Huguenot graduates faced dangerous pioneer situations. Matilda Keck Goy, for example, buried her husband and child on the banks of the Zambezi. She then proceeded to the Free State with only her remaining child and African helpers, having to walk hundreds of miles and running out of food.

The importance of the Huguenot training for Afrikaner missionary women can be seen clearly in the history of the Nyasaland Mission, the first foreign field of the Dutch Reformed Church. All the founders of the Nyasaland Mission married Huguenot women, and numerous single women served there. Martha Murray, Martha Zondagh, Bertha Helm, Lettie Stegman, Mrs. A. C. Murray, Mrs. Blake, Mrs. Margaret Vlok, Annie le Roux, and Jane Soyland had all gone to Nyasaland by 1898. In 1886, the Rev. A. C. Murray, nephew of Andrew, volunteered to be the pioneer missionary to Nyasaland, paid for by the subscription of DRC clergy. On his way to the field, he spoke at the Huguenot Missionary Society and appealed for workers. During his first furlough, he married Huguenot-trained Lydie Lautré, daughter of a French missionary in Basutoland. The second Nyasaland pioneer who joined Murray was the Rev. T. C. B. Vlok, who married Margaret Blake of Huguenot. In 1892, Robert Blake joined the work and soon married Maria Jacobs of Huguenot. Martha Murray of Huguenot was the first single woman missionary there and opened a school for girls. Of the first eight DRC missionaries in Nyasaland, all four of the women — three wives and one single woman — were graduates of Huguenot Seminary. Surely this fact underscores the need for serious attention to the missiological assumptions of the school. When Mrs. Vlok died of fever in 1896, she became the first DRC missionary to die in Nyasaland.

Another great center of Huguenot women was Mashonaland, the other foreign mission of the Dutch Reformed Church. In 1891, the Reverend Andrew Louw set out by ox wagon, arriving two months later at the Zimbabwe ruins, and three miles from there founded the Morgenster Mission. Before he departed from the Cape, Louw spoke at the Huguenot Missionary Society, telling of his call to mission work and the opposition he had experienced, and asking for prayer. A moving letter from his mother, of the Northern Paarl missionary society, was read, telling of her sacrifice in giving her oldest son to the so-called heathen. Since Mrs. Louw was the first vice-president of the Vrouesendingbond, one must speculate that she influenced her son's call to missions. Louw's wife was Francina "Cinie" Malan, a Huguenot graduate. Among her other duties, Mrs. Louw undertook linguistic work and produced a grammar in the Chikaranga dialect. She and her husband translated the Bible into Chikaranga, a dialect of Shona. Single women from Huguenot joined the Louws at Morgenster, including Maria van Coller, who kept the official mission diary. American-trained women from Huguenot College thus served as missionaries in all the major missions of the Dutch Reformed Church in the late nineteenth century — Zoutpansberg and Saulspoort in the northern Transvaal, Nyasaland, and Rhodesia.

In order to prepare students specifically for missionary work, Huguenot began a mission study class in 1890. Abbie Ferguson funded the class from money she had received for her birthday. The purpose of the class was to give special training in biblical studies and missionary methods to those who had volunteered for mission work. The Student Volunteer Movement had come to Huguenot from the United States in 1890, with its emphasis on systematic mission study and the signing of a declaration, "I am willing and anxious, God permitting, to be a missionary among the heathen." The first volunteer mission band at Huguenot Seminary contained fifteen. In 1890 a missionary convention was held at Wellington that united twenty-one student volunteers from Huguenot with twenty-five from the men's missionary institute in Wellington and three from the theological seminary at Stellenbosch. In 1896 the student volunteers constituted themselves into the Students' Christian Association for South Africa, a branch of the World's Students' Christian Federation.

In 1904 the missionary training class at Huguenot had become so large that it became a separate missionary training school called Freidenheim, under the care of the Dutch Reformed Church. Its director was an American woman, Miss C. E. Waite, who had worked at the Moody Bible Institute in Chicago for eleven years. By the time Freidenheim was founded, Huguenot had already placed approximately fifty women in the mission field. Freidenheim continued the missionary traditions of Huguenot Seminary, training the vast majority of Dutch Reformed missionary women during the twentieth century.

The spinning off of a separate missionary training institution along the lines of Moody Bible Institute indicated that the pioneer missionary phase of Huguenot College was coming to an end. In 1898, Huguenot College had emerged from the upper grades of Huguenot Seminary, with an emphasis on secular education and the ability to grant the B.A. degree. The transformation from seminary to college was the same path taken by Mount Holyoke when in 1880 the students began to challenge the Mary Lyon rules and in 1888 it became a college. Following the Boer War, Huguenot and all its branches saw a great increase in applications, since Afrikaners wished their daughters to receive education in English but not be trained by teachers from England. In postwar South Africa, the secularization of Huguenot gradually replaced its image as an old-fashioned seminary and missionary-training institution with that of a modern college. Huguenot physics professor Sue Leiter wrote in the Mount Holyoke class letter of 1917 about the new generation of Huguenot students: "The girls are mostly English and Dutch, and are like college girls the world over. It is not a missionary institution. The girls resent its being so designated as much as we used to resent being addressed as young ladies of Mount Holyoke Seminary."

Conclusions

In the formative period of South African missions, American women missionary teachers were a major influence in the creation of a missionary movement among Dutch Reformed women. American women introduced an educational system that facilitated the conversion and commitment of their pupils to cross-cultural missionary outreach. As Anna Bliss overheard one Huguenot student say of the school in 1896, "When I came here I said there were three things I would never do. I would never teach a class of black children, nor join a temperance society, nor become a missionary; now I have done the first two, and I am afraid I will be compelled to do the third. When I hear Miss Ferguson speak about missions...I feel my life caught up in a power beyond my will to control" (quoted in G. Ferguson 1927:80). As students went out from Huguenot Seminary or one of the other "Mount Holyoke" schools as missionaries, they took with them the missionary commitment, evangelical theology, self-reliance, voluntaristic ethos and Americanized education they had received at school. In terms of mission theory, the Huguenot missionaries shared the view of late-nineteenth-century American women's missionary societies that the role of women in missionary work was to teach women and children. In late nineteenth-century South Africa, American-run Huguenot Seminary was the place to go if a Dutch Reformed woman wanted to become a missionary or if an ordained missionary man wanted to find a wife.

Important questions remain, however, on the relationship between American influence and the growing missionary consciousness of the Dutch Reformed Church. American influence was certainly the catalyst for the organization and mobilization of DRC women, but without the support of mission-minded pastors and the impact of missionary daughters and sisters on the Huguenot students, American influence alone would have been inadequate to launch the missionary movement. Additional research needs to be done on the nature of the partnership between American women and the Dutch Reformed Church, especially since so many clergy and missionary daughters were sent to Huguenot. Even more research needs to be done on the mission activities and mission theories of the Afrikaner women who went as pioneer missionaries, and on the impact of their educational approach on the missions of the Dutch Reformed Church. Could the contributions of women be the reason why Dutch Reformed missions supported large numbers of schools early in the twentieth century? This paper is only one small piece of what needs to be written, namely, a history of Dutch Reformed women in mission in its full social, political, and intellectual context.

- 9 -

THEOLOGY OF RELIGIONS

THE EPITOME OF MISSION THEOLOGY

Gerald H. Anderson

The thesis of David Bosch's monumental book *Transforming Mission* is that there are "paradigm shifts in theology of mission" running through a succession of six epochs in mission history from the first century to the twentieth. Each epoch, he says, reflects a paradigm of mission that is different from any of its predecessors. But "a paradigm shift always means both continuity and change, both faithfulness to the past and boldness to engage the future, both constancy and contingency, both tradition and transformation...both evolutionary and revolutionary" (Bosch 1991a: 366). The transition "from one paradigm to another," he says, "is not abrupt" (188); the agenda is always "one of reform, not replacement," with "creative tension between the new and the old" (367).

Emerging Ecumenical Missionary Paradigm

Next to his masterful exposition of New Testament models of mission in the epoch of the primitive church, Bosch gives greatest attention to the latest (sixth) epoch and what he calls "the emerging ecumenical missionary paradigm," which began to appear after the Second World War and is marked by "a growing sense of disaffection with the Enlightenment and a quest for a new approach to and understanding of reality" (Bosch 1991a:185). He describes seven changes in the world that are shaping the new emerging "postmodern" or "ecumenical" paradigm (188–89), and then devotes 142 pages to a discussion of thirteen elements of an emerging pattern of mission in this epoch. "We find ourselves, at the moment," he says, "in the midst of one of the most important shifts in the understanding and practice of the Christian mission" (xv), and therefore "mission must be understood and undertaken in an imaginatively new manner today" (367).

Bosch suggests that thirteen elements form part of the "emerging ecumenical missionary paradigm" in the latest epoch of church history: (1) mission as

Gerald H. Anderson is Director of the Overseas Ministries Study Center, New Haven, Connecticut, and Editor of the *International Bulletin of Missionary Research*.

113

the church-with-others; (2) mission as *missio Dei* ("God's mission"); (3) mission as mediating salvation; (4) mission as the quest for justice; (5) mission as evangelism; (6) mission as contextualization; (7) mission as liberation; (8) mission as inculturation; (9) mission as common witness; (10) mission as ministry by the whole people of God; (11) mission as witness to people of other faiths; (12) mission as theology; and (13) mission as action in hope.

An Unresolved Problem

Of all these elements, Bosch singles out one in particular as paramount in importance for a theology of mission in this epoch, namely, mission as witness to people of other faiths. He identifies this as one of the "largest unresolved problems for the Christian church" (1991a:476–77). This involves the theology of religions — *theologia religionum* — which is the discipline that deals with understanding other religions in the light of Christian faith. This is what shapes our attitude and approach to people of other faiths and determines much of what we think and do in terms of mission, evangelism, dialogue, service, and other forms of Christian witness (see Anderson 1993).

Although this is eleventh in Bosch's list of elements in an emerging ecumenical missionary paradigm, he recognizes that the theology of religions "is the epitome of mission theology" (477), for if this is not properly established, everything else will be in jeopardy.

A New Church Struggle

While the theology of religions has always been important, it is especially critical today because there is a growing internal threat of radical relativism in much mission theology with potentially devastating consequences. Lutheran theologian Carl E. Braaten describes the situation — at least on the American scene — in terms of a new church struggle, not as dramatic as the threat encountered in Hitler's National Socialism, but equally serious in terms of undermining the integrity of the gospel and the church (Braaten 1992: 50–51).

The issue at stake is the centrality of Jesus Christ and his atoning work on the cross, and the universal salvific significance of this event, as revealed in the New Testament. Braaten illustrates what we are facing in the theological struggle today:

> John Hick represents the liberal Protestant view that allows Christians to hold to Christ as their unique Savior without necessarily claiming as much for others. Christ may be my personal Lord and Savior, but this does not mean that he is the only savior or the only lord for all other religions. To cling to Christ as the one and only Word of God, as Barth and the Barmen Declaration assert, is branded "theological fundamentalism...." To be sure, Jesus is one of the ways in which God meets the world of human experience, but it is arrogant bigotry to claim, as Barth does, that Jesus is God's unique way of dealing with the salvation of the world.

Braaten gives further examples of the problem:

> Other voices in modern theology, like Tom Driver, Rosemary Ruether, and
> Dorothy Sölle, are claiming that the uniqueness, normativity, and finality
> of Jesus Christ account for the sins of Christianity — its sexism, racism,
> and anti-Semitism. The scandal of particularity that insists on a once-for-
> all Christ is supposedly the breeding ground of intolerance, supremacy,
> imperialism, and what these theologians call "Christo-fascism. . . ." These
> theologians are asking for a paradigm shift from a theology in which
> Christ is the center to one in which he is one of the satellites in a galaxy
> of religious superstars. (1992: 51–52)

A similar effort to relativize the theology of religions in the emerging paradigm of theology of mission is found in *The Myth of Christian Uniqueness*
where John Hick, Gordon Kaufman, Langdon Gilkey, and others propose a
shift in Christian belief of such magnitude that they describe it as "the crossing of a theological Rubicon" (Hick and Knitter 1987: vii). They propose that
Christians should abandon claims about the uniqueness of Christ and Christianity, or about having any definitive revelation, and accept instead that there
is a plurality of revelations and a parity of religions, with Christianity just
one among many religions through which people may be saved (see Anderson
1993:201–3).

In view of this theological threat, Braaten warns that "Christian theology
is today teetering on the brink of suicidal confusion. . . . The question whether
there is the promise of salvation in the name of Jesus, and in no other name,
is fast becoming a life-and-death issue facing contemporary Christianity. In the
churches this issue will become the test of fidelity to the gospel, a matter of
status confessionis more urgent than any other" (Braaten 1992: 2, 89).

Mainline Decline

A study of radical relativism in the theology of religions and its impact on
the life and mission of a major American denomination can be seen in the
United Methodist Church, which is the largest member church in the National
Council of the Churches of Christ in the U.S.A. First, a look at the views of
two prominent American United Methodist theologians. Schubert M. Ogden
is University Distinguished Professor of Theology at Southern Methodist University, Dallas, Texas. In 1990 he gave the Samuel Ferguson Lectures at the
University of Manchester, which were published under the title *Is There Only
One True Religion or Are There Many?* (Ogden 1992). In four short chapters
Ogden reviews and rejects as inadequate the three usual options in a theology
of religions.

Exclusivism, Ogden says, "is an incredible theological position, being incapable of validation in terms of common human experience and reason, but also
because it is deeply inappropriate to Jesus Christ" (1992:53). Ogden, a process theologian, discounts the authority of Scripture and makes no reference

to any scriptural text except a passing comment about the two great command-ments. He maintains that "historical-critical study of scripture has undercut any claim that Jesus Christ was already proclaimed prophetically in the Hebrew scriptures" (42).

Inclusivism, Ogden says, allows that all individuals may be saved by Christ and that all religions can be more or less valid means of salvation. But Og-den considers this also an extremely conservative position because "Christian inclusivists continue to maintain that Christianity alone can be the formally true religion, since it alone is the religion established by God in the unique saving event of Jesus Christ" (31). Thus it is another form of Christian monism, like exclusivism, which he rejects.

On *pluralism* in theology of religions (à la John Hick), Ogden ends up "skeptical rather than negative," because "the position that there are many true religions is logically as extreme as the contrary position of exclusivism that there can be only one" (79).

Beyond these three positions, Ogden offers a fourth option as "the relatively more adequate option open to us." He describes his fourth option as "*pluralistic inclusivism,*" in contrast to "*monistic* inclusivism," and calls it a "complete break with Christian monism, whether exclusivistic or inclusivistic" (82). What char-acterizes Ogden's fourth option? Its difference from pluralism is only one word: whereas pluralism maintains that there are many true religions, Ogden says that there *can be* many true religions. His difference with the two monistic options is that they deny what he affirms, namely, "that religions other than Christianity can as validly claim to be formally true as it can" (83–84). In Ogden's option there is no place — no need — for an evangelistic mission to people of other faiths.

John B. Cobb, Jr., now retired, was for many years professor of theology at the School of Theology in Claremont, California, a United Methodist semi-nary. In *Circuit Rider,* a journal for United Methodist clergy, he published an article, "Salvation: Beyond Pluralism and Exclusivism," that gives his views on the theology of religions.

Cobb, also a process theologian, points out the strengths and weaknesses of exclusivism, inclusivism, and pluralism. He then describes "another view," not unlike Ogden's "fourth option," as his own position. It "locates salvation in the future as that toward which history moves...is anticipated in Jesus Christ...but in its fullness it is not yet here." This salvific future, he says, "will contain the contributions of other religious traditions as well as Christianity," because each religion has "its own irreplaceable role to play in the economy of God's salvation of the world." Cobb shares "the view that we move to-ward the fullness of God's purpose for humankind as we learn from others and are thus transformed.... This means that Jesus Christ and our witness to him play a unique role in the salvation of the world. But it does not mean that other religious communities have nothing to contribute to that salvation" (Cobb 1993: 7–8).

Ogden believes there can be many true religions; Cobb maintains that each of the major religions has "its own irreplaceable role to play in ... God's salvation of the world." Like Ogden, Cobb never refers to the Bible in these discussions. They assume, it appears, that the Bible has nothing to contribute to a theology of religions.

While not all United Methodist theologians would agree with Ogden and Cobb, the position of radical relativism that they represent in the theology of religions is widespread in the denomination. A few years ago I was appointed by the Council of Bishops of the United Methodist Church to serve on a commission of pastors and seminary professors to formulate a biblical and theological statement on mission for the guidance and instruction of church members. In the course of our work I tried, without success, to persuade the commission to mention in our document, alongside other views, that Jesus said, "No one comes to the Father except through me" (Jn 14:6); that Acts 4:12 says "there is salvation in no one else" — and to discuss our understanding of these New Testament texts today in the context of religious pluralism. When that failed, I suggested — by way of protest — that perhaps the commission would prefer to say that the church no longer believes these statements to be true and to explain why. But the members of the commission were unwilling to make any reference to these New Testament texts at all. In fact, in this statement of 8,000 words the only reference to people of other faiths is in one paragraph near the end which speaks about "our life in the broader community of world religions and contemporary ideologies." In this situation, the statement declares, "God is preveniently present to all people," and "United Methodists witness to all persons about the Lordship of Jesus Christ." But it does not suggest that all persons need to have faith in Jesus Christ or that faith in Jesus Christ is supremely different, or to be preferred to any other faith. In the context of religious pluralism, there is no suggestion that any individuals will be lost without faith in Christ, no urgency, only a cautioning that "as religious traditions interact, we are called to listen with sensitivity to those of differing faith while presenting Christ in the spirit of Christ." The call to humility is important, but a call to boldness, equally important, is missing. The statement, titled "Grace upon Grace," was adopted by the General Conference of the United Methodist Church in 1988 as the theology of the church in regard to mission.

Membership in the United Methodist Church in the United States (8.7 million in 1992) has not increased by one member since 1968. To the contrary, the church has lost more than two million members since 1968, an average net loss of 80,000 members per year or 220 members every day for twenty-five years. Between 1965 and 1975, 4,000 small congregations disappeared. In 1993, 21 percent of United Methodist congregations reported worship attendance of fewer than 25 persons (Schaller 1993: 10). The United Methodist active missionary task force from the United States serving overseas decreased from 1,580 in 1960 to 344 in 1993 (General Board of Global Ministries 1993:125–50). The head of the World Division for United Methodist global ministries reported in 1993 that they were operating with a substantial financial deficit, that "reserve funds...are exhausted," and that to balance the budget in 1994 "twenty current missionaries must retire or not continue in missionary service." He reported that "there are fewer than 5,000 of the 36,000 local United Methodist churches participating in any form of world mission personnel support" (Harman 1993). Bishop Kenneth L. Carder says, "The United Methodist Church confronts a sickness of life-threatening proportions.... The sickness originates in theological amnesia and missional anemia" (Carder 1993: 7).

More than anything else, the cause of decline in the United Methodist Church and in other so-called mainline ecumenical denominations, in the judgment of many observers, is a radical relativism in theology that has become pervasive in these denominations since the 1960s (Anderson 1991: 132–36). James H. Burtness, an American Lutheran theologian, has observed that

> the single most striking fact in the life of our mainline U.S. churches these last twenty years is the rapid erosion of concern about whether people believe in Jesus.... The point is not that people no longer believe in Jesus. The point is that those who do believe care less than they did twenty years ago about whether those who do not believe come to the point where they do, and that this lack of care is not simply thoughtlessness, but rather an energetic rejection of such care. (Burtness 1982: 190–91)

A recent study of members in the Presbyterian Church (USA) reported that almost 60 percent of active Presbyterians believe that "all the different religions of the world are equally good ways of helping a person find ultimate truth." While most members "prefer" Christianity to other faiths, they are "unable to ground their preference in strong truth claims.... They are hard put to offer theological reasons why anyone should remain a Presbyterian, or even a Christian" (Johnson, Hoge, and Luidens 1993: 15–16). Thomas W. Gillespie, President of Princeton Theological Seminary, says, "The Presbyterian Church (USA) belongs on the list of endangered species. At the present rate of decline, our church will be only a fond memory by the year 2027 A.D."

David Bosch's Contribution

In the midst of this theological malaise, David Bosch has pointed the way toward a theology of religions for the present epoch that can help to shape a new missionary paradigm. First, in *Transforming Mission* (1991a:478ff.), Bosch describes three "fundamental positions": exclusivism, fulfillment, and relativism, followed by a critique "from the perspective of a postmodern missionary paradigm." In his critique, these three models "are found wanting," because they "leave no room for embracing the abiding paradox of asserting both ultimate commitment to one's own religion and genuine openness to another's." This leads him then to set forth eight perspectives needed in a theology of religions, especially in the interrelationship between dialogue and mission: (1) to accept the coexistence of different faiths; (2) to recognize the important role of interfaith dialogue, which presupposes witnessing to our deepest convictions while listening to those of our neighbors; (3) to recognize that God has gone before us and prepared the way for dialogue and mission, therefore Christians should approach other faiths and their adherents reverently and with respect; (4) a need for humility in dialogue and mission; this "also means showing respect for our forebears in the faith, for what they have handed down to us"; (5) to recognize that each religion is fundamentally different and they are not equally valid; (6) to recognize that dialogue "is neither a substitute nor a subterfuge for mission"; they are not the same nor are they necessarily opposed to one another; each has its own integrity in Christian witness; (7) to recognize that conversion to Christ involves not only eternal salvation, but "the responsibility to serve God in this life and promote God's reign in all its forms"; and (8) to accept that we cannot resolve the "abiding paradox" between our faith in God as revealed uniquely in Jesus Christ, and the confession that God has not left himself without a witness even among people who do not know of the biblical revelation, an apparent incompatibility between the possibility of salvation outside the church and the necessity of the church and missionary activity.

It was in his comments on this last point that Bosch explained how Christians should admit that we do not have all the answers and should be prepared in dialogue and mission to take risks and anticipate surprises "as the Spirit guides us into fuller understanding." This is not agnosticism, he said, but humility. "It is, however, a bold humility — or a humble boldness. We know only in part, but we do know. And we believe that the faith we profess...should be proclaimed" (1991a:489).

David Bosch had nearly finished writing *Transforming Mission* when he attended the World Council of Churches' World Conference on Mission and Evangelism at San Antonio, Texas, in May 1989, on the theme "Your Will Be Done — Mission in Christ's Way." At the conference, he was asked to draft the report of Section One on "Turning to the Living God," which included the subtopic "Witness Among People of Other Living Faiths." In reading that report one can see the stamp of Bosch's vision as it would later appear in *Transforming Mission*. Here are a few excerpts from Section One in the San Antonio report:

> True witness follows Jesus Christ in respecting and affirming the uniqueness and freedom of others.... Such an attitude springs from the assurance that God is the creator of the whole universe and that he has not left himself without a witness at any time or any place. The Spirit of God is constantly at work in ways that pass human understanding. [quoting from "Mission and Evangelism: An Ecumenical Affirmation," WCC 1982]
>
> We cannot point to any other way of salvation than Jesus Christ; at the same time we cannot set limits to the saving power of God. At times the debate about salvation focuses itself only on the fate of the individual's soul in the hereafter, whereas the will of God is life in its fullness even here and now.
>
> We affirm that witness does not preclude dialogue but invites it, and that dialogue does not preclude witness but extends and deepens it. Dialogue has its own place and integrity and is neither opposed to nor incompatible with witness or proclamation.
>
> We are well aware that these convictions and the ministry of witness stand in tension with what we have affirmed about God being present in

and at work in people of other faiths; we appreciate this tension, and do not attempt to resolve it. (CWME 1989: 351–52)

There has been no better statement for a theology of religions from any church or mission agency since the San Antonio conference, and it was due in large part to the work of David Bosch.[1]

A Missing Piece

I did not discover until 1993 that Bosch had written a 220–page study guide, *Theology of Religions*, which was published by the University of South Africa in 1977. Some of the material and ideas were later adapted in *Transforming Mission*. For instance, in *Theology of Religions*, Bosch was already describing the theology of religions as "a central issue of missiology" and urging that "our approach to other religions must be a combination of boldness and humility" (1977b:210).

Part of an important schema he developed in *Theology of Religions*, however, does not appear in *Transforming Mission*. In *Theology of Religions* Bosch described "the four dominant interpretations" or "approaches" or "ways" or "solutions" in a theology of religions, and he devoted a chapter to each. They are: relativism, fulfillment, exclusivism (although he does not use this term), and "a fourth way." He described the "fourth way" as that of "an abiding paradox," of "continuity as well as discontinuity," a Christian "yes as well as a no" toward the non-Christian religions (Bosch 1977b: 123). The concept of "a fourth way," as such, does not appear in *Transforming Mission*, although some features — such as the emphasis on an "abiding paradox" — appear in the eight perspectives mentioned above that he outlined for a theology of religions. One aspect of his "fourth way," however, is never mentioned in the later book, namely, the categories of *continuity* and *discontinuity* in the relationship between God's revealing and redeeming activity in Christ and his activity among people of other faiths. This is surprising because they have been important categories in discussions among Protestants in the twentieth century about the theology of religions. There is no clue from Bosch about why they were omitted or why he did not include "a fourth way" as found in *Theology of Religions*.

Whither Mission?

At the end of *Transforming Mission*, David Bosch asks, "Whither Mission?" As for the theology of religions, we have to say — as David Bosch suggested — that all is not clear, not all the crucial issues have been settled, there are loose ends, untidiness, an "abiding paradox," risks, and we should anticipate surprises. But we are not dismayed, for we have assurance in the great commission from the risen Lord, "Lo, I am with you always, to the close of the age" (Mt 28:20).

---

1. For Catholic statements see the statements of the Pontifical Council for Interreligious Dialogue, "Dialogue and Proclamation" and Pope John Paul II's missionary encyclical, *Redemptoris Missio* (William Burrows, Maryknoll, N.Y.: Orbis Books, 1993).

– 10 –

A Seventh Paradigm?

Catholics and Radical Inculturation

William R. Burrows

Introduction

David J. Bosch's achievement in *Transforming Mission* is a *summa missiologica* that enables us to look further and think more deeply about the Christian vocation to mission in the contemporary world. It helps particularly in re-envisioning Christian relations with persons of other religious and philosophical traditions. In that context, the unifying question in this essay is how Christians can find ways to share, manifest, and proclaim their faith in manners that reflect the respect that members of one tradition must extend to members of other traditions. I see this required by a world where differences are real but also where common humanity requires humility in the face of mystery greater than available theological categories can comprehend.

Viewing the tremendous success of *Transforming Mission*, I have grown concerned lest it be treated as the *end* of conversation about Christian vocation rather than as an aid to orient ourselves for voyages into uncharted territories. Since Christian vocation and understanding of Christian mission in the world are unfinished books in which each generation, in the freedom of God's Spirit, must write new chapters, only this latter approach is proper.

Accordingly, the most important task in articulating Christian wisdom is to discern the Spirit's invitation to creativity in areas of life, mission, and apostolate that lie ahead of us. In that process, taking account of the Bible, Christian origins, and doctrinal statements from the past and present are important. More important, though, is living as contemporary-era Christians whose challenges are easily as great as the mission that Bosch sees as the mother of the New Testament.

The historical and exegetical chapters that form the bulk of *Transforming Mission* show Bosch's synthetic abilities, and they have been the parts most commented upon. Chapters 10 through 13, though, show other qualities — including the ability to entertain cognitive dissonance that defied his synthetic temperament's desire to overcome it. What follows aims at teasing out themes in

William R. Burrows is Managing Editor of Orbis Books and in charge of acquisitions in the areas of mission and evangelization, theology of religions, and ecotheology. He has worked in Papua New Guinea and in urban African-American Catholic parishes in the United States.

these last chapters, especially those contained in the sections on mission as contextualization, as liberation, and as inculturation (Bosch 1991a:420–57). Overall, this essay suggests that to make better sense of Bosch's chapters on a postmodern theology of mission, a "Catholic Inculturation Paradigm" needs to be added to his six models. When this is done, something important is brought into greater relief when one reads Part Three: "Toward a Relevant Missiology." The key element I hope to bring into relief is a *model or paradigm of mission entailing an embodied, inculturated, liberating manifestation of the Christ brought about by spiritual transformation.* This goes some way, I hope, to correct what I call an "over-objectification" of the Christian message that typifies many understandings of proclamation.

To begin, I draw attention to the following theme in Chapter 10, "The Emergence of a Postmodern Paradigm":

> Rationality has to be expanded. One way of expanding it is to recognize that language cannot be absolutely accurate, that it is impossible finally to "define" either scientific laws or theological truths. (353)

What is implied in this exhortation shows a philosophical side of Bosch's thinking that I have seldom heard discussed. I refer to the way in which — although they react *against* the Enlightenment — many Christians are held more deeply in the Enlightenment's thrall than they know, exemplifying ironically the adage, "you should choose your enemies carefully, for you shall soon be like them." Conservatives — among whom I include many Catholic restorationists as well as many Protestant Evangelicals and Fundamentalists — end up as wounded by modernity's inability to deal with mystery as the progressives, liberationists, and liberals they love to hate. Even when believing themselves to be firmly "biblical," the work of George Marsden (see 1991) shows they are to a great extent entrapped in narrow, objectivist readings of the Bible — interpretations that owe more to the scientism they reacted against than the rich multi-dimensionality of biblical texts and traditions on mission.

To get to the end of my argument on how "a radical Catholic inculturation paradigm" deserves consideration as a seventh paradigm, I must ask the reader to detour through three discussions — the first on "warfare" in Christian identity; the second on "over-objectification" of mystery as a cause for missiological superficiality; the third on "spirit" in the world. All three discussions are essential to get to part four, though I am sympathetic to anyone who feels they make the chapter too long and beg forgiveness in advance for a certain convolution of my argument.

Remnants of "Missionary Warfare" in Christian Identity

Much of what I deal with below revolves around consequences identified by Bosch as stemming from the medieval and early modern Catholic heritage of a "missionary war" motif (Bosch 1991a:220–30), to which are added the involvement of Christians in patterns of unequal relations between religious traditions, along with unequal international economic and political relations. These patterns, Bosch believed, persist in both blatant and subtle ways in the modern and contemporary missionary movement (the Catholic modern period beginning in the early sixteenth century; the Protestant modern period beginning in the late eighteenth).

The issue revolves around whether received understandings of Jesus as the Christ are suited for interreligious conversations across the boundaries of faith. The problem lurking in the background is foreshadowed in the words taken from Bosch above — attempts to define mission and dialogue within limits of a theological rationality limited by modern objectivist epistemologies may stunt our understanding of what God is about in our age.

A caveat is necessary. I raise the missionary war motif not to bash the missionary movement, but to suggest that a surrender dynamic intrinsic to the dialogue of faith, an element in divine-human relations with analogues in other religious traditions — as well as genuine evangelical roots — has been subverted. I shall go on to suggest how that subversion can be replaced by attitudes more authentically "Christic" in a transformation made necessary if Christians are to achieve true mutuality in relation to other religious traditions.

Unless Christians want to be ridiculous in ways that have nothing to do with Paul's doctrine of the foolishness of the cross (1 Cor 1:18–31), more effective ways of manifesting and proclaiming faith in the Christ need to be found. In that context, re-envisioning Christian self-understanding is vitally important, lest we find ourselves forced to choose between the false alternatives of biblicist fundamentalism or relativist skepticism.

As Bosch summarizes the evidence, and as Troeltsch shows so convincingly in his monumental study of the social teaching of the churches (1976), the church's medieval social ideal in the West was to create a Christian civilization. To do so entailed overcoming the chaos that followed the fall of the Roman Empire. In a process with origins in the collapse of the Western Empire in 410 c.e. and extending through the first centuries of the Protestant Reformation, the church sought to make princes and kings follow ecclesiastical leadership. When Augustine's *De Civitate Dei* was understood well — and often it was not — Augustinian theology's perception of a gulf between the city of God and the ambiguous capacity of history to embody God's Kingdom chastened the church; when Augustine was misunderstood, sacerdotalism reigned.

It seems fair to observe that such nuances were lost when just war theory was cited to warrant wars between Christians and pagans in efforts such as Charlemagne's to establish a new Holy Roman Empire or in a later age's attempt to discipline heretics such as the thirteenth-century Albigensians. The necessity to justify the large-scale killing of Muslims during the Crusades took Christians a step further down the road of seeing non-Christian societies as objects of conquest. Finally, there is no way to hide the fact that the irenic spirit of a few souls like Francis of Assisi and Raymond Llull did not characterize the attitude of Western Christians as a whole toward Islam. Rather, their example is the exception that proves the rule that the six centuries of Christian-Muslim encounter leading up to 1492 and the birth of the modern Catholic missionary movement are a virtually unrelieved history of disastrous relations. That history imprinted itself indelibly on the character of Western Christianity, both Catholic and Protestant.

The missionary war motif carries over into the colonial era. Particularly as Spain and Portugal conquer their "New World," the recent ouster of Muslims from Spain was fresh in memory. The very enthusiasm with which the name of Bartolomé de las Casas was invoked during recent commemorations of the five hundred years since the beginning of the conquest of the Americas by the two Iberian powers is a powerful reminder of just how exceptional de las Casas was (see Gutiérrez 1993).

My point in reciting this is straightforward. Western Christianity has till recently tended to understand the Lordship of Christ, interreligious relations, missionary efforts, and conversion to Christianity — at least implicitly — in military terms. In that conceptual framework the goal of mission is to lead non-believers to surrender to Christ and to create civilizations dominated by Christian values. The fact that biblical terms are utilized at one level in describing mission and conversion, in my opinion, only conceals the fact that a recessive gene in missionary ideology produces results more like those of conquistadors than of the Nazarene founder of our faith.

All that said, we have also learned from Lamin Sanneh (1989 and 1993) (1) that the relationship between Christian mission and colonial regimes was often much more complex than many moderns believe; and (2) that the freeing dynamic of the Gospel often subverted imperialist goals of both missionaries and colonial powers. Furthermore, local people were always *active* participants in shaping the message they received. The picture of passive local peoples bribed by rice-proffering missionaries — so popular among secular academics and propagated in countless novels and films — is as phony as the reciprocal myth of native innocence. Still, even if peoples like the Quechua, the Igbo, and the Chimbu discerned a liberating message in the Gospel, many Christian missionaries and their supporters were perhaps less subtle of intellect. The ultimate victims of missionary war versions of mission theology, as a result, may well be the "sending" churches whose narrow construals of certain doctrines have cut them off from reciprocal relations and friendships with those to whom they went to minister. How is this possible?

A wise spiritual director once told me that human beings are generally not done in by their weaknesses as thoroughly as they are by an excess of their virtues. I have found frequent reason to reaffirm that adage. Applying it to the history of Christian relations with other religious traditions, what is the "virtue" Christians have too vigorously practiced? Zeal for particular angles of vision on truth? Is it possible that simplistic uses of true-false logic have robbed both secular and Christian Westerners of entrée into freeing habits of heart and mind?

Is Over-Objectifying the Christ-Event the Root Problem?

In the case of Christian theology, I wish to suggest that what Bosch calls an "objectivist framework imposed on rationality" (1991a:353) fatally truncates the capacity of Christians to deal with mystery. At the same time, it tricks secularists into believing that politics, social work, science, and technology, shorn of the encumbrance of religious superstition, can create a new humanity. In particular, is it possible that over-objectification of biblical themes on the finality of Christ may have resulted in positivist approaches to doctrine?

What do I mean by *positivist* or *over-objectified* approaches? (1) Extracting and applying logically propositions from events and symbols such as the death of the redeemer without regard to the overall narrative structure in which the symbol is embedded. (2) Applying such objective propositions universally without sensitivity to the problems of going from first-order religious language closely linked to events, symbols, words, and persons in one socio-historical context to second-order doctrinal language in different contexts. This, I believe, leads to an attitude that holds, in effect, that scriptural propositions and doctrines can function "meta-culturally" and "meta-historically" to mediate religious transformation.

The question, overall, is whether Christian theology is sufficiently nuanced in interpreting the nature of the divine-human relationship revealed in the death of Jesus when it extracts a proposition like the following and applies it logically across the universe: *an act of personal faith in the sacrificial death of Jesus is the necessary and constitutive means of salvation.* One could as easily take themes such as the Lordship and finality of the Christ or the incarnation of the *logos* in the Christ. In a different direction, one could examine how Hebrew Testament condemnations of idolatry were extended, say, to African divination rites. In this essay, though, there is space only to look at one such doctrine and its impact on the Christian theology of mission and vocation.

The symbol of the death of the God-man is a focal point in the New Testament's kaleidoscopic portrayal of Jesus as liberating humankind from sin and death and as revealing the heart of Godself. It is, moreover, so powerful an event and symbol both of divine love and human evil that if Jesus' death is seriously misconstrued and falsely objectified, it will necessarily lead to dangerous consequences.

At one level, historians and exegetes see Jesus' death — if I may conflate a host of studies well summarized by invoking those of John Dominic Crossan (1991) and Raymond Brown (1994) — as occurring for one set of reasons from a Jewish perspective and for another from a Roman. But for the followers of Jesus who produced the New Testament, his death as a criminal was a scandal that had to be dealt with theologically, since it upset every comfortable human standard of understanding God analogically.

As diverse as New Testament christologies and soteriologies are — ranging from strict, redemption-accomplished-by-vicarious-sacrifice theories to seeing Jesus as the representation of the character of God — the Christ-event as epitomized in the death of Jesus is a matter of life and death. Basic families of interpretations of the death of Jesus coalesce around the words "transactional" and "revelatory." The former see a transaction taking place between persons of the Trinity on Calvary whereby divine justice, offended by human sin, was satisfied by the sacrificial death of Jesus. The latter revolve around the death of Jesus as representative of the universal state of humankind and of the character of divine-human relations. Transactional theories have predominated in Christian history. Revelatory theories have tended to find favor in recent years.

In classic transactional accounts of the death of Jesus and its importance for human salvation, explicit surrender in faith to the God of Jesus is necessary for salvation. While various escape clauses are often brought forward to account for belief that God can and will save "invincibly ignorant good pagans," such exceptions function to strengthen the general rule (that there is "salvation in no other name" — Acts 4:12), not to weaken it.

Under objectivist doctrines of the operation of unmerited grace — in the context of a Christendom ideal for the social order — if non-Christians or heretics impeded the church in the proclamation of these important facts, the use of princely power to wage just wars to overcome resistance, to imprison heretics, or to compel obedience to received doctrines was readily justified as representing the pursuit of the common good required of Christian princes. And from that insight justifying the right of Christian nations to rule the rest of the world was an easy step.

On the one hand, such doctrines draw attention to the fact that a more robust form of Christianity believed the Christ to be the savior of humankind from a dire fate. Much contemporary theology seems to go wobbly when asked whether humanity suffers from a malady that requires "salvation," and in that wobbliness, I suspect, is revealed a great deal of agnosticism. On the other hand, the use of coercion in direct or indirect missionary wars bears little resemblance to the paradigmatic revelation of the manner in which God saves — the death of Jesus on the cross and new life being conferred in the depths of ignominy.

When what we used to call "faith knowledge" is prostituted, what Bonhoeffer called "cheap grace," made available by "believing" in information about the cross and the death of Jesus, becomes the constitutive means whereby the guilt of believers is expunged and God's justice is satisfied by the sacrifice of Jesus. I term this an over-objectification of doctrine or biblical teaching. Instead of the narratives pointing to a divine-human dialogue, they function in the same way as an impersonal law of nature. In such an objectified belief system, the way is paved for arrogance and false senses of privilege. Despite the biblical pedigree of doctrines such as the "universal finality of Christ," do over-objectifications of the salvation mediated solely by Jesus *reify* and *instrumentalize* the mystery of what took place at Calvary?

David Bosch will have none of this in the present era, as one brief quote makes clear: "... the cross is also a critical category. It tells us that mission cannot be realized when we are powerful and confident, but only when we are weak and at a loss" (1991a:525). He is even more forceful in one of his last speeches, "The Vulnerability of Mission" (1994). Yet liberals, in rejecting such soteriologies, and conservatives, in insisting on them, both fall unwittingly into the trap set by rigid uses of propositions and logic that ignore deeper — paradoxical, ironic, mystical — dimensions of the life, death, and resurrection of Jesus. In a process of real death to self, the fully adult Christian moves beyond mere belief in certain facts.

This kind of changed selfhood — corporate/cultural and individual — imaged in the Bible raises the fundamental problem of missionary war, unequal relations between faiths, and colonial-era understandings of mission which influence how many Christians relate to persons of other traditions. Said briefly, they have so little to do with real transformation in the Spirit of Jesus. The irony is that in liberal rejections of transactional redemption theologies as barbaric and mythological, and in conservative defenses of them against modernist corrosions of biblical truth, both camps may only be displaying the inability to deal adequately with mystery with which one-dimensional modernity has saddled Western culture.

My suspicion is that the death of Jesus strikes deeper chords in those who have ears to hear than what *doctrines* of the significance of that death can mediate. What is needed is a theology of Christian vocation and mission that recognizes the need to develop ears for mystical and spiritual meanings revealed by the events of Calvary and in God's continual suffering in humanity. Such "truths" are not easily reduced to abstract categories such as those traditionally used to describe the effects of the life and work of Jesus for subsequent ages. What am I after? Not a theology that itself warms hearts, though that is a worthy ideal. Rather, a theology that recognizes that *conversion* is the narrow gate through which one enters into communion with God in the faith-knowledge, hope, and love that are the foundation of vocation to mission.

Much more than *information* about the necessity of faith in the Christ for salvation is being recounted in the gospels. In Johannine theology, for instance, the scandal of the death of Jesus is central to the Gospel. Still, units of Johannine text devised to frame the death and resurrection are highly mystical. Reading units such as Chapters 13–17, 18–19, 20, and 21 in a single sitting shows a fast-moving narrative that "composes" events leading up to, comprising, and away from the crucifixion. When John chapters 1–12 are read in the light of the latter chapters, again as narrative parts of a single book, the mystical-spiritual-sapiential nature of the composition of events is clear. We have something more here than "pure history." That uncanny "more" includes an invitation to total personal involvement with the person of Jesus and the transformation made possible in the Spirit.

When, as is done by Richard Cassidy (1992), the entire Johannine corpus is shown to be a body of early Christian literature redacted into its present form during persecutions in Asia Minor as antidotes to Roman "theologies" of the Emperor, particular texts take on new meaning. John 14:6 ("No one comes to the Father except through me") is not merely a proposition underpinning Christian exclusivism. John 15:5b (". . . apart from me you can do nothing" — i.e., embody God's life-giving relation to your fellows — is much more than a proof text for Jesus as the sole source of divine grace. Rather, this small flock, members of an insignificant Jewish sect, are reminded, in the face of concrete threats to their individual and corporate life, that in adhering to the Jesus who had found God precisely in death, they too will find the path to true life. How different this is from finding in such texts warrants to condemn other faiths as idolatrous.

The message of the Johannine texts cited above is deeply Christic and important in an age where gurus of personal fulfillment would seduce us to self-salvation regimens. The universal claim Christians make on the basis of the cross is, in the context of spiritual consumerism, a teaching about the nature of life and death and the possibility of transformation by God found in embracing rather than fleeing death. Seen as part of the wisdom tradition that John clearly means to embrace in making Jesus in 1:1–18 the incarnation of *hokmah-sophia-logos,* the death of Jesus is far richer as a revelation of "life-through-death" than as a transaction between members of an offended triune deity. Transactional theories make sense in cultures where mediation and sacrifice are part of people's intellectual furniture. They are less effective in bringing people into contact with Christian "truth" in other cultures, such as that characterizing much of modern North America.

The claim that God is the source of all life and that this life is available only through embracing the transformation made possible in death *is* a universal claim made with warrants and backing in the life, death, and resurrection of Jesus. But it is not *exclusivist* in a narrow sense. It can be truly good news for all the world.

Still, for many who are presented with objectivist notions of truth by modernity, being faithful to the Bible offers no other alternative than accepting or rejecting theologies of blood sacrifice and expiation as the sole valid interpretation of Calvary. On the other side of that coin, many who have found elements of beauty in other religious traditions believe that exclusivist doctrines generated by objectivized interpretations of Calvary as I have recited are wrong; and that therefore Christianity must be wrong. Ashamed when examples of missionary arrogance are recited, they rush to dissociate themselves from such arrogance. Commonly they feel that faith and hope in Jesus as more than an example or forerunner of social revolution and liberation from other-worldly mumbo-jumbo is over-belief. This, too, betrays an over-objectivist mind-set.

Spirit in the World

What has gone wrong in Christian relations with other traditions may be simply but accurately stated when one observes that the churches have largely worked from a *categorical,* Father-Son theology of Christian existence and not a Trinitarian understanding of the economy of salvation. The Spirit, largely ignored in theologies of mission, introduces a *non-categorical,* mysterious dimension into religious life. Although theology in the West has generally confined the Holy Spirit to the status of mysterious energy making for the efficacy of ecclesiastical activities, "Spirit" functions biblically as a name that moves beyond and disrupts attempts to define Jesus or mission in straightforward language. "Spirit" injects an uncontrollable, effervescent element into the structure of Christian existence — a dimension scarcely explored by theology. Recovering the ability to factor the mysterious event (not primarily conceptual) character of the process of generation of new life into our understanding of Christian mission and vocation, I believe, is central to Christianity recovering its health and being able to deal more vitally with other traditions.

Spirit as the enlivening presence of God invites us to see history as the locus of God's being and action. God-as-Spirit, blowing where *it* will (Jn 3:8), cannot be pinned down, nor can its mediation of divine presence and action be neatly confined to the churches' institutional life, although its fruits can be discerned (Gal 5:16–22). Yet, if I am right, most Western church teaching about the Spirit is little more than an afterthought used to explain God's activity in the church in connection with Jesus, ignoring the mystery of the Spirit as an equal modality or *persona* of the divine nature.

Purely Jesusological pneumatology can lead to putting overmuch faith in seemingly objective biblical and theological categories, while ignoring one of the most important bodies of truth in the New Testament — that imaged in stories such as the one of the disciples on the road to Emmaus (Lk 24:13–50) who meet Jesus in a borderline between ordinary and extraordinary experience — in a liminal, non-categorical presence. There is, I believe, an "event-character" to Christian "truth" that theology needs to acknowledge and is powerless to mediate.

The Emmaus text is a literary transition between Luke's first and second books. It is also a prime example of the event-character of the manifestation of the Christ that leads to new life in faith, hope, and love. In the Acts of the Apostles, the Holy Spirit becomes the dominant partner in mission, the one in whom Luke sees ongoing generations of Christians experiencing the presence of the eschatological kingdom (Stanley 1965). God, in Stanley's convincing rendering of the Lukan, Trinitarian economy of the Spirit, is revealed at places and times not controlled by church or preacher. The call of Saul and the mission of Paul in spreading the Gospel of the Christ are the paradigm of that dynamic. In Paul's exemplification of missionary vocation, the human role is normally instrumental in the process of conversion to the Christ, but subordinate to the divine. What Luke-Acts as a whole reveals is that human activities, whether providing relief (Acts 11:27ff.) or in Paul's celebrated sermon at the Areopagus (Acts 17:22–34), are at the service of a process that enables others to hear God with the heart, a process led by the Spirit (Acts 28:25–28). This theme is prefigured in texts such as Ezekiel 36:24–27, upon which Luke draws, where a new heart gives one the ability to discern realities beyond the categories of space and time.

Now the language with which I ended the last paragraph is clearly not satisfactory to persons who believe that the language of faith is meaningless. What I must answer, however, is that with David Tracy (1981:6–28), I distinguish three publics (or audiences) for theological language: (1) society at large, (2) the academy, and (3) the church. I am using an inner-church language that the liberal church has itself almost abandoned! Furthermore, I agree fully with Tracy's earlier discussion (1975:79–81) about the need to "correlate" theological language with the experience and language of the world at large and with the academy in a new form of fundamental or apologetic theology. Relating Christian claims to experience seems to me essential if the world of faith is not to be relegated to a mere language game played by persons who hold certain private convictions that have no warrants in everyday reality. Making such correlations, however, is not what I am about in the present piece. Here I use highly metaphorical inner-Christian language to denote the fact that:

- Christian experience leads believers to see with new eyes, hear with new ears and understand, hope, and love with a new heart; and that
- this experience is Christomorphic — deriving its basic character from Jesus the Christ, who lived as a first-century Jew, was crucified, and was raised by God from the dead.

One does no favors to conversation partners in other traditions to pretend that Christians make no claim for an experience of, belief in, and hope for a particular kind of transcendent reality mediated by Jesus the Christ, a reality that in transcending all else paradoxically includes everything truly human. Conversion leads to exactly this kind of faith, hope, and love, or it is something other than fully Christian — being in the world in one vital sense while not of it in another.

At a second stage, a distinction between ontological and temporal priorities in mission is important. Ontologically, divine action in grace gives one new eyes to see. Temporally, however, the divine-human concursus is one in which one must first take the risk of following Christ (for example, by helping alleviate the suffering of a neighbor), only afterward discovering that God was leading all the while. In that structure of self-transcending existence, Christian life revolves primarily not around human activities but around responding to divine love and then mediating the mystery of God's presence, love, and promise of salvation. These are central to the Christian vocation to mission. They also mark a structure of existence that results-oriented Westerners are apt to pay lip service to and then forget, lest it impede their compulsion to do important work in which they seek a victory over evil much like victory in warfare. The problem is, in the context of the overall argument of this chapter, that the victory of Christ is perhaps more paradoxical and less straightforward. The resurrection was real, but it was also a *transitus* of Jesus from historical existence to a liminal state wherein his presence is mediated by the Spirit. And victories in the economy of the Spirit are apt to be as paradoxical and liminal as that of Jesus.

"Inculturation" as an Alternate Paradigm?

Insights triggered by David Bosch, Andrew Ross, Raimon Panikkar, and Aloysius Pieris offer ideas of a different model of Christian self-understanding than those dominant in ordinary missiology. In the pages that follow, I attempt to spell out what this may mean in the context of David Bosch's missionary paradigms.

Background

Andrew Ross has spent many years researching the history of Jesuit missions in Japan and China in the sixteenth through the eighteenth centuries. As his research into Alessandro Valignano, Matteo Ricci, Adam Schall, and their associates has progressed, I have had the privilege of hearing him speak formally and informally about what he has learned. Still later, I was able to read successive drafts of his book *A Vision Betrayed: The Jesuits in Japan and China 1542–1742* (1994).

Ross has convinced me that a seventh paradigm needs to be added to David Bosch's six. I shall call it a "Catholic Inculturation Paradigm," and characterize it briefly as one marked by a *radical vision of what is entailed in interfaith and cross-cultural dialogue that leads to the contextualization and inculturation of Christianity.* While I shall not say it on every page, when I say "inculturation" I am including in that term both "dialogue" and "contextualization," since they are components of a single process.

Viewed historically, the Catholic Inculturation Paradigm follows and modifies the Medieval Catholic Paradigm. It antedates and then runs parallel with the Protestant Reformation Paradigm. It had its own encounter with the Enlightenment. In its initial phases, its proponents were formed in Jesuit colleges that were inculcating the new Christian humanism through the extensive Jesuit educational network. This philosophy profoundly influenced basic attitudes toward faith and culture for generations of missionaries. The eighteenth-century squelching of mission practices rooted in the missiology of Matteo Ricci and his successors in China and the throttling of modernism in the last decades of the nineteenth and early part of the twentieth centuries, however, meant that this paradigm was largely repressed until the Second Vatican Council. In addition, since this humanist-influenced missiology was so strongly identified with the Jesuits, who were anathema to the circles of Protestants from which came the Modern Protestant Paradigm, many issues in Catholic inculturation debates were, I suspect, not faced by Protestants until recently. Given their propensity for objectivist readings of the Scriptures and tradition, Evangelicals, Fundamentalists, Pentecostalists, and — ironically — *the Vatican* find the hermeneutics lurking behind Catholic ideas on the permissible limits of inculturation difficult to swallow.

A good deal of the disagreement on inculturation's limits stems from the very different way in which the new learning that led to the Enlightenment influenced different strata within the various churches. Catholic missionary orders patterned on Jesuit models generally embraced ideals of Christian humanism that are fertile ground for fairly radical inculturationist viewpoints. In these orders, questions on inculturation raised within the horizon of a sacramental view of Christian life (as opposed to a more proclamation-oriented Protestant view) never stopped being discussed. Reading Andrew Ross's *A Vision Betrayed,* I realized that even men such as myself, who received initial formation for missionary life in the Society of the Divine Word (the SVD) prior to Vatican Council II, were told by virtually everyone who spoke on the subject that Ricci was right and the Papacy had been wrong. Criticisms were couched carefully, since the SVD was careful not to dissent publicly from official teaching and discipline; still, I never heard anyone defend the decisions of the Papacy. My point? *The Catholic Inculturation Paradigm had an important, though largely invisible, life in the mainstream of Catholic missiology, a place that Bosch seems to have missed.*

What Robert Schreiter has noted in regard to problems involved in sorting out the criteria of authentic local theologies (1985:96–101; see also 119–21) leads me to observe that *who* decides what is a valid local theological development may predetermine *what* will be counted as acceptable. One example may suffice. While there were great efforts expended to cover disagreements between African bishops and the Papacy on the 1994 African Synod in Rome, matters ultimately came down to a firm Vatican decision to seize the initiative on planning the Synod, thus reducing the chance that inculturationists would be in charge of an African Synod in Africa (see African 1996). In a troubling exemplification of deconstructionist insights into the role of power in establishing what counts as "truth," Vatican policies ignore the fact that the same Catholic principles used to enforce official disciplinary practices also allow quite different practices. Should liberty not be given to local churches to make decisions? Power, however — not persuasion — often wins, and when it does the legitimacy of the hierarchy suffers.

While I paint with a broad brush, I see the Catholic Inculturation Paradigm as an attempt to work out what Schreiter calls "local theologies" — with a relatively high degree of decision-making power at the local level. I commend Schreiter's work to persons interested in careful analysis. Stephen Bevans's *Models of Contextual Theology* (1992) is a very accessible exposition of basic approaches to contextualization (and inculturation) involved in this process. In large measure, this radical contextualization-inculturation-dialogue paradigm aims at transcending the lingering effects of the medieval paradigm's missionary war implications. Anthony Gittins's *Bread for the Journey* (1993) may be read as an extended meditation on attaining a spirituality of mutuality in interfaith and cross-cultural conversation in mission. Paul F. Knitter's three major books (1985, 1995, and 1996) bring all this to bear on interreligious questions from a perspective that paradigmatically epitomizes this Catholic inculturationist paradigm.

Returning to Asia and my historical case study, I summarize Ross's exquisitely nuanced work in five paragraphs, which I hope render accurately several of his most important insights as they bear on the Catholic Inculturation Paradigm.

The Asian Jesuits as an Historical Case Study

1. Alessandro Valignano, appointed Jesuit Visitor in the East in 1574, became acquainted with ambiguous aspects of Jesuit missions in Japan as a second generation of missionaries and converts built on and coped with Francis Xavier's methods. Faced with the need to give guidance to Jesuits who were to go to China, Valignano wanted to insure that they understood Chinese philosophy, religion, culture, and language, lest they make the kind of choices in terminology and misunderstandings of customs that had weakened an otherwise very successful mission in Japan. He counseled his men to become fully Chinese, to the point of giving up allegiances to European kings and of transferring political allegiance to the Chinese Emperor, thus completely severing the relationship between Christian faith and European crown power. It was radical in the sixteenth century, a step that the rest of the missionary church had a hard time taking in the twentieth.

2. In Matteo Ricci, Valignano found a man with the temperament and talent to lead this endeavor. As the Japan mission went into decline as a result of both

internecine Christian feuds and being caught up in Japanese political turmoil and xenophobia, Ricci and his successors spent long years gaining access to the imperial court and in study of Chinese classics. While not discouraging Chinese converts to Christianity, they believed that generations of study by themselves and their successors would be necessary before the "Way of Christ" could be taught fully in ways appropriate to China. They embarked on exactly this plan.

3. While Catholic missions virtually everywhere else in the world at this time followed a paradigm that saw non-Christian religious and cultural traditions as elements to be conquered, redirected, or extirpated — a version of the missionary war syndrome — dialogue with Chinese culture and intellectual traditions was carried on by Ricci and his successors as *a conversation between equals*. It was precisely the judgment of equality between cultures that became the stumbling block for their mendicant order rivals and that ultimately brought about their condemnation.

4. The key to whether this inculturation or contextualization of Christianity would be successful rested in the blend of practical mysticism and activism that ideally mark Jesuit-inspired apostolic life. Trusting this mystical activism, however, was ultimately deemed too unpredictable and dangerous for the Papacy to allow to continue. Ignatian rules for discernment, when coupled with immense respect for learning, offer ways in which creativity can be brought into contact with ecclesial criteria. Included in that discernment is a recognition of the event-character of Christian discovery of God's particular invitation in concrete circumstances. Outsiders often forget how Ignatian spirituality was designed to give scope to exactly this kind of Christ-rooted willingness to explore new paths.

5. In manners redolent of contemporary complaints that inculturationists are really shameless syncretists, Ricci and his followers were accused of betraying authentic Christian faith in their attempts to conform their message to Chinese cultural and intellectual forms. Eventually the political climate changed, their experiments were stopped, and the promise of a radically Chinese form of Christianity was dashed.

Reflections

In retrospect, one sees that Ricci had embarked on a program of reconceptualizing Christian identity for the Chinese world in ways as radical as the Hellenization that was Christianity's first major hermeneutic and inculturational milestone. It would be anachronistic to say that the Jesuits in China were consciously carrying on what we today call "inculturation," but *mutatis mutandis* that was the effect of their entire posture, and they were doing it at a depth analogous to that of early Greek and Latin Church Fathers.

In our own day, it is fairly well known, though not often said publicly, that Vatican officials suspect Asian and African theologians writing on mission issues, especially Indian Catholic theologians, of being engaged in post-Christian syncretism. If one views theologies of liberation and feminist theology as forms of inculturation, papal condemnations take on a different light. The question to be addressed to each side in the current impasse is whether they have truly submitted their agenda to a radical discernment process. In addition, the question of *critical* discernment needs to be addressed. Some inculturationist voices are extreme, and one should not believe that our generation will be the first not to produce false prophets. That a proposed step is a way of adapting Christianity to culture is not the same as saying it is dynamically Christian. Discernment is necessary, and the task of ecclesial authorities is not easy.

It is clear that Pope John Paul II's rhetorical questions in *Redemptoris Missio* article 4, on whether missionary work is still relevant or necessary, are motivated by judgments that inculturationists and liberationists go too far. Chapter two of the same encyclical (articles 12–20), on the Kingdom of God, moreover, is written to show that proclamation of Christ is intrinsic to mission and cannot be replaced by vague witness of Kingdom values, which the Pope fears some recommend. These are views that many associate with Latin American and Asian Catholic theologians. Still, all African, Asian, and Latin American theologians whose work I know or with whom I have personally talked deny that the Pope has fairly characterized their positions. They feel, in addition, that channels for frank discussion of these issues are closed and that a kind of creeping infallibilism restricts conversations on inculturation and what constitutes justifiable ecclesial pluriformity.

Pieris and Panikkar: Contemporary Exemplars of Catholic Inculturationism

The case for the Catholic Inculturation Paradigm in Asia, where it is unlikely that such traditions as Hinduism, Buddhism, Islam, Confucianism, and Taoism will ever be "overcome" by existing forms of Christianity, is illustrated in the life and work of Aloysius Pieris and Raimon Panikkar. (An analogous case for a dynamic engagement with cultural-historical currents can be as easily documented in Africa or Latin America, or among North American women, African-Americans, Hispanics, or Asians.)

For the record, it should be noted that both Pieris and Panikkar have personally expressed to me their dislike of the term "inculturation" and reluctance to be associated with it. I still see it as useful, when its definition is expanded to include the results of dialogue and shared praxis.

Aloysius Pieris, director of the Tulana Research Center, is a Sri Lankan Jesuit, an heir to the traditions of the great Japan and China Jesuit tradition, as well as the South Asian Jesuit tradition of Roberto de Nobili. Pieris holds graduate degrees from the University of London and the Gregorian, and has taught in many prestigious schools. He lives today, however, in a humble center where he carries on studies in ancient Buddhist texts, aids disadvantaged peoples, works to promote peace, and generally carries on within an interfaith community a life that blends spiritual practices of Buddhism and Christianity. Pieris's two published books (1988a and b) and a third, which is in press (1996), show profundity in both spiritual and scholarly dimensions.

Raimon Panikkar is a veritable United Nations in one person — Indian and Catalan; philosopher, student of science, scholar of Indian texts, Christian theologian, social critic, and ecologist; Christian, Buddhist, and Hindu; priest and mystic. Panikkar has written scores of books and articles in a dozen or more European and Asian languages, among which *The Cosmotheandric Experience* unifies in a single vision insight into how the depths of human experience entail simultaneous participation in the Divine, the Cosmic, and the Human. He now lives in a tiny mountain village near Barcelona where he is finishing at a prodigious rate books begun during his distinguished academic career in the United States.

While their personalities and styles are different, one important element illustrative of the Catholic Inculturation Paradigm shines through. Both Pieris and Panikkar refuse to separate within their personhood Christian, Buddhist and/or Hindu elements, and neither concedes to accusations that they bifurcate, synthesize, or syncretize these traditions. They can and will *distinguish* between them, but each believes that the worlds mediated by these religious traditions are — at our present stage of knowledge and conceptual abilities — incommensurable. Still they maintain that they are existentially compatible on a different plane. In conversation, I have asked them if the phrases "plural religious consciousness" or "plural identity" render what they experience. They smile benevolently and say that perhaps these terms can describe how they belong to more than one tradition simultaneously. I don't believe, though, that they think it describes *everything* they experience. I need a label. They seem quite happy to live without one.

What is one to make of such men? On the one hand, as a Protestant Evangelical friend observes, if medieval Catholic missionaries believed as they do, Europe might never have been converted. On the other hand, to know Pieris and Panikkar is to know also that their Christian identity — if unconventional — is deep and authentic. Christ and Asian traditions, it seems, have changed them in ways that many Western Christians feel uncomfortable with.

Since we are dealing with questions of mission, it is well to say clearly that one of the areas that makes Western Christians uncomfortable is their view that there is virtually no chance of wholesale conversions of Asians to Christianity within any foreseeable time frame. In fact, neither would see it as a desirable goal, if the Christ to whom Asians would convert were the one they find some churches proclaiming — an over-objectified Christ who is believed to be captured adequately in certain litmus-test propositions. These are, admittedly, very strong views.

Both go on to venture the guess that Asian religious traditions are having at least as great an effect on Christians as Christianity is having on Asians — and probably making as many converts. Pieris, in a recent article (1993: 33–35; reprinted in Pieris 1996), states categorically that he does not believe that the "Euro-ecclesiastic Christ of the official church" can succeed except in "a few well-defined areas." Why? Because, he says, conversions commonly occur between cosmic religions (sometimes called "tribal," "local," or "primal") and metacosmic religions (such as Christianity, Buddhism, or Islam). They do not occur, except in relatively rare instances, from one metacosmic tradition to another. Pieris recognizes that this is not an absolute truth, but he cannot imagine circumstances that will alter it in the foreseeable future. He does, though, see a future for an "Asian Christ" (37–42) who will be revealed over time in a dialectic process of resolving at least four deeply rooted conflicts (42–46) wherein the poor and marginalized struggle for full human dignity. Pieris's Asian Christ is a liberator, but not visibly connected with the church.

To go into Pieris's or Panikkar's christologies and accounts of the possibilities of plural religious consciousness would take pages and pages, and still not do justice to them. What I must remain content with is, first, to recommend that their works be read and, second, to suggest that they are not recommending something radically new. The process was, in fact, initiated by Alessandro Valignano's directions to Matteo Ricci to enter fully into Chinese habits of mind and heart. Moreover, although we will not develop the matter here because of the complexity of the entire raft of problems raised by de Nobili's Brahman status and the caste system, the life and work carried on in India by Roberto de Nobili also helped pave the trail trodden by both Pieris and Panikkar.

While what I believe can be proved or disproved only *a posteriori,* the achievements of persons such as Panikkar and Pieris may someday be pointed to as marking the way: (1) toward the expansion of rationality called for by David Bosch in his outline of what should constitute a postmodern theology of Christian mission; (2) toward embracing "mystery" and dealing with it in non-reified manners in theology; and (3) toward enabling Christian wisdom to deal with intuitions of the character of existence that go beyond our common logical categories. I suspect that only in some such way of encouraging the unfolding of this inculturation paradigm will we meet the Spirit preparing hearts to meet Christ on the way to new Emmauses.

Drawing Conclusions

In the world emerging from the Cold War and Western ascendancy in so many areas of life, *verbal proclamation* of Christ may not be the best way for Christians to carry on mission. We live in a world of such verbal and noise pollution, of claim and counterclaim, of consumerism and religious salesmanship that preaching may indeed be a counterwitness. In that context, then, if one is Christian and believes the Gospel is Good News to all humankind, it could well be that *embodied manifestation* of the Good News will enjoy priority. One Mother Teresa may indeed be worth a thousand sermons or leaflets distributed.

A perspective on why Catholics are typically taken with "manifestation" as opposed to "proclamation" may be found in David Tracy's monumental *The Analogical Imagination* (1981). This book is the best source I know for a discussion of how a (typically) Protestant concentration on "proclamation" needs to be kept in tension with a (typically) Catholic concentration on "manifestation." Tracy's point overall is that Christianity needs both manifestation and proclamation. In that context, the Catholic Inculturation Paradigm I have been speaking of can be interpreted as a concretization of the sense that lives, sacraments, and events can manifest the presence and action of God in ways that complement and sometimes replace the word that proclaims God's presence and action. I have profited immensely from contact with Protestant Evangelicals over the years. I hope they will find in the sometimes fuzzy mystical manifestation preoccupations of Catholics similar food for thought.

It is my judgment that letting the Spirit transform one's entire personhood and communities and then putting the transformed self and community at the service of God is the most effective way to witness to Christ in our day. It goes far deeper than liberal exhortations to give good example. Rather, it exemplifies another Augustinian adage, *cor ad cor loquitur* ("heart speaks to heart"), recalling that religious knowledge is intersubjective and mediated by sacramental encounters. Recognizing that dynamic, though, puts churches in an uncomfortable position, for the initiative is truly then in God's hands.

Responding to these insights from spirituality and mysticism entails Westerners letting go of controls, for embodied manifestation will largely have to be done by local Christians. Mission will cease to be something done by Northerners *for* their brown, black, red, and yellow brothers and sisters or vice versa. Letting go of old habits may be made easier for Western Catholics in that they will have very little choice. The dearth of vocations to traditional fulltime ministries — especially to life in religious orders and as priests — insures that there will be insufficient Westerners to control the process in the South.

Christian efforts to manifest Christ in Latin America, Africa, and Asia will be carried on by Latin Americans, Africans, and Asians — or they will grind to a halt. More important, changes underway in both the Third World and in the traditional homelands of Christianity in the First make geographical conceptions of mission largely outmoded. Despite Pope John Paul II's careful nuances in *Redemptoris Missio* (articles 31–40), mission *ad gentes* is everywhere, and the boundaries between pastoral work, new evangelization, and "mission" are blurred. Christianity has become a diaspora faith in many parts of the world, and cultural-historical reasons will keep present forms of Christianity from making substantial progress in Asia. I suspect that a form of post-liberal, evangelical and liberationist Catholicism — one that embraces insights from the women's movement, liberation theology, interreligious dialogue, and our growing understanding that humankind is part of the world of nature — will evolve. That form of Christian life will carry on an embodied manifestation of Christ, or Catholicism will become irrelevant.

I move to shakier ground when I say that I also suspect that the future of mission by Protestants will be shaped largely by analogous inculturationist movements. I realize fully that mainline churches appear to be tottering and uninterested in mission, except as a commitment to changing social conditions. I know, too, that immense numbers of foreign Evangelical, Pentecostalist, and Fundamentalist missionaries, especially from the United States, are active in Latin America, Africa, and Asia. These Protestants are important in bearing explicit witness to and proclaiming their construals of the biblical message about Jesus. The whole church should be happy they are at work. Still, it takes an immense suspension of historical judgment to believe that *their* converts will not do to *their* construals of the Christian message what every group of converts to Christ has always done — *embody* the message in forms of inculturation that will be every bit as radical as those which some conservative churches today vehemently oppose. African Independent Christianity, for instance, is perhaps the liveliest and most vital form of Christian mission in the world today, and its life takes place in categories that have very little to do with "normal" Christian pathways.

The Christian future will be like the past, we can be sure, in at least one way if in no other. It will surprise us. David Bosch's last three chapters — despite his great desire to harmonize dissonant strands of thought and action — show that he understands that. It was his greatness, in the final analysis, to recognize that the Spirit blows us where we know not. I hope that my attempt to bring into relief implications of the Catholic Inculturation Paradigm will help us anticipate the surprises we have in store.

Placing Critical Issues in Relief

A Response to David Bosch

Christopher Sugden

Introduction

I recommended *Transforming Mission* as a textbook before I had read it. I was attracted to David Bosch's book not only from knowledge of his earlier work, but by the prospect of having within one volume a decent missiology updating the reader on current missiological thinking that took account of context, of the relation between evangelism and social concern, and treated the biblical writings as sources for missiological reflection. Much of this had already been written in other disparate sources. Bosch brings it together between two covers. While marking papers in mission at Oxford University over the last two years I have noticed a marked change: in 1992 everyone was reading and quoting Newbigin. This year, everyone was quoting Bosch.

But they may not have read him cover to cover; 500 close-type, densely argued pages is heavy work. The measure of the book's quality is that it is possible to read it on two levels — in gobbets for the excellent summary of the important issues — interfaith dialogue or mission in the Reformation period, for example. At another level the whole work displays Bosch's major thesis that in the current century we have entered a new paradigm of mission which is historical, inductive and pluralist.

Bosch takes the thesis that Thomas Kuhn developed in order to describe the way people develop scientific theories: scientists operate with a framework of given presuppositions called a paradigm. Bosch uses it as a heuristic device to understand what people take for granted in the way they think about Christian mission. The way is open for us to evaluate whether his description of any particular paradigm operating at any particular time is consistent and adequate.

According to Bosch, the current period is marked by a paradigm which is historical, inductive and pluralist and includes foci of the unity of the church, the mission of God, and the missionary dimension of all theology. Saayman

Christopher Sugden directs the Oxford Center for Mission Studies in Oxford and is active internationally in the attempt to help theological education, especially by extension, in the Global South.

A longer version of this essay was prepared for a September 1993 meeting of the British and Irish Association for Mission Studies.

(1992) and Baillie (1993) identify aspects of the reality of present-day mission that are not covered in Bosch's description. That is part of the continual process of modifying the paradigm. But we should beware of reifying the paradigm, which Bosch tends to do when he criticizes evangelicals on the grounds that they do not follow the current paradigm in the area of the unity of the church. "The paradigm shift which is in evidence in the ecumenical movement is absent among evangelicals" (Bosch 1991a:461). He actually defines this as meaning that evangelicals have an understanding of spiritual unity prior to visible unity. It could be equally the case that the paradigm might be described in different ways. For example, the period since 1989 has seen the collapse of highly centralized universal organizations politically and in the Christian world. Both the WCC and the Lausanne Committee have experienced severe difficulty, as Bryant Myers points out (1992). The Lausanne Committee has, to all intents and purposes, greatly retrenched, and following the Canberra Conference, the WCC reorganized itself in the face of considerable criticism at Canberra, not least from the Orthodox and Evangelicals (see Maldanado 1993). The new paradigm is plurality and networking. Organizational unity may not so easily belong to the new paradigm.

Bosch's thesis can undoubtedly be critiqued and revised. This does not imply a weakness. It means we can build on the foundation he has laid and follow the signposts he sets up.

First it is instructive to ask whether his description of the current paradigm covers all the evidence. Saayman and Baillie draw attention to the omission of the role of women in mission, both in history and today; the growth of the Pentecostal Movement, especially in Latin America where consensus among observers is that Pentecostals are achieving among the poor at least as much if not more than liberation theologians and activists whom Bosch discusses at length; the developments in liturgy both in the Catholic and Protestant traditions; the developing concern for the environment as part of Christian mission; the role of Christian non-governmental organizations in the relief and development field; and I would add and develop later, the role and contribution of Two-Thirds World Evangelicals.

Second, does he give criteria for evaluating the components of the current paradigm? or for critiquing the post-modern culture that is replacing modernity? Baillie asks whether the current paradigm is the result of Christian reflection or of the impact of the culture on the church.

Third is Bosch's approach a history of ideas approach, or does he adequately describe and evaluate the institutions which expressed and promoted these paradigms? The substance of this critique is that though Bosch might identify a shift in paradigm in the realm of ideas from modern to post-modern and thus the window of opportunity for a church in mission to be a significant contributor to defining what is human (Bosch 1991a:362), modern ideas are enshrined in three institutions of modern capitalism, the modern bureaucratic state and the knowledge industry of universities and the media. Os Guinness, James Hunter and John Seel pointed out at a 1993 Lausanne Consultation on Modernity that just because the ideas of the Enlightenment have been shown to be inadequate does not mean that the institutions that have heavily invested in modernity will go into voluntary liquidation.

Bosch's Contribution

Bosch's case is that there is a missionary dimension to all theology:

> Mission was... an expression of the very being of the church.... Just as the church ceases to be church if it is not missionary, theology ceases to be theology if it loses its missionary character.... We are in need of a missiological agenda for theology rather than just a theological agenda for mission; for theology... has no reason to exist other than critically to accompany the *missio Dei.* ... mission [is] the subject with which theology has to deal. (Bosch 1991a: 494–95)

Bosch is particularly helpful in identifying the source of the lack of missionary dimensions to theology:

> For many centuries there was only one discipline of theology without subdivisions.... Under the impact of the Enlightenment this one discipline subdivided into two areas; theology as practical know-how necessary for clerical work, and theology as one technical and scholarly enterprise... theology as practice and theory.... "Practical" theology became a mechanism to keep the church going, whilst the other disciplines were examples of pure science. (489–90)

The supposed objectivity of the Enlightenment insisted that study of any discipline be autonomous and objective. This required detachment. Those who were engaged in and committed to the mission activity of the church clearly could not be detached and objective. So they were disqualified from engaging in the scientific study of the church and her beliefs.

The major break with this tradition of "pure science" in theology came, according to Bosch, from the birth of Third World theologies which insisted that all theology (like all other disciplines) is contextual. The supposed objectivity and universality were only the expressions of the interests of the context in which they were formulated. This attack at the level of ideas may have undermined the claims of Western theology to arbitrate over Third World theologies (456). But can it help address those practical situations which continue to be the cause of the Two-Thirds World being held in thrall? This is why a practical critique of Bosch as will be adduced later is most important.

Bosch's case and his analysis of the lack of a missiological dimension in so many theologies is particular apposite in the UK today. There is a process in hand whereby mission teachers in theological colleges and university faculties are examining ways in which to recover the missionary dimension of theology. The urgent point is that leaders and teachers of the church need to develop the skills to discover ways in which to think missiologically about their situations, and to use their week by week teaching to enable congregations to engage missiologically with their surroundings in everyday life. This is to be achieved not by special classes in mission as a bolt-on extra, but by encouraging the study of, for example, the Old Testament in such a way that a study of the religion of the patriarchs provides resource material for reflecting on living among those of other faiths.

It is for this reason that mission theology must be practical — it must enable Christians to engage with their surroundings. This begins to generate part of the critique of Bosch, for which his own writing serves as an impulse. What practice does Bosch's theology actually encourage? This is the basis of the critique we will examine.

Critique in Context

There are three possible levels in which to offer a critique. As Bosch points out, all theology is done in context. So we ask from what context and to what context is he speaking? With whom is he discussing? In his own setting he remained at some personal cost a member of the Dutch Reformed Church in South Africa. He was also chairperson of the National Initiative for Reconciliation (NIR), which was formed in South Africa after the June 1985 "emergency."[1]

At a second level is the critique from those who could be classed as or identify themselves with the marginalized in South Africa. As we shall point out later, the epistemological perspective of the poor is important in the biblical writings.

The third level is the intercultural and international critique. David was engaged in dialogue through the journal *Missionalia* and attendance at conferences with the community of Christian mission leaders from churches and mission organizations addressing the issues of Christian mission. The engagement of those from different cultures and contexts provides the setting for enriching our viewpoint, freeing us from a ghetto mentality, and enabling the church to engage in a process by which necessarily contextual theologies in each context can yield a theology that transcends context.

These levels overlap. A critique from the marginalized is also an intercultural critique. His book is an engagement with mission paradigms from different cultures in time and space. But since a person's prime location is his or her own context, this study will focus on the critique that has been offered by marginalized black and white evangelicals on the essence and implications of David's missiology in theology and practice in South Africa.

---

1. The original National Initiative for Reconciliation Conference was called by Michael Cassidy of Africa Enterprise. Its aims were as follows: (1) to gather together the scattered Children of God and especially Christian leaders, to bring love and light into the situation of polarization and darkness in South Africa; (2) to assemble in humility and repentance, penitence and prayer so that we might in Faith and Hope affirm and work out God's redemptive purpose for South Africa at this time; (3) to encourage the demonstration of true discipleship by practical and relevant action to announce the Good News and discern His guidance for Church and State; (4) to bring encouragement to the Body of Christ so that it may stand and live as a Community of Hope. Accompanying the aims was a statement that claimed the NIR was ideologically free and politically neutral: "A Third Way forward must be found in which socio-political solutions emerge from Christian repentance, reconciliation, reflection and resolution" (Statement of purpose of NIR, quoted in Balcomb 1990:103 and Appendix).

Critiques from the South African Context

The sources for my critique from the South African context include several who attended the September 1993 meeting of the British and Irish Association for Mission Studies, where this paper was presented. They include the Rev. George Ngwenya from Soweto, an office bearer in Concerned Evangelicals. Mr. Ngwenya is doing post-graduate research at the Oxford Center for Mission Studies, comparing the missiology of David Bosch and Archbishop Desmond Tutu. Concerned Evangelicals is a grouping of black and white Evangelicals who came together in the wake of the June 1985 Emergency. Their initial task was to produce the document "Evangelical Witness in South Africa," partly as a process of self-criticism in response to the Kairos Document. That task has expanded to include theological education at the Evangelical Theological House of Studies (ETHOS) on the campus of the University of Natal in Pietermaritzburg for black pastors who, because of their stance on apartheid, have been ejected from seminaries run by white-led mission churches. Concerned Evangelicals also identify themselves internationally with that stream of the evangelical ecumenical movement which Bosch refers to in *Transforming Mission* (1991a:461).

A second source of South African views on Bosch's theology is Dr. Tony Balcomb, who comes from a South African English background, is a member of Concerned Evangelicals and is the dean of studies at ETHOS. His doctoral work at the University of Natal under Professor Cochrane was on "Third Way Theology, a Critical Analysis of the South African Church's Struggle for Significance During the Decade 1980–90." This focused particularly on the process of the National Initiative for Reconciliation, of which David Bosch was the chairman.

Bosch's role in the changes within the Dutch Reformed Church must not be overlooked. Once this church abandoned giving its theological rationale for apartheid, the government soon began modifying its position. Bosch was a very early critic of the DRC position from the perspective of justice within the DRC. The impact and contribution that this had must be measured by others.

Ngwenya points out that the issue of justice is not the only or even the fundamental issue to be addressed. First, apartheid was itself a way of solving a number of issues clustered about the issues of land, peoplehood, state and nation. Historically, in the nineteenth century, the Boer people sought an identity and a life for themselves outside the encroaching British Empire in South Africa, partly because they wished to keep their slaves. They interpreted their experience in the categories of the Exodus as they engaged in the Great Trek and sought a new land as a separate people. Bosch brought the critique of justice to their solution. But the theological questions of who owns land and what constitutes a nation remain as an agenda for missiological reflection. For example, the questions raised are: What are the rights of the original inhabitants of land (in this year of indigenous peoples)? What are the rights of those who have from the point of view of the indigenes usurped the land and from their own point of view developed it? What counts as a nation — European-imposed political divisions or the bonds of race and blood across imposed political barriers? These are urgent issues for the church to address in South Africa, since the answers the church has given in the past have been discredited. Are they to be replaced by answers that deny Christian faith?

Reconciliation or Restitution

A major issue to be addressed is the issue of the relation between reconciliation, repentance and restitution. On the one side, according to Balcomb, the theological concern of the leaders of the NIR was for reconciliation. The NIR itself offered to be the framework and meeting ground where people of all views could come and seek reconciliation with one another so as to better address the common issues facing the country. On the other side, those who framed the Kairos Document and those who formed Concerned Evangelicals hold that reconciliation is a good rather than a prerequisite, and can only be achieved through proper restitution and recompense for the theft of land, for inhuman and degrading treatment, and myriads of injustices experienced by the blacks at the hands of the white community.

John de Gruchy (1986) suggests that in fact reconciliation and restitution are complementary strategies. Balcomb suggests that the division between them exists at a number of levels. For Balcomb it represents a tension between those on the one side who have power, fear losing it, fear conflict, and regard the exercise of power as necessarily forceful and possibly violent, and those on the other who do not have power and seek it; this involves a tension between understanding power as either necessarily coercive (as Bosch does, 1991a: 442), and therefore to be avoided by Christians, or as constructive and cooperative. It represents a tension between on the one hand a view that interprets society in functional terms and puts a high priority on order, and on the other a view that sees society in conflictual terms. For Ngwenya, the NIR put reconciliation before social justice. Seen in this perspective, in light of the asymmetry of power between the white and black community, the call for reconciliation by the white Christian community rather than an active promotion of empowerment is seen as yet further evidence of the domination of one particular power group, and of a failure by the NIR to engage in an adequate analysis of the South African context.

This is a debate which Bosch alludes to. He writes:

> Since Christians believe that the decisive battle has been won by Christ, they may believe in the possibility of forgiveness, justification and reconciliation. In view of the harsh realities of oppression and exploitation such reconciliation will be costly... the element of conflictual analysis in liberation theology should not be an alternative to reconciliation but an intrinsic dimension of restoring community between those who are now the privileged and underprivileged. (1991a: 442)

Here is the hard issue and the tension: on the one hand reconciliation is by grace and constitutive of the church. On the other, set within the social reality of the South African situation, this is easily distorted by the culture in a way that is incompatible with the Christian concern for justice.

The Church and Social Change

This tension represents a debate about the nature of the church, the nature of God's work in the church, the nature of God's work outside the church, and the engagement of the church with the realm of politics. Ngwenya is critical of Bosch's view because, even if the church is identified as an alternative community, if the church is the focus of God's activity to bring change in any situation, no way forward is suggested about what the church should *do* in the concrete situation. Willem Saayman records Nicol's critique: "There is a basic tension between the distinctiveness, uniqueness and weakness of the church and his desire that she should stimulate real social change" (Saayman 1992:46; quoting Nicol 1990:86).

For Bosch, "The church is an ellipse with two foci: its worship and prayer on the one hand and its engagement with the world on the other" (1991a:385). The church's identity sustains its relevance and involvement (385). "There is a legitimate concern for the inalienable identity of the church and there should not be any premature amalgamation and confusion between it and the world" (386). "Even if secular history and the history of salvation are inseparable they are not identical" (387). "Salvation history is not a separate history, a separate thread unfolding itself inside secular history. There are not two histories, but two ways of understanding history" (508). Bosch is hesitant to identify God at work in history. The lesson he draws from the heresy of the theological justification of apartheid, as of the German Christian movement in the 1930s, secularism in the sixties and the development of socialism in the postwar period is that "all these signs of the times have been discredited, to the point of being an acute embarrassment to those who hailed them so enthusiastically" (429). He rejects the view that facts of history reveal where God is at work, but assents that the facts illuminated by the gospel do reveal where God is at work.

> Where people are experiencing and working for justice, freedom, community, reconciliation, unity and truth, in a spirit of love and selflessness, we may dare to see God at work . . . this enables us to make decisions, even if they are relative in nature, since our judgments do not coincide with God's final judgment. (429–30)

In the NIR process, there was a special concern to avoid the two extremes of the nationalists and the liberationists. Balcomb (1990) interprets this as showing that, having identified with the forces that established apartheid, the church did not wish to expose itself to a similar fate by identifying with the forces that sought to overthrow apartheid. Apartheid is thus an evil political policy that will be replaced by another evil political policy if its overthrow is supported.

Balcomb further identifies that the motif used to reinforce discontinuity with political programs was that of the alternative community. This was not intended to militate against any engagement whatsoever, but to qualify and monitor that engagement; to provide a framework to relativize the aims of political programs. Balcomb's critique is that the approach was essentially theoretical. "The fact that there were not demonstrable models of the alternative community meant inevitably that . . . any use . . . would have to be on the level of abstract theory rather than empirical reality." Cochrane objects that "an ideal Church never experienced in practice is more likely to breed cynicism, bitterness and despair rather than concretely situate a real hope" (Balcomb 1990: 67, quoting Cochrane 1987:225).

Balcomb suggests that Bosch would find it very difficult to escape this critique because for him liberation is "of another other" (Bosch 1977a). The otherness of the church and the otherness of the kingdom means the otherness of the church's involvement in society, and the otherness of true liberation. "He was unable to elucidate in any significant way what constituted this otherness in the concrete realities of society. This would be to enter into terrain where the church should not interfere (Balcomb 1990:70). This fear was partly based on the notion that as soon as the church does this, it attempts to impose theological values on the world and makes itself vulnerable to the dangers of identifying with a particular political ideology. Bosch writes, "The Church as an eschatological community may not commit itself without reservation to any social, political (or economic) project," (1991a:387). Balcomb draws the following conclusion: "While Bosch repudiated neutrality by saying that the church should be "intensely interested" in the affairs of this life he clearly warned that this interest should go no further than announcing Christian principles" (Balcomb 1990:70). Balcomb sees the working out of these principles in the case study of the National Initiative for Reconciliation in a neutrality that meant siding with the powerful. Balcomb also identifies this position in the "Kerk en Samelewing" document of the Dutch Reformed Church, where the church attempted to disassociate itself from apartheid by stressing the church's uniqueness. But it could not bring itself to legitimate the struggle against apartheid. Bosch held the same position. Thus for Balcomb, the essential problem with Bosch's view of the church is that the uniqueness of the church was more important than the church's prophetic function in society.

Balcomb then asks in whose interests it is to affirm the distinctiveness of the church. While Bosch clearly shows prophetic concern for the poor and oppressed, he holds that the work of the church is to soften the sharp edge of differences between peoples and races into diversity (Bosch 1977a:16). Balcomb suggests that Bosch, a careful master of language, was more concerned to be heard by members of his own church than by those sensitive to such contradictions.

Bosch's use of the term "the third race" for the church must be understood in the context of his own DRC's use of the term "people's theology" to legitimize apartheid. The alternative community motif is to deabsolutize his own people's theology. Nicol defends Bosch on grounds that Bosch was working against white domination in the way he knew best. Balcomb suggests that as a critic of the powerful, Bosch was indeed prophetic. But to the extent this avoided a legitimation of the struggle of the oppressed, the question is raised: "Is the moral decision to delegitimize the structures of power for the powerful equal to the moral decision to delegitimize the processes of empowerment for the powerless?" (Balcomb 1990:74). Is it legitimate, in other words, to equate distance from the violence of the oppressor with distance from the violence of the oppressed in resistance? Balcomb invites consideration of the further factors, that the protagonist of delegitimization was a member of the powerful group. Balcomb likens this to taking part in the suppression of a weaker group and then withdrawing from the conflict and refusing to act with the weaker group on the basis that the weaker may eventually become the stronger. He likens this process in turn to deciding that AIDS is a serious but incurable disease, so let us find preventions against similar diseases in future (rather than seeking to combat AIDS now).

The Epistemological Position of the Poor

The question is whether this decision primarily to address the position of the powerful matters. Bosch has considerable and important material in *Transforming Mission* on the place of the poor in the mission of the church. But, as Balcomb points out, Bosch does not embrace what to Balcomb and this writer is an important aspect of that material. That is that the meaning of the term "Good news to the poor" is that what the gospel means *to the poor* determines what it means *for everyone*. It can be shown, for example, that the meaning of the good news for the poor is that people gain a new identity and peoplehood in Christ — those identified as sinners are reidentified as "lost" sheep of the house of Israel, and in Paul later those who were no people, and aliens to the commonwealth of Israel, receive a new identity as members of the household of God. With identity as a key concept, we can notice that the content of Jesus' call to the rich in Luke 12 was not to seek their identity through grace in their possessions (see Samuel and Sugden 1991). Recall the text, "A man's life does not consist in the abundance of his possessions" (Lk 12: 14). In the history of the church, when the gospel has been formulated by what it means to the rich, it tends to omit precisely those factors that are important for the poor.

By omitting discussion of this putative epistemological privilege, Bosch omits the importance of solidarity with the poor, not only for their benefit, but for the mutual benefit of the non-poor. Such a perspective would perhaps have encouraged him to take further steps in the struggle of the disenfranchised majority against apartheid. It was my privilege to go as a guest of Caesar Molebatsi, the founding chairman of Concerned Evangelicals, with an international delegation to meet with David Bosch and members of his faculty in the University of South Africa in Pretoria in 1989 to discuss the situation in South Africa. I remarked after the discussion that I was disappointed at the somewhat dismissive attitude David evinced in regard to the work of black evangelicals and their statement, "Evangelical Witness in South Africa." This was only a subjective response, and is only anecdotal evidence, but it bears upon my sense that David Bosch was still on a journey in this regard, as indeed we all are. Bosch's note on this in *Transforming Mission* is instructive:

> In the context of the apartheid system and the experience of repression
> and police brutality during a state of emergency, evangelicals felt forced to

respond, that they were called to a ministry of proclaiming Christ as Savior and of inviting people to put their trust in him, but they were equally
convinced that sin was both personal and structural, that life was of a
piece, that dualism was contrary to the gospel, and that their ministry had
to be broadened as well as deepened. (1991a:407)

This is interesting for what it does not say about Evangelical Witness, which was
a forceful argument for evangelical involvement in the struggle against apartheid,
and on the need for repentance in collusion with it.

Further, despite his words about the need to listen to theologies from the
Third World (456), his discussion of such theologies is limited to those that he
is able to undermine for an over-optimistic confusion of the activity of God and
the process of history in liberation theology, not those that would come close
enough to his position to actually modify it. Thus he gives no serious attention to the missiologies from the two-thirds world evangelicals pioneered by the
Latin American Theological Fraternity. He does not recognize that the whole
trend of evangelicals since Lausanne 1974 to unite evangelism and social concern in the mission of the church started with the presentations of René Padilla
and Samuel Escobar from Latin America at Lausanne, a process documented
from 1966 to 1983 by Padilla and Sugden (1986).

Padilla concludes that the process by which evangelicals around the world
came to understand the integration of evangelism and social concern was from
the reflection of those two-thirds world Christian communities engaged in this
ministry. These were often mediated to the West by relief and development
agencies (who get no mention in Bosch's survey) who themselves were able to
build up a considerable constituency of support of a theology that they inherit
from but never attribute to the two-thirds world.

Bosch dismisses the term "two-thirds world" as failing to encompass social
and economic realities (1991a:432), whereas the original place that this term
appears and is defined in print (Samuel and Sugden 1984) clearly states that it
refers to those who live in situations of poverty and powerlessness and shows
that it is a self-definition of people in such contexts. It is hardly proper for
someone outside that context to find fault with people's own self-designation.
The critique of those who define themselves in such terms of the EATWOT
fraternity is that they live with a victim mentality and fail to take seriously the
presently experienced victory of the gospel.

Bosch's discussion of western development as modernization cites Wayne
Bragg in a presentation made in 1983 (Bosch 1991a:433). Bragg's critique was
derived from his experience with the Latin American Theological Fraternity,
was a critique that fraternity had made for a number of years, and indeed Bragg's
presentation was at a consultation called and directed by Two-Thirds Evangelical Church leaders in 1983. The very integration reached at that consultation,
in which "for the first time in an official statement emanating from an international evangelical conference the perennial dichotomy was overcome" (407),
was due to the input of the Two-Thirds World participants. Later, Bosch talks
about the need for interculturation, that all theologies need each other. This

has been said consistently by Two-Thirds World Evangelical theologians since at least 1982. (See, for example, the Conference Findings in Sharing Jesus in the Two-Thirds World, which took place in 1982.) This may all sound like nit-picking. But the plain fact is that many concerns Bosch records have been raised for a number of years by Two-Thirds World Evangelicals. But they are not cred-ited with them. Instead, while there is an exhortation to have an exchange of theologies, this is going to be through Western students studying in the third world as well as Two-Thirds World students studying in the West (456). There is no hint that there might be current theologians who would be able to react to Western theologians on their own terms, and no suggestion that already existent Two-Thirds World Evangelical theology might engage with Western theology. Where it has in the last twenty years, that process is accredited to Western mis-sionaries and writers in Bosch's pages. It falls into a pattern of the way in which the West gathers information, packages it, and reprocesses it as its own. All the Two-Thirds World church has are its perspectives, insights and theological re-flections. It is therefore specially sensitive when it sees a process taking place which it likens to stealing its clothes. This may seem innocuous in the free trade of ideas. But the ability to generate ideas depends on considerable effort and energy in activity and reflection. The question faces all Western missiologists and historians of mission: in our trade and practice are we genuinely empow-ering those whom we are engaging in partnership with by engaging with their ideas? The classic example is the Western research scholar gathering informa-tion for a dissertation on the church in India which will end up on the shelves of a university in Europe. How can scholars in Indian and African churches be enabled to develop their own research? How can interaction between Two-Thirds World contexts be encouraged? For example, black Christians in South Africa have long wanted Christians from Latin America to come and engage with them missiologically, but the resources are never available. What are the ethics and rights of property over their information and the data they yield? What are the ethics of attribution?

There are a number of significant lacunas in David's description of the world mission scene: the issue of church and state in Africa; the nature and practice of Christian leadership; the funding of Christian mission; the impact of moder-nity of the West on the rest of the world and the production of schizophrenic societies; resistance of Islam to Christianity emanating from the West and thus the call already issued for a moratorium on Western missionaries to Islam and the facilitating of Two-Thirds World mission there. The significance of these lacunas and the stealing of Two-Thirds World clothes is that the picture is given that only now is the field opening up for issues in the Two-Thirds World to impact Western mission; that the process has yet to get underway. The fact is that so-called "mission in reverse" has been happening for over twenty years. The Two-Thirds World has been researching in the West theologically and has identified important missiological issues and questions. Yet they do not appear in Bosch's horizon.

The immediate impact of this lacuna is to lessen the value of *Transforming Mission* as an adequate description of contemporary missiology and to suggest that Bosch does not adequately dialogue with the mission concerns of those who now make up the majority and the center of gravity of the world church.

For reasons suggested in this presentation, there is more to be said about the theology, practice and mission of the church in the Two-Thirds World as a contributor to the current paradigm of mission than Bosch has allowed: the epistemological priority of the poor; the categories of covenant and family; the integration of evangelism and social action; the understanding of the relation between reconciliation and restitution; the understanding of power; the role of Pentecostalism. I still regard Bosch as required reading, but I would also require other reading along lines suggested in this chapter as well.

– 12 –

Transforming Missionaries
Implications of the Ecumenical Paradigm

Margaret E. Guider

In this chapter I argue that the transformation of mission, as envisioned by Bosch's postmodern ecumenical missionary paradigm, is predicated, at least in part, on the transformation of missionaries. Building on this premise, I seek to show that those responsible for the initial and ongoing formation of missionaries must come to terms with the fact that the postmodern ecumenical missionary paradigm requires much more of individual missioners and missionary-sending societies than a willingness to think new thoughts or engage in new forms of ministry. My thesis is that the emerging ecumenical paradigm requires of missionaries an inner capacity to meet the complex demands of mission in an increasingly complex world and that this capacity is determined as much by the evolutionary dynamics of human development as the discretionary dynamics of the human will.

In Part Three of his book *Transforming Mission*, David Bosch sets forth a series of timely and thought-provoking ideas under the title "Toward a Relevant Missiology" (1991a: 467–74). As such, Bosch's work provides a catalyst for critical and sustained reflection on the theoretical and practical implications of the postmodern missionary paradigm. However, with the exception of a brief discussion of the function and identity of the missionary in the section entitled "Mission as Ministry by the Whole People of God," Bosch does not deal directly with one of the most serious missiological questions of the postmodern era: what are the psycho-spiritual demands of the postmodern missionary paradigm on missionaries themselves?

In an effort to respond to this question, I seek to make available several insights from constructive developmental theory for missionaries who, despite their enthusiasm for Bosch's emerging ecumenical missionary paradigm, often find themselves overwhelmed by its actual demands. To explain this phenomenon, I draw upon the work of Robert Kegan, a psychologist recognized for his research in the area of adult development (Kegan 1994). I believe Kegan's findings merit our attention and consideration for three reasons. First, for those of

Margaret Eletta Guider, a member of the Sisters of St. Francis (Joliet, Illinois), is Associate Professor of Religion and Society at Weston Jesuit School of Theology, Cambridge, Massachusetts. She has worked in Brazil and lectures widely on mission and church-society questions.

us who share Bosch's conviction that we are at a critical turning point in the history of world Christianity, Kegan's insights make it possible for us to recognize how the transformation of Christian mission in the twenty-first century is inextricably linked to the integral transformation of Christian missionaries and their respective missionary-sending societies. Second, Kegan's research alerts us to the fact that many of us may be cognitively and emotionally undermatched to meet the actual demands of the postmodern missionary paradigm. Third, when examined in the context of Bosch's overall analysis, Kegan's insights enable us to reflect more thoughtfully about the implications of shifts in Christian mission and what they mean in the individual and collective lives of missionaries.

Inherent in the thesis of this chapter is the conviction that we should not presume that most missionaries have the inner capacity to meet the complex demands of mission in the *modern* world, even less the demands of the *postmodern* world. If valid, this thesis requires us to grapple with two findings that are rarely taken into account by many of us who advance the theory of the emergent ecumenical missionary paradigm without fully understanding the reasons why we feel "in over our heads" as we endeavor to practice what we preach. These findings can be summarized as follows: (1) we are unaware of how much we do not know about how individuals give meaning to the theory and practice of missionary activity, and (2) we do not realize that the capacity to meet the demands of the emerging ecumenical missionary paradigm is not predicated only on *what* missionaries know, but also on *how* they know what they know.

Though the traditional disciplines of theology, history and cultural anthropology make it possible for missiologists to articulate what we know about the emerging ecumenical missionary paradigm, these disciplines do not necessarily provide us with a theoretical framework for comprehending more fully how we know what we know about this paradigm. Competent as we may be at knowing *what* we know, we tend to know less about *how* we know what we know. Moreover, when one understands fully the insights of developmental psychology, it is clear that I cannot — by an act of my will — bring about within myself the requisite psycho-spiritual growth necessary to cope with our complex world. A different kind of transformation is necessary.

If Bosch's analysis is correct, the postmodern world will require far more of missionaries than the modern world ever did. If Kegan's analysis is correct, we cannot assume that missionaries will have the inner resources to meet theses demands. If my thesis is correct, we do well to attune ourselves to the practical implications of these two analyses as soon as possible. In the following pages, I reflect upon some of the reasons why.

The Turning Point: Coming to Terms with *How* We Know What We Know

Last year at an annual gathering of professors of mission, a discussion of *Transforming Mission* generated vigorous interactions. They reflected a wide diversity of opinions about the adequacy and appropriateness of the emerging ecumenical missionary paradigm for Christian mission in the twenty-first century. The conversation raised a number of questions for me as well as my teaching colleagues regarding the biases and assumptions that inform our respective approaches to individuals preparing or renewing themselves for missionary activity. Furthermore, the conversation alerted me to how much we do not know about the ways in which others give meaning to their knowledge and experience of mission. It was evident to me that what we knew about mission was not really the point of the conversation. At issue was how each of us knew what we knew. Our conversation disclosed more than a diversity of opinion among missiologists. It reflected what developmental psychologists would characterize as a display of distinct orders of consciousness.

As a concept, an order of consciousness does not focus on what a person knows, but rather on how the person knows what he or she knows. In short, it takes into account how the individual structures knowledge. It suggests an evolving inner capacity to make meaning of what the individual knows or experiences in an increasingly more complex fashion. The five distinct orders of consciousness are described as follows by Kegan (1994:314–15):

1. first order consciousness indicates the capacity to perceive reality in ways that are immediate and atomistic.

2. second order consciousness indicates the capacity to understand one's world in terms of durable categories. It is demonstrated by concreteness, a point of view and a categorical self.

3. third order consciousness indicates the capacity for cross-categorical meaning-making. It is demonstrated by abstractness, ideals, values, mutual relationships and inner states/reflective emotions.

4. fourth order consciousness indicates the capacity to generalize across abstractions in terms of complex systems. It is demonstrated by the ability to subordinate, regulate and create (rather than be created by) one's values and ideals, thus taking them as the object rather than the subject of knowing.

5. fifth order consciousness indicates the capacity to generalize across complex systems so as to organize reality in terms of a multiplicity of complex systems (a trans-system). It is demonstrated by the ability to move a complex system from subject to object.

This terminology is abstract and technical. I hope to make its implication and ask the reader to bear with me as I do. First, for purposes of clarification, the ethos of third order consciousness may be characterized as premodern, fourth order consciousness as modern, and fifth order consciousness as postmodern.

By way of background information, it may be helpful to recall the work of Jean Piaget on the inner structures that govern how infants, children, and adolescents know what they know. Piaget has mapped the evolutionary changes that take place in the human person at different stages of human development from infancy through adolescence. What we are about here is advancing an analogous theory that similar transformations continue to occur throughout adulthood. The fact that the onset of such evolutionary changes in adults cannot be predicted, nor assumed to be inevitable, raises the question in some people's minds about the plausibility of such an idea. For the sake of argument, however, I recommend that we take this theory on its own terms and consider the possibility that, over the course of the adult life span, any given missionary could evolve from a third order consciousness to a fourth order consciousness, and possibly even a fifth order consciousness.

Let me be more precise. From the dawn of the modern missionary era until our own times, historical evidence suggests that missionaries have gone forth to preach the gospel with unwavering confidence in the durable categories of what may best be characterized as premodern Christianity — a Christianity unscathed and unchanged by the scrutinies and challenges of modernity. Missionary conviction about the redemption of humanity by Jesus Christ, the absolute necessity of grace for salvation, the religious supremacy of Christianity, and the melding of Christianity with Western culture were intact and unquestioned. The lessons of time, however, make us aware that, as missionaries learn new languages and become more familiar with the lifeways of other peoples, some are moved by a desire to understand more fully the cultures, economies, social networks, and religious traditions of the people whom they have grown to love and serve with reverence and respect. Often these very missionaries are among the first to perceive the incompleteness of their own limited perspectives and experiences. The expansion of their missionary consciousness, however, is a costly venture that frequently comes at the price of their former certitude in absolutes that once served as the principle and foundation of their missionary vocations. Unlike missionaries who do not call into question the relativity of their own beliefs and experiences, emerging modern missionaries tend to be interested in insights gleaned from anthropology, ethnography, and the history of religions. Frequently they set the findings of these social-scientific studies in creative tension with those arising out of historical-critical studies of the Bible and theology. For many emerging modern missionaries, the studies that they started in the service of enlarging the "durable categories" of premodern Christianity end up making them wonder if the inherited traditions can ever be true in the same way they were once thought to be. In the process, a "first naïveté," to borrow Paul Ricoeur's famous term, is inevitably lost.

With reference to Kegan's schema, missionaries who move through and beyond the first naïveté face another set of adaptive challenges as they deal with abstractions drawn from knowledge of complex systems and insights into how persons and cultures create meaning. The modern psycho-spiritual crisis in which these missionaries often find themselves is one of trying to relate all this complex information to the durable categories of premodern Christian faith in a meaningful way. The crisis is deepened as they try to live out in their day-to-day lives what they have tried to think through in their minds. In the evolution from a premodern missionary consciousness to a modern missionary consciousness, the dynamic process that first gave rise to the possibility of living in the modern world brings about the necessity of coming to terms with the challenges of a postmodern world.

Though many of us can imagine the postmodern missionary paradigm in terms of a world in which we see the necessity of whole new kinds of trans-system categories, it is not clear how many of us have the inner structures to support a postmodern move into a world wherein a whole new kind of rationality and relationality are required in the passage through confusion to Ricoeur's "second naïveté," where the world becomes whole once again. If the multiple vectors Bosch identifies in his postmodern ecumenical missionary paradigm require of missionaries a personal transformation roughly equivalent to entrée into Kegan's fifth order of consciousness, how many of us will find ourselves "in over our heads," tossed and towed under a sea roiled by currents that few if any can chart, much less swim in?

Building on these comments and questions arising out of our *Zeitgeist*, I would like simply to say that my reason for drawing upon an evolutionary understanding of adult development is to illustrate how the diversity of opinions regarding the future of Christian mission, as expressed in the debates of professors of world mission studies, mirrors both the experiences of missionaries as well as the ways in which missionaries give meaning to their experiences. For example, there are those missionaries whose belief in authority, tradition and revelation has not been unravelled by historical consciousness or critical theory. Their understanding of the permanent validity of the missionary vocation is characterized by confidence, certitude and clarity of purpose. This understanding, however, is not a universally shared experience, particularly among missionaries who have taken seriously the demands of postmodernity as proposed by David Bosch. For these individuals, missionary self-understanding is characterized also by experiences of vulnerability, anger, malaise, insecurity, resentment and uncertainty, to name but a few. Though undoubtedly there are many attribution theories to account for this reality, I would like to explore one possible explanation that may be best expressed in the form of a question: what happens to missionaries who operate out of third order consciousness when the world in which they minister demands fourth order consciousness and, perhaps increasingly, fifth order consciousness?

This question helps focus the hypothesis that the causes of division that polarize or paralyze so many missionary societies may have more to do with how people think rather than what they think. The question also draws attention to the fact that these conflicts could be a function of individuals operating out of different orders of consciousness. I contend that efforts to grapple with this question may provide us with important insights into the adaptive challenges facing missionaries and missionary societies, regardless of their ecclesial identification or denominational affiliation.

To the extent that Bosch's description of the emerging ecumenical missionary paradigm articulates these adaptive challenges, it is fair to say that *Transforming Mission* holds the potential for redefining what may best be described as the visible curriculum for the initial and ongoing formation of missionaries in many regions of the world. The question posed above, however, urges us to recognize that as we move into the third millennium of Christianity, Bosch's visible curriculum is not the only curriculum that we will need to master. There also exists another curriculum that may best be described as the "hidden curriculum" of the increasingly postmodern modern world in which we live.

Mastering the Visible Curriculum of Missionary Formation and the Hidden Curriculum of the Postmodern "Modern" World

Historically, the expectations and standards of the visible curriculum for missionary formation have changed in scope and orientation, as Bosch's book readily discloses. Whatever religious leaders or ecclesial authorities have mandated as the specific design and content of missionary formation, there is a premodern — a tribal or traditional — dimension of the visible curriculum that seems to be a constant. Even at the close of the twentieth century, the visible curriculum of the emerging ecumenical missionary paradigm maintains this character. This fact is illustrated most pointedly by what might be characterized as Bosch's ambivalence, one I suspect that many of us share, about the degree to which the competing claims and fragmented nature of the contemporary world should set the agenda for Christian mission in the next millennium.

For the most part, it is fair to say that many missionaries find the visible curriculum of the emerging ecumenical mission paradigm tenable, albeit to various degrees. I assume this is the reason many of us continue to promote world mission in theory and practice. I assume also that it is the reason we feel justified in distinguishing those whom we entrust with the tradition and charism of our respective missionary societies as masters of this visible curriculum. Such confirmations of mastery, as many of us understand them, serve as indicators of the qualities and competencies of those identified as missionaries. At best, we hope that the mastery of theory and practice will enable us to be knowledgeable, prudent, enthusiastic, dedicated and resourceful. At least, we trust that our mastery of the visible curriculum is some assurance of the adequacy and appropriateness of our readiness to respond to what we believe to be divine inspiration.

As for the hidden curriculum that informs and influences the initial and ongoing formation of missionaries, it may be best understood in terms of the demands of modern life and the even more rigorous demands of postmodern life. The exigencies of this curriculum are defined and determined by the expectations of the contemporary world. To master this curriculum, one must have a capacity for holding together the complex dynamics of modern or postmodern life in a meaningful way. For example, from studies in history of religions, one learns of the riches of Buddhism, and in mission work in Thailand one concretely experiences both its richness and its contradictions. One grows in habits of mind and heart that respect Buddhists. Yet there in the background are the theological categories of Christian tradition. Add to this picture the fact that your children in Thailand may be finding your Christian anthropology quite simplistic in the light of the richness of Thai culture. Still you have to keep a sending mission board happy and perhaps partake in the education of new missioners for your church, all the while trying to keep alive communication with your wife or husband.

Kegan's insight on our situation of "being in over our heads" begins to take on new dimensions in the light of such realities. The kind of mastery that will allow a missionary to say he or she is at peace in the midst of such category confusion is well beyond the reach of most of us.

Given such a scenario, it is no wonder that when our sister and brother missionaries fall victim to disillusionment, depression, isolation and lethargy associated with missionary burnout (see Freudenberger 1980 and Maslach 1982 as cited in Kegan 1994:171), we who are designated as leaders within our respective missionary institutes, congregations, and associations find ourselves questioning not only our abilities to lead, but the whole notion of leadership itself (Heifitz 1994).

Understandably, the phenomenon of missionary vulnerability and malaise calls into question the adequacy of the visible curriculum, regardless of its design and content. In turn, we who help shape and promote the visible curriculum may feel challenged to assume responsibility for addressing the apparent inadequacies of this curriculum. The fundamental problem with our attempts to do so, however, is that our efforts to innovate, adjust or adapt the visible curriculum may be misdirected or inconsequential. The reason for this is that the unsettling realities of missionary life that we are inclined to attribute to the inadequacies of the visible curriculum may actually have more to do with the missionary's inability to meet the demands of the hidden curriculum, a curriculum that may be so hidden that missionaries, whether ordained or lay, secular or religious, women or men, may fail it without ever knowing what they did not know.

As we ponder the lives of many missionaries, some of whom may be our elders, peers or more youthful companions, I believe Kegan's metaphorical suggestion that we are in over our heads provides a way to perceive our reality in light of the demands of the hidden curriculum. It gives us insight into our need for reassessing the accuracy and adequacy of our preferred modes of problem analysis and causal attribution. It also provides us with an interesting perspective on the meaning of "mastery."

In taking seriously Kegan's premise that most adults live in historical-cultural contexts that increasingly demand postmodern emotional and cognitive skills, it is important to discover what such adults need to master in order to avoid getting in over their heads. We also need to recognize how some of these insights may apply specifically to missionaries failing to meet the expectations that modernity and postmodernity demand of them.

In addition, we should realize that the applicability of this theory to sociocultural contexts outside the United States of America and Canada is open for discussion and debate. It may be helpful to consider the degree to which the demands of modernity, as they are understood and experienced in the West, accompany, challenge and influence shifts of consciousness taking place in other cultural contexts for ministry in other regions of the world. In any case, one of the demands missionary life places upon Euramericans is that they need to function effectively in both a host culture, in which they work, and their native culture, from which they draw various kinds of support and to which most will return when their cross-cultural missionary service is finished.

Minimally, the hidden curriculum of the contemporary world requires missioners to meet and master the following expectations and demands. They are quite different from those our missionary forebears had to meet; indeed, to contemporary (but premodern) missioners, they will appear to concretize the collapse toward the very subjectivism they fear has ruined contemporary Christianity (see Kegan 1994:152–53).

1. To invent or own our ministry (rather than see it as owned and created by religious authorities, ecclesiastical officials or institutional administrators).

2. To be self-initiating, self-correcting, self-evaluating (rather than dependent on others to frame the problems, initiate adjustments, or determine whether things are going acceptably well).

3. To be guided by our own visions of mission (rather than be without a vision or be captive of the authority's agenda).

4. To take responsibility for what happens to us as missionaries externally and internally (rather than see our present internal circumstances and future external possibilities as caused by someone else).

5. To be accomplished masters of our particular missionary role, function or career (rather than have an apprenticing or imitating relationship to what we do).

6. To conceive of the religious institution or ecclesial organization from the "outside in," as a whole; to see our relation to the whole; to see the relation of the parts to the whole (rather than see the rest of the religious institution/ecclesial organization and its parts only from the perspective of our own part, from the "inside out").

Though admittedly these expectations and demands may not be in line with some centers of authority that influence and determine the visible curriculum of our respective missionary societies and institutes, these expectations are in line with the demands that modern life places on adults.

At a theological level, of course, it is important not to beg a question that is presumed in what I have said and will say. We cannot answer it here, but — and due deference to the sincerely held beliefs of "conservative" missioners demands it — whether any of this is ultimately important requires a positive answer to the following question: are the demands of modernity and postmodernity to be taken as legitimate, or are they the results of Christianity that has lost its roots in transcendence?

If the demands of modernity and postmodernity are legitimate — as I think they are, subject to careful qualification — it seems reasonable to conclude that a missionary's incapacity to meet the expectations and demands of the hidden curriculum may be one of the primary factors contributing to his or her experiences of vulnerability, malaise and uncertainty about the future.

As we reflect upon the consequences of a missionary's capacity or incapacity to master the hidden curriculum, it is important to recognize that the demands of modern life have claims on all our institutes and on us all.

Though the hidden curriculum may be less hidden in some circumstances than others, it is possible to acknowledge that there are individuals who have the inner capacity to master the hidden curriculum, others who do not, and some who find themselves somewhere in between.

Coming to terms with this also requires us to admit that this inner capacity may not be something that can be acquired through an act of will. It is not necessarily predicated on intelligence, ability, experience or commitment. Essentially it is the result of many interactive processes, some of which are evolutionary in nature. As is the case with every evolutionary process, the evolving of consciousness from one order to the next may be furthered by a challenging life event or enhanced by a supportive environment. Still, it is not completely clear why, given the same circumstances, some individuals continue to grow and evolve while others do not.

If we are willing to grant that at least fourth order consciousness is necessary for missionaries to meet the demands of mission in a postmodern modern world, and that without it we may find ourselves in over our heads, we must also be willing to think through the implications of this finding. In order to do so with some measure of wisdom and grace, it may be helpful to begin by not assuming that we ourselves have mastered the hidden curriculum. It also may be helpful to acknowledge the fact that we cannot control the process of how others make meaning of their missionary identity, their lives, and their world. It could be potentially liberating for everyone concerned to recognize, at least theoretically, that the apparent failure or refusal of some people to see things the same way as others may not be the result of mean-spiritedness, willfulness, belligerence, ignorance, insensitivity or prejudice. It may not be the case that they simply refuse to see things the way others see them. Rather, it may be that the ways in which they make meaning, along with the inner structures that support and determine this process, may be very different.

Understanding the Process of Making Meaning

As we hold together the imperatives of Bosch's postmodern ecumenical missionary paradigm and the insights of Kegan's analysis of adult development, the implications of these imperatives and insights are as challenging as they are problematic, particularly for those of us entrusted with the responsibility of educating and updating individuals who desire to commit themselves to sharing in the mission of Jesus Christ. It goes without saying that these imperatives and insights merit our attention and reflection. Still, given the exigencies of Christian mission in an increasingly postmodern modern world, are there appropriate ways to support and challenge individuals who represent different orders of consciousness?

Clearly, this question highlights the fact that our efforts to take account of the differing orders of consciousness present in any given group of missionaries is not as simple as saying:

> Those of you who want me to teach you the facts you need to know about the history of Christian mission, move to the right side of the room. Those of you who would like to discover how to do mission theology by exploring the tradition in light of your own experiences of mission, working in small self-selected groups and receiving relevant input and encouragement from me, move to the left side of the room. Those of you who would like to engage in a process of examining various theological systems through comparative study and ongoing dialogue regarding living faiths and ideologies, move to the front of the room. Those of you who would like to reflect critically on missiology from the vantage point of other systems of thought and the social sciences of your choice, so that you can later assist the rest of us in acquiring insight into where we as missionaries succeed and where we fail, move to the balcony.

As a caricature, this scenario captures the awkwardness of our efforts to take up the challenge of transforming theory into practice. As a parable, however, it offers us a bit of wisdom as we missionaries journey together into the next millennium. It enables us to get a better grasp on the demands that the modern world makes on adults who are missionaries and helps us understand why the tendency of so many to construct their lives and missionary identities in certain ways may be more a function of nature than ideology.

As we survey the broad spectrum of missionaries, whether young or old, inexperienced or seasoned, it is important to recognize that individual actions or attitudes are not always what they appear to be. A missionary who displays what appears to be an independent nature characteristic of a fourth order consciousness may in fact be manifesting a veiled form of third order counter-dependence. What may appear to some as a dependent individual representative of a third order consciousness may in fact be a form of fourth order inter-dependence. What appears to be a missionary's ability to think critically may be nothing more than an example of persuasive parroting. We must be alert to the fact that there are individuals who may grasp the theoretical discourse of a fourth or fifth order consciousness. However, their inability to handle complexity and ambiguity at a relational level discloses the fact that they have yet to reach the threshold of such consciousness. Needless to say, more of us may be giving new meaning to the term "false" consciousness than we would like to admit!

Conclusion

Among those of us who assume responsibility for the initial and ongoing formation of missionaries, there is no doubt that our eyes have been opened by the work of David Bosch. His postmodern ecumenical missionary paradigm is an ongoing reminder of the imperatives of Christian mission as we enter the next millennium. What I have attempted to do in this essay is allow the insights of Robert Kegan to open our eyes to the demands which an increasingly post-modern modern world makes on missionaries, individually and collectively. In summary, these insights include the following points:

1. The so-called "inner capacity" of an individual missionary to meet the demands of an increasingly postmodern modern world may be best understood in terms of "orders of consciousness." These orders of consciousness are indicators of the ways in which individuals make meaning of their lives in light of the ever-increasing complexities of relationships and responsibilities of adulthood.

2. Research demonstrates that in order to meet the mental demands of modern life, a fourth order consciousness is necessary. Research also demonstrates that more than half of professionally trained adults organize their lives according to principles reflective of a third order consciousness (see Kegan 1994:185–97, 368–75).

3. It is important to underscore that orders of consciousness are not predicated on levels of intelligence, experience or commitment. The movement from one order of consciousness to another is essentially an evolutionary process of human development. The movement cannot be forced. An order of consciousness cannot be taught. It cannot be achieved through an act of human will. An order of consciousness is not determined by content, but by structure, the inner structure of the human person that governs the ways in which he or she makes meaning out of the content of his or her life.

In conclusion, I cannot emphasize strongly enough that though these insights are potentially helpful and valuable, they represent perspectives that in and of themselves are constrained by certain biases and limitations. Sobering as this realization may be, it is nonetheless a fitting reminder that our ability to challenge and support missionaries in transforming their lives is ultimately a matter of nature and grace, a matter that no missionary paradigm or developmental theory will ever explain completely.

- 13 -

DAVID J. BOSCH
AS AN ECUMENICAL PERSONALITY

Emilio Castro

My first encounter with David Bosch was in the context of the World Council of Churches' Commission on World Mission and Evangelism, of which I had the privilege of being the Director from 1973 to 1983. CWME, of course, carried into the WCC the agenda of the International Missionary Council "to help the churches in the proclamation of the gospel of Jesus Christ in word and deed so that all may believe and be saved." In a sense, then, the CWME context was the natural place to meet David Bosch, a missionary of the Dutch Reformed Church to its African part and a missiologist.

Bosch was a delegate from the Republic of South Africa to the World Conference on Evangelism in the Church held in Melbourne, Australia, in May 1980 on the theme "Your Kingdom Come." He was also at the Fourth World Conference on Evangelism held in San Antonio, Texas, in 1989 on the theme "Your Will Be Done: Mission in Christ's Way." Apart from presence at WCC meetings, he also — until his untimely death during Holy Week 1992 — served on the editorial board of the *International Review of Mission,* a publication of WCC. So he was a friend of the WCC and made his contribution to this principal arm of the ecumenical movement.

It was natural for Bosch, a missiologist, to collaborate with the WCC with respect to its work on mission and evangelism. But from another perspective it was a surprise, if not a miracle, especially as the relationship between the WCC and the government of the Republic of South Africa was anything but friendly. The history of the chilly relationship goes back to the Cottesloe meeting which the WCC sponsored in 1960 to seek the response of WCC member churches in South Africa to the tragic massacre that took place at Sharpeville. The statement that came out of that consultation was unpalatable to the South African government. But what did it say?

It contained four striking points: (1) prohibition of mixed marriages is unscriptural; (2) colored peoples should have direct representation in parliament; (3) no believer in Christ may be excluded from the church on grounds of color or race; and (4) spiritual unity of all must be visibly expressed. These affirmations

Emilio Castro, pastor and onetime president of the Evangelical Methodist Church of Uruguay, served as Director of the WCC Commission on World Mission and Evangelism and as General Secretary of the WCC.

were obviously contrary to apartheid. The first irony is that the statement was drawn up largely by theologians of Nederduitse Gereformeerde Kerk (NGK) of the Dutch Reformed family, although it had a policy of segregated churches. The other irony was that the NHK excluded blacks from membership.

The NHK's response was to withdraw from membership of WCC. The NGK at first accepted the Cottesloe statement but later rejected it, apparently under pressure from Prime Minister Hendrik Verwoerd, the architect of contemporary apartheid. Against that background, Bosch's continued open involvement in the WCC programs was a courageous demonstration of his ecumenical commitment. But it was apparently a reasoned position.

Bosch had convinced himself of the great weakness in Protestantism in respect of the centrality of the unity of the church. He writes:

> I have seen, in my own denomination, how a weak ecclesiology has opened the door to racially segregated churches and what this has done to the credibility and evangelism of the Church. I have seen other denominations, particularly Anglicans and Roman Catholics — where their white members were also racially prejudiced, no less than the Dutch Reformed Church members, yet they found themselves incapable of giving up the unity of the Church. That unity was not something on which they decided one could decide. It was a given, it was part of the gospel itself. (Bosch 1988:20)

In this statement Bosch signals the primary ecumenical issue of the *Una Sancta* which has been identified as an inherent weakness in Protestantism. For example, Paolo Ricca writes:

> It is very difficult, maybe even impossible, to speak for European Protestantism, because there is no place, no structure, no occasion where European Protestantism comes together and speaks together. There is no General Assembly of European Protestantism nor a kind of "Kirchentag" of European Protestant Churches. There is no unifying body, not a common paper or magazine. European Protestantism as such never comes together, never speaks together, never acts together — one could say that European Protestantism does not exist as one unified body. Does it exist as one soul? Are there many Protestant souls? It is a question about the follow-up (which did not happen) the Leuenberger Konkordie, through which Lutheran and Reformed Churches joined together in full ecclesial fellowship. Protestant churches were not able to give themselves structures of unity or even recognizable "meeting points" (as every airport does). (Ricca 1986:41–42)

Bosch recognizes the difficulty of apartheid, a peculiar combination of religion and racial prejudice, because of the consistent injustices it perpetrates against peoples of color. At the root of it is the fact that "subconsciously these Afrikaners tend to arrogate the epithet 'Christian' only to White South Africans (preferably Afrikaners)" (Bosch 1984b:14). Thus the deep cause of the tragic racist situation of South Africa was the weak ecclesiology which did not exactly capture the *Una Sancta*. It follows from this that a recovery of the *Una*

Sancta is a *sine qua non* of the healing of Afrikaner civil religion. Any other approach will be cosmetic. I dare to suggest that the National Conference of Church Leaders in South Africa held at Hunter's Rest, Rustenburg, Transvaal, from November 5–9, 1990, on the theme "Toward a United Christian Witness in a Changing South Africa" may be read as a dawning of that realization.

This sense of the ecumenical imperative he demonstrated by remaining within the DRC but in his own quiet way enabled several Africans to make it good in the face of all-pervasive apartheid. As one *In Memoriam* puts it,

> for many people tough rhetoric and breaking radically with a wicked system are the only way to share one's disapproval of a hated system. I learnt from his style that not all revolutionaries are given to tough and loud talk; some beat the system from within; realism is as important in resistance as revolutionary rhetoric. Because he adopted the approach of fighting quietly and creatively from within the *status quo* his integrity was sometimes impugned. But I am persuaded he was genuine. (Pobee 1992a:252)

It was clear from his style that the unity of the church, as of his denomination, was of priority concern.

However, his commitment to unity did not mean sacrificing commitment to what is right, as his numerous publications and support of disadvantaged peoples demonstrate. There is another aspect of this which we dare not lose sight of because of what it says of ecumenical methodology.

Ecumenical methodology proceeds by making connections between the local and the universal. This we wish to demonstrate in a number of ways.

At the Melbourne Conference mentioned above, we got into some tense moments. In the course of a statement on South Africa, a Pakistani asked for a similar statement on USSR intervention in Afghanistan, to which the Russian delegates had objected. Bosch had supported the concern for Afghanistan and the conference was truly torn down the middle. The next session Bosch broke the impasse with a proposal which was, by and large, accepted. It ran as follows:

> We wish to state that the mentioning of specific countries and situations in the resolutions of this conference is partly to be attributed to current events in those countries. We recognize, however, that there are other countries where foreign powers are intervening militarily, and governments which oppress, exploit, imprison and kill innocent people. We may be able to identify some of those countries and peoples. Others, however, we dare not identify for the simple reason that such a specific identification by the Conference may endanger the position — even the lives — of many of our brothers and sisters, some of whom are participating in this Conference. We therefore confess our inability to be as prophetic as we ought to be, as that may, in some instances, entail imposing martyrdom on our fellow believers in those countries — something we dare not do from a safe distance. We know that many of them suffer under different regimes for their faith in Jesus Christ and urge that freedom of conscience be respected as well as other human rights. At the same time, we want to assure our unnamed brothers and sisters in many unnamed countries that we have not

forgotten them; we identify strongly in their suffering for the Kingdom of God. (CWME 1980:251)

Bosch was the architect of this resolution. It is a paragon statement of ecumenism. In it we seek convergence, which is characteristic contemporary ecumenical style — convergence between strangers and opposing factions; a commitment to the perspectives that choices are not always between right and wrong but sometimes also between the lesser of two evils; an open admission that ecumenical commitment to the prophetic ministry has to be matched with realism; and a commitment to unity in spite of whatever adjustments need to be made. His architectural construct helped save the unity of the meeting.

There are other ways in which Bosch made interconnections. His contribution to the Rustenburg Conference (Bosch 1991f) illustrates a number of those things. To that let us proceed presently.

First, he recalled that "Calvinism . . . forms the substractum of Anglicanism as well, as it does of other traditions, such as Methodism" (129). Thus while he does not sweep under the carpet the differences between Reformed, Presbyterian, Anglican and Methodist denominations, he makes the inter-connection between them through Calvinism. Thus they may not regard one another as total strangers but as siblings who should not be in opposite camps but work together at their commonalities.

First, he argued for the convergence between Calvinism and liberation theology, first because for the two "the involvement of believers in the world was not an addition to theology. Social ethics did not belong to a different category, divorced from theology" (131). Rediscovering some of the antecedents of liberation theology in Calvinism is a powerful rebuttal of those who have tried to dismiss liberation theology as politics donning theology. But the alliance also becomes a powerful critique of the Enlightenment's privatization of religion and buttresses that rediscovery made by liberation theology in our times.

Second, he argued that liberation theology, like Calvinism, expresses "concern for the victims of society in essentially the same manner: not by applying bandages, but by identifying the causes of the wounds inflicted on people and by seeking to effect changes in respect of the structures of injustice. . . . Not that Calvinism or the Reformation tradition reduces theology to politics. Rather, theology has to do with the knowledge of God and His glory. But precisely because Calvinists regard politics as one fundamental sphere within which God reveals His glory and should be worshipped, they lift politics into the realm of theology" (131). These two examples of how Bosch does the interconnection between Calvinism and liberation theology is a remarkable contribution to the pursuit of ecumenical theology. To date there has been a gulf fixed between theologies of the North and those of the South. Some dare to call the theologies of the North "classical" theology. Here in Bosch's arguments we can see a way to break the impasse: liberation theology is, after all, no aberration; it is faithful to the spirit of Calvinism. This is all a healthy reminder that the way theologies have been stated in the North are not the last word: there is room for new ways without which ecumenical theology is not possible.

David Bosch's commitment to ecumenism, particularly as it is lived in the WCC, is not uncritical. The clearest illustration of this is what he had to say on the CWME San Antonio Conference. He writes:

> I returned from San Antonio with a good deal of frustration and perplexity. But I also returned with the firm conviction that there is no substitute for the World Council of Churches, but this amorphous body of believers with its strange blend of arrogance and uncertainty, of faith and doubt, is playing a role no other existing Christian organization can ever hope to play. I therefore submit that those Christian churches who stand aloof from the WCC and what it does are doing a disservice to themselves and are thereby impoverishing the "community" we should all be seeking. (Bosch 1989c:137–38)

What a fine testimony of commitment to the ecumenical vision! It is a critical commitment — no starry eyes, ready to accept weakness but also not ready to lose sight of the strength.

In the same article, David Bosch discloses why he was committed to the WCC and the ecumenical movement in spite of the mess it looks like. The key is the ecumenical theme of community which he discerned behind the sectional reports of the San Antonio Conference. He writes:

> The documents echoed the search and longing for community in many different ways: Christians being called to community with those who suffer injustice, hunger, and oppression; with those of other faiths whom we are to see as people whom God also loves and with whom he has also had a history; with those of secular society who have been cut loose from their anchors but are still craving for fellowship; for communion — which they then sometimes find in the most bizarre cults imaginable; and with fellow Christians of a bewildering variety of backgrounds, cultures and confessions; who are called to unity in faith, love and hope. Perhaps then, the search for community will turn out to be a major missiological theme during the 1990s. (137)

Coming from a church which had turned its back on the WCC and a nation which had an ideological commitment to racism, his welcome to the idea of community, transcending sectarian interest and tribal captivity, is a powerful testimony to his ecumenical commitment.

Enough has been said to demonstrate that David J. Bosch was an ecumenist who had the courage to remain in his tradition while not retaining the divisive elements of his ecclesial and national backgrounds. He let the ecumenical vision penetrate through to him. And he also courageously made his contribution to the ecumenical movement. Though his life ended too soon, there is cause for rejoicing because he left behind a goodly heritage. The key to it is perhaps because he understood all too well that mission and ecumenism are inextricably linked, that vibrant mission is a test of ecumenism.

BIBLIOGRAPHY

Part 1
Works of David J. Bosch

1954 "Verkondig die Koninkryk" (Proclaim the Kingdom), *Deo Gloria*, 51–53.

1971 Preface to *Church and Culture Change in Africa. Lux Mundi* 3. Pretoria: N. G. Kerk Boekhandel, 7.

1972a "The Case for a Black Theology," *Pro Veritate*, 11–4, 3–9.

1972b "Systematic Theology and Missions: The Voice of an Early Pioneer," *Theologia Evangelica* 5:3:165–89.

1973a "Die lewe van die sending-werker" (The Life of a Missionary), *Pro Veritate*, I: vol. 11–11 (March), 7–10; II: vol. 11–12 (April), 13–16; III: vol. 12–1 (May), 10–14; IV: vol. 12–2 (June), 18–20; V: vol. 12–3 (July), 21–24.

1973b "God through African Eyes," in H.-J. Becken, ed. *Relevant Theology for Africa*. Mapumulo, Natal: Lutheran Theological College, 68–78.

1973c "God in Africa: Implications for the Kerygma," *Missionalia* 1 (April): 3–21.

1973d "Missionêre dilemma in Afrika: die probleem van die kwade" (A Missionary Dilemma in Africa: The Problem of Evil), *Theologia Evangelica* 6 (September): 173–98.

1974a "Currents and Crosscurrents in South African Black Theology," *Journal of Religion in Africa* 6–1, 1–22.

1974b *Het evangelie in Afrikaans gewaad* (The Gospel in an African Robe). Kampen: J. H. Kok.

1974c "Navolging van Christus in Suid-en Suid-Wes-Afrika Vandag" (Following Christ in South- and South-West Africa Today), in M. Buthelezi et al., eds. *Swakopmund Konferensie van die Christelike Akademie*. Johannesburg: Christian Academy, 13–22.

1975a "Missiological Developments in South Africa," *Missionalia* 3 (April): 9–30.

1975b "Onderweg na 'n *theologia Africana*" (En Route to *Theologia Africana*), in I. H. Eybers et al., eds. *Teologie en Vernuwing*. Pretoria: UNISA, 160–79.

1975c "The Church in South Africa — Tomorrow," *Pro Veritate* 14 (August), 4–6; vol. 14 (September): 11–13.

167

1975d "The Church as the 'Alternative Community,' " *Journal of Theology for Southern Africa* 13 (December): 3–11.

1976 Review of Anderson, Gerald H. ed., *Asian Voices in Christian Theology* (Maryknoll, NY: Orbis Books), *Missionalia* 4 (August): 53.

1977a "The Church and the Liberation of Peoples?," *Missionalia* 5 (August): 8–39.

1977b *Theology of Religions.* Pretoria: University of South Africa.

1978 "Renewal of Christian Community in Africa Today," in *Facing the New Challenges: The Message of PACLA, December 9–19, 1976.* Nairobi: Africa Enterprise: 92–102.

1979a *A Spirituality of the Road.* Scottdale, PA: Herald Press.

1979b "Currents and Crosscurrents in South African Black Theology," in Gayraud S. Wilmore and James H. Cone, eds. *Black Theology: A Documentary History, 1966–1979.* Maryknoll, NY: Orbis Books, 220–37.

1979c "Racism and Revolution: Response of the Churches in South Africa," *Occasional Bulletin of Missionary Research* 3: 3–20.

1979d "The Kingdom of God and the Kingdoms of This World," *Journal of Theology for Southern Africa* 29 (December): 3–13.

1980a *Witness to the World: The Christian Mission in Theological Perspective.* Atlanta: John Knox; London: Marshall, Morgan & Scott.

1980b "Salvation — Tomorrow and Today" (A Response to Adrio König), *Missionalia* 13: 20–26.

1980c "Thy Will Be Done on Earth," *International Review of Mission* 69: 303–5.

1980d "Forgive Us...as We Forgive," *International Review of Mission* 69: 330–31.

1980e "The Melbourne Conference: Between Guilt and Hope," *International Review of Mission* 69: 512–19.

1981 "Kerk en politiek in die Suid-Afrikaanse konteks" (Church and Politics in the South African Context), in Nico J. Smith, et al., eds. *Stormkompas: Opstelle op soek na 'n suiwer koers in die Suid-Afrikaanse konteks van die jare tagtig.* Kaapstad: Tafelberg, 24–37.

1982a *The Church as Alternative Community.* Potchefstroom: Instituut vir Reformatoriese Studies.

1982b "Church Unity Amidst Cultural Diversity," *Missionalia* 10: 16–28.

1982c "How My Mind Has Changed: Mission and the Alternative Community," *Journal of Theology for Southern Africa,* no. 41 (December): 6–10.

1982d "Theological Education in Missionary Perspective," *Missiology* 10:1 (Jan.):13–34.

1983a "An Emerging Paradigm for Mission," *Missiology* 11:4 (Oct.):485–510.

1983b "Nothing but a Heresy," in John de Gruchy and Charles Villa-Vicencio, eds. *Apartheid Is a Heresy.* Cape Town: David Philip; Guildford: Lutterworth, 24–38.

1983c "Prof. Bosch on Church-state Relationship," *Ecunews* 2, February: 24–30.

1983d "Die religiösen Wurzeln der gegenwärtigen Polarisation zwischen Weisz und Schwarz in Südafrika" (The Religious Roots of the Contemporary Polarization between Whites and Blacks in South Africa), *Zeitschrift für Mission* 10: 98–105.

1984a "Missionary Theology in Africa," *Journal of Theology for Southern Africa* 49 (December): 14–37.

1984b "The Roots and Fruits of Afrikaner Civil Religion," in J. W. Hofmeyr and W. S. Vorster, eds. *New Faces of Africa: Essays in Honor of Ben [Barend Jacobus] Marais.* Pretoria: Unisa.

1984c "The Scope of Mission," *International Review of Mission* 73: 17–32.

1986a "Afrikaner Civil Religion and the Current South African Crisis," *Transformation* 3 (April): 23–30.

1986b "The Afrikaner and South Africa," *Theology Today* 43: 203–16 (identical to 1986a).

1986c "Processes of Reconciliation and Demands of Obedience — Twelve Theses," in B. Tlhagale and I. Mosala, eds. *Hammering Swords into Ploughshares: Essays in Honor of Archbishop Mpilo Desmond Tutu.* Johannesburg: Skotaville Publishers, 159–71.

1986d "Wat baat sending en evangelisasie ons?," in *Sodat my huis vol kan word. Reformatoriese Perspektiewe op ons evangelisasieroeping vandag.* Potchefstroom: Potchefstroomse Universiteit, 193–202.

1987a "The Problem of Evil in Africa: A Survey of African Views of Witchcraft and of the Response of the Christian Church," in Pieter G. R. de Villiers, ed. *Like a Roaring Lion... Essays on the Bible, the Church and Demonic Powers.* Pretoria: Unisa, 38–62.

1987b "Theologies of Mission," in H. L. Pretorius et al., eds. *Reflecting on Mission in the African Context: A Handbook for Missiology.* Bloemfontein: Pro Christo Publications, 41–55.

1987c "Evangelism: Theological Currents and Crosscurrents Today," *International Bulletin of Missionary Research* 11 (July): 98–103.

1987d "Vision for Mission," *International Review of Missions* 76: 8–15.

1988 "Church Growth Missiology," *Missionalia* 1 (April): 13–24.

1989a "Mission in Jesus' Way: A Perspective in Luke's Gospel," *Missionalia* 17:1 (April), 3–21.

1989b Review of F. J. Verstraelen et al., eds., *Oecumenische Inleiding in de Missiologie: Teksten en Konteksten van het Wereld-Christendom* (Ecumenical Introduction to Missiology: Texts and Contexts of World Christianity), *Missionalia* 17 (April): 70–74.

1989c   "Your Will Be Done? Critical Reflections on San Antonio," *Missionalia* 17 (Aug. 2): 126–38.

1990a   *Goeie nuus vir armes...en rykes: Perspektiewe uit die Lukasevangelie* (Good News for Poor...and Rich: Perspectives from the Gospel of Luke). Pretoria: Unisa.

1990b   "Mission in the 1990s," *International Bulletin of Missionary Research* 14: 149–52.

1991a   *Transforming Mission: Paradigm Shifts in Theology of Mission.* Maryknoll, NY: Orbis Books.

1991b   "Die NG Kerk se noue verbintenis met die Afrikanervolk" (The DRC's Close Link with the Afrikaner People) in Etienne de Villiers and Deon Kitching, eds. *Derdegelui vir môre: Die NG Kerk voor die uitdagings van 'n nuwe tyd* (Last Warning Sign for Tomorrow: The DRC Confronted by the Challenges of a New Era). Kaapstad: Tafelberg, 87–93.

1991c   "Church Perspectives on the Future of South Africa," in Louw Alberts and Frank Chikane, eds. *The Road to Rustenburg: The Church Looking forward to a New South Africa.* Cape Town: Struik Christian Books, 140–48.

1991d   "A Calvinist Perspective on the Future of Democracy in South Africa," in Klaus Nürnberger, ed. *A Democratic Vision for South Africa: Political Realism and Christian Responsibility.* Pietermaritzburg: Encounter Publications, 188–95.

1991e   "The Changing South African Scene and the Calling of the Church," *Mission Studies* 8 (no. 16): 147–64.

1991f   "The Future of South Africa: A Reformed Perspective," in Louw Alberts and Frank Chikane, eds. *The Road to Rustenburg: The Church Looking forward to a New South Africa.* Cape Town: Struik Christian Books, 129–39.

1992   "The Vulnerability of Mission," *Vidyajyoti* vol. 56/11: 577–96.

1993a   "Reflections on Biblical Models of Mission," in James M. Phillips and Robert T. Coote, eds. *Toward the Twenty-first Century in Christian Mission.* Grand Rapids, MI: Eerdmans Publishing Co., 175–92.

1993b   "God's Reign and the Rulers of This World: Missiological Reflections on Church-State Relationships," in Charles Van Engen, Dean S. Gilliland, and Paul Pierson, eds. *The Good News of the Kingdom: Mission Theology for the Third Millennium.* Maryknoll, NY: Orbis Books, 89–95.

1994   "The Vulnerability of Mission," in James A. Scherer and Stephen B. Bevans, eds. *New Directions in Mission and Evangelization 2: Theological Foundations.* Maryknoll, NY: Orbis Books, 73–86.

Part 2
General Bibliography of Works Cited

African Faith and Justice Network
1996   *The African Synod: Documents, Reflections, Perspectives.*

Alberts, Louw and Frank Chikane, eds.
1991   *The Road to Rustenburg: The Church Looking Forward to a New South Africa.* Cape Town: Struik Christian Books.

Anderson, Gerald H.
1991   "Toward A.D. 2000 in Mission," in Dean S. Gilliland, ed. *The World Forever Our Parish.* Lexington, KY: Bristol Books, 125–40.
1993   "Theology of Religions and Missiology: A Time of Testing," in Charles Van Engen et al., eds. *The Good News of the Kingdom: Mission Theology for the Third Millennium.* Maryknoll, NY: Orbis Books, 200–208.

Appiah-Kubi, Kofi and Sergio Torres, eds.
1979   *African Theology En Route.* Maryknoll, NY: Orbis Books.

Assimeng, Max
1986   *Saints and Social Structures.* Tema: Ghana Publishing.

Ayandele, E. A.
1989   *The Missionary Impact of Modern Nigeria 1841-1914.* London: Longmans, Green & Co.

Baillie, T. J.
1993   "Models and Methods for the Current Missionary Paradigm." M.Th. in Pastoral Theology. Cardiff: University of Wales.

Balcomb, A. O.
1990   "Third Way Theologies in the Contemporary South African Situation," in M. Hofmeyer, K. Kritzinger and Willem A. Saayman, eds. *"Wit Afrikane?" 'n Gesprek met Nico Smith.* Johannesburg: Taurus.

Banana, Canaan S.
1982   *Theology of Promise: The Dynamics of Self-Reliance.*

Barrett, D. M.
1968   *Schism and Renewal in Africa.* Nairobi: Oxford University Press.

Barth, Karl
1962   *Church Dogmatics: The Doctrine of Reconciliation.* Edinburgh: T. and T. Clark.

Berkhof, Hendrikus
1964   *The Doctrine of the Holy Spirit.* Richmond, VA: John Knox Press.

Bevans, Stephen B.
1992   *Models of Contextual Theology.* Maryknoll, NY: Orbis Books.

Blough, Neal
1993   "Messianic Mission and Ethics: Discipleship and Good News," in W. R. Shenk, ed., 178–98.

Boer, J. H.
   1979   *Missionary Messengers of Liberation in a Colonial Context: A Case Study
          of the Sudan United Mission.* Amsterdam: Rodopi.

Boesak, Allan Aubrey
   1976   *Farewell to Innocence.* Maryknoll, NY: Orbis Books.
   1978a *Black Theology, Black Power.* Oxford: A. R. Mowbray & Co. (origi-
          nally published in 1976 under the title *Farewell to Innocence* [Kampen:
          J. H. Kok]).
   1978b "The Relationship between Text and Situation, Reconciliation and
          Liberation in Black Theology," *Voices of the Third World* 2 (no. 1):
          30–40.
   1980   "Mission to Those in Authority: Letter from Dr. Allan Boesak to the
          South African Minister of Justice" (August 24, 1979), *International
          Review of Mission* 69 (January): 71–77.

Boshoff, C. W. H.
   1977   "Church and Mission and the Liberation of Nations in the South
          African Context," *Missionalia* 5 (August): 47–57.

Braaten, Carl E.
   1992   *No Other Gospel! Christianity Among the World's Religions.* Minneapo-
          lis: Fortress Press.

Bright, John
   1953   *The Kingdom of God.* Nashville: Abingdon.

Brown, Raymond
   1994   *The Death of the Messiah,* 2 vols. Garden City, NY: Doubleday.

Burtness, James H.
   1982   "Does Anyone Out There Care Anymore Whether People Believe in
          Jesus?" *Dialog* 21, no. 3: 190–94.

Buthelezi, Manas
   1972   *Towards an African Theology.* Lectures given at the University of
          Heidelberg, Germany.
   1976   "The Relevance of Black Theology: Apartheid in the Church Is
          Damnable Heresy," *AACC Bulletin* vol. 9: 34–39.

Carder, Kenneth L.
   1993   "A UMC Prognosis: Naming the Diseases and Finding the Cures,"
          Circuit Rider 17, no. 7: 7–9.

Cassidy, Richard J.
   1992   *John's Gospel in New Perspective: Christology and the Realities of Roman
          Imperial Power.* Maryknoll, NY: Orbis Books.

Cobb, John B., Jr.
   1993   "Salvation: Beyond Pluralism and Exclusivism," *Circuit Rider* 17,
          no. 1: 7–10.

Cochrane, J. R.
 1987   *Servants of Power: The Role of the English-speaking Churches in South Africa 1903–1930.* Johannesburg: Ravan Press.

Comaroff, Jean and John
 1991   *Of Revelation and Revolution: Christianity, Colonialism, and Consciousness in South Africa,* vol. 1. Chicago: University of Chicago Press.

Comblin, José
 1979   *Sent from the Father.* Maryknoll, NY: Orbis Books.

Commission on World Mission and Evangelism (CWME)
 1980   *Your Kingdom Come: Mission Perspectives.* Geneva: World Council of Churches.
 1989   "San Antonio: Report, Section One," *International Review of Mission* 78, nos. 311/312: 345–56.

Cone, James H.
 1986   *A Black Theology of Liberation.* Maryknoll, NY: Orbis Books.

Cone, James H. and Gayraud S. Wilmore
 1972   "The Future and . . . African Theology, Part 2," *Pro Veritate* 10-10:18–24.

Conferencia general del episcopado latinoamericano
 1992   *Santo Domingo Conclusiones.* Lima: Conferencia Episcopal Peruana.

Crossan, John Dominic
 1991   *The Historical Jesus: The Life of a Mediterranean Peasant.* San Francisco: HarperSanFrancisco.

Cullmann, Oscar
 1963   *The Christology of the New Testament.* Philadelphia: Westminster Press.

de Gruchy, John
 1986   "The Church and the Struggle for South Africa," cited by Kevin Livingston, "A Missiology of the Road." Ph.D. Thesis, University of Aberdeen, 1989: 454.

Desroche, Henri
 1979   *The Sociology of Hope.* London: Routledge and Kegan Paul.

Douglas, Wm. M.
 1981   *Andrew Murray and His Message.* Grand Rapids, MI: Baker Book House.

Driver, John
 1983   "Mission: Salt, Light and Covenant Law," *Mission Focus* 11:3 (Sept.): 33–36.
 1993   "The Kingdom of God: Goal of Messianic Mission," in W. R. Shenk, ed., 83–105.

DuPlessis, J.
  1919   *The Life of Andrew Murray of South Africa.* London: Marshall Broth-
          ers.

Durand, J. J. F.
  1981   Response to Prof. J. A. Heyns, "'n Teologie se perspektief," *Storm-
          kompas:* 21–23.
  1985   "Afrikaner Piety and Dissent," in C. Villa-Vicencio and J. de Gruchy,
          eds. *Resistance and Hope: South African Essays in Honor of Beyers Naudé.*
          Cape Town: David Philip.

Dussel, Enrique, ed.
  1992   *The Church in Latin America 1492–1992.* Maryknoll, NY: Orbis
          Books.

Eboussi-Boulaga, F.
  1984   *Christianity without Fetishes: An African Critique and Recapture
          of Christianity.* Maryknoll, NY: Orbis Books (French original,
          1981).

Éla, Jean-Marc
  1986   *African Cry.* Maryknoll, NY: Orbis Books (French original, 1980).
  1988   *My Faith as an African.* Maryknoll, NY: Orbis Books; London:
          Geoffrey Chapman (French original, 1985).

Emerson, Mabel
  n.d.   "Tribute to Caroline E. Frost." South Hadley, MA: Mount Holyoke
          Archives.

Farquhar J. N.
  1913   *The Crown of Hinduism.* New Delhi: Oxford University Press.

Ferguson, Abbie
  1898   "Rev. Andrew Murray, D.D.," *The Huguenot Seminary Journal,* no. 3.

Ferguson, George P.
  1927   *The Builders of Huguenot.* Cape Town: Maskew Miller.

Fisk, Fidelia
  1866   *Recollections of Mary Lyon, with Selections from Her Instruction to the
          Pupils in Mount Holyoke Female Seminary.* Boston: American Tract
          Society.

Freudenberger, H. J.
  1980   *Burnout: The High Cost of Achievement.* Garden City, NY: Anchor
          Press.

Freund, B.
  1984   *The Making of Contemporary Africa.* Bloomington, IN: University of
          Indiana Press.

General Board of Global Ministries
  1993   *Prayer Calendar 1993.* New York: United Methodist Church.

Gittins, Anthony J.
1993   *Bread for the Journey: The Mission of Transformation and the Transformation of Mission.* Maryknoll, NY: Orbis Books.

Goba, Bonganjalo
1988   *An Agenda for Black Theology: Hermeneutics for Social Change.* Johannesburg: Skotaville Publishers.

Green, Elizabeth
1979   *Mary Lyon and Mount Holyoke: Opening the Gates.* Hanover, NH: University Press of New England.

Groenewald, E. P.
1952   "Die Stand van die Teologiese Wetenskap in Suid-Afrika," *Die Kerkbode,* 12/3/52.

Gutiérrez, Gustavo
1973   *A Theology of Liberation.* Maryknoll, NY: Orbis Books (Spanish original, 1971). Fifteenth Anniversary Edition, 1987.
1983   *The Power of the Poor in History.* London: SCM.
1993   *Las Casas: In Search of the Poor of Jesus Christ.* Trans. Robert R. Barr. Maryknoll, NY: Orbis Books.

Guy, J.
1983   *The Heretic: A Study of the Life of William John Colenso.* Johannesburg: Ravan Press.

Harman, Robert J.
1993   "Some New Beginnings: Report to the Missionary Conference, World Division, General Board of Global Ministries," July 29. Unpublished manuscript photocopy.

Heifitz, Ronald
1994   *Leadership Without Easy Answers.* Cambridge, MA: Harvard University Press.

Hick, John and Paul F. Knitter, eds.
1987   *The Myth of Christian Uniqueness: Toward a Pluralistic Theology of Religions.* Maryknoll, NY: Orbis Books.

Hitchcock, Edward, comp.
1852   *The Power of Christian Benevolence Illustrated in the Life and Labors of Mary Lyon.* Northampton, MA: Hopkins, Bridgman & Co.

Horowitz, Helen
1984   *Alma Mater: Design and Experience in the Women's Colleges from Their Nineteenth-Century Beginnings to the 1930's.* Boston: Beacon Press.

Huguenot Missionary Society
n.d.   "Constitution of the Woman's Missionary Union of South Africa," *Minutes.* Cape Town: Nederduitse Gereformeerde Kerk Archives.

Huguenot Seminary Journal
1874, 1875, 1898 South Hadley, MA: Mount Holyoke College.

Hurley, Denis
    1973   "Apathy in the Church: The Need for Reform," *Pro Veritate* 13 (April 15): 7–13.
Jacobs, Sylvia M.
    1987   *Black Americans and the Missionary Movement in Africa.* Westport, CT: Greenwood Press.
John, T. K. O.
    1993   "Issues in Inculturation," *East Asian Pastoral Review*, vol. 30/3, 260–82.
Johnson, Benton, Dean R. Hoge, and Donald A. Luidens
    1993   "Mainline Churches: The Real Reason for Decline," *First Things*, no. 31 (March): 13–18.
Kane, Herbert J.
    1983   *Understanding Christian Missions* (3rd ed.) Grand Rapids, MI: Baker Book House.
Kegan, Robert
    1994   *In Over Our Heads: The Mental Demands of Modern Life.* Cambridge, MA: Harvard University Press.
Knitter, Paul F.
    1985   *No Other Name? A Critical Survey of Christian Attitudes toward the World Religions.* Maryknoll, NY: Orbis Books.
    1995   *One Earth, Many Religions: Multifaith Dialogue and Global Responsibility.* Maryknoll, NY: Orbis Books.
    1996   *Jesus and the Other Names: Christian Mission and Global Responsibility.* Maryknoll, NY: Orbis Books.
Koyama, Kosuke
    1984   *Mount Fuji and Mount Sinai: A Critique of Idols.* Maryknoll, NY: Orbis Books.
Kraus, C. Norman
    1993   *The Community of the Spirit.* Scottdale, PA: Herald Press.
Kritzinger, J. N. J.
    1990   "Liberating Mission in South Africa," in J. N. J. Kritzinger and W. A. Saayman, eds. *Mission in Creative Tension: A Dialogue with David Bosch.* Pretoria: Southern African Missiological Society.
Kritzinger, J. N. J. and Willem A. Saayman
    1990   *Mission in Creative Tension: A Dialogue with David Bosch.* Pretoria, South Africa: Southern African Missiological Society.
Kuitse, Roelf S.
    1993   "Holy Spirit: Source of Messianic Mission," in W. R. Shenk, ed., 106–29.
Küng, Hans
    1967   *The Church.* New York: Sheed and Ward.

Ladd, George Eldon
1964   *Jesus and the Kingdom.* New York: Harper and Row.

Lascaris, André
1993   *Zuid Afrika in verandering. Een gesprek met Albert Nolan* (Changing South Africa: A Conversation with Albert Nolan), *De Bazuin* (October 22): 16–17.

Lernoux, Penny
1980   *Cry of the People.* New York: Doubleday.

Livingston, Kevin
1990   "David Bosch: An Interpretation of Some Main Themes in His Missiological Thought," *Missionalia*, vol. 18/1, 3–19.

Lohfink, Gerhard
1984   *Jesus and the Kingdom.* Philadelphia: Fortress; New York: Paulist Press.

Lombard, T. E.
1981   "Reaction to Bosch's Contribution 'Kerk en politiek in die Suid-Afrikaanse konteks' (Church and Politics in the South African Context)," *Stormkompas* (1981): 37–40.

Makhubu, P.
1988   *Who Are the Independent Churches?* Johannesburg: Skotaville.

Maldanado, I. E.
1993   "Building Fundamentalism from the Family in Latin America," in Martin E. Marty and R. Scott Appleby, eds. *Fundamentalism and Society.* Chicago: University of Chicago Press, 214–39.

Marsden, George M.
1991   *Understanding Fundamentalism and Evangelicalism.* Grand Rapids, MI: Eerdmans.

Maslach, C.
1982   *Burnout: The Cost of Caring.* Englewood Cliffs, NJ: Anchor Press.

Mbiti, John
1978   " 'Cattle Are Born with Ears, Their Horns Grow Later': Towards an Appreciation of African Oral Theology," in Alison Bares, ed. *Christian Theology and Christian Education in the African Context.* Geneva: Lutheran World Federation, 35–51.

McClendon, James William, Jr.
1994   *Systematic Theology: Doctrine,* vol. 2. Nashville: Abingdon Press.

McGovern, Arthur F.
1989   *Liberation Theology and Its Critics: Toward an Assessment.* Maryknoll, NY: Orbis Books.

Meiring, P. G. J.
1981   "In die konteks van Afrika," *Stormkompas:* 8–14.

Mignone, Emelio F.
  1986   *Witness to the Truth: The Complicity of Church and Dictatorship in Argentina, 1976–1983.* Maryknoll, NY: Orbis Books.

Míguez Bonino, José
  1975   *Doing Theology in a Revolutionary Situation.* Philadelphia: Fortress.

Milingo, Emmanuel
  1984   *The World in Between: Christian Healing and the Struggle for Spiritual Survival.* London: C. Hurst; Maryknoll, NY: Orbis Books; Gweru: Mambo Press.

Miller, Larry
  1993   "The Church as Messianic Society: Creation and Instrument of Transfigured Mission," in W. R. Shenk, ed., 130–52.

Minear, Paul S.
  1960   *Images of the Church in the New Testament.* Philadelphia: Westminster.

Mkhatshwa, Smangaliso
  1991   "Church Perspectives on the Future of South Africa," in Louw Alberts and Frank Chikane, eds. *The Road to Rustenburg,* 140–48.

Mofokeng, Takatso Alfred
  1983   *The Crucified among the Crossbearers: Toward a Black Christology.* Kampen: J. H. Kok.
  1990   "Mission Theology from an African Perspective: A Dialogue with David Bosch," in J. N. J. Kritzinger and W. Saayman, eds. *Mission in Creative Tension,* 168–80.

Moltmann, Jürgen
  1967   *Theology of Hope.* London: SCM.
  1974   *The Crucified God.* New York: Harper and Row.

Mosala, Itumeleng J.
  1989   *Biblical Hermeneutics and Black Theology in South Africa.* Grand Rapids, MI: Eerdmans.

Mosala, Itumeleng J. and Buti Tlhagale, eds.
  1986   *The Unquestionable Right to Be Free: Essays in Black Theology.* Johannesburg.

Mphahlele, E.
  1977   "South Africa: Two Communities and the Struggle for a Birthright," *Journal of African Studies* 4 (Spring): 21–50.

Murray, Andrew
  1898   "The Mount of Sources," in *The Huguenot Seminary Journal,* no. 3.

Mushette, Ngindu
  1979   "The History of Theology in Africa: From Polemics to Critical Irenics," in Kofi Appiah-Kubi and Sergio Torres, eds. *African Theology En Route.* Maryknoll, NY: Orbis Books, 23–35.

Muthukya, S. M.
n.d.   *Africanization of Christianity.* Nairobi: East Africa Christian Alliance.

Muzorewa, Gwinyai Henry
1991   *An African Theology of Mission.* Lewiston/QueenstonLampeter: The Edwin Mellen Press.

Myers, Bryant
1992   "A Funny Thing Happened on the Way to Evangelical/Ecumenical Cooperation," *International Review of Mission* (July).

Neill, Stephen
1959   *Creative Tension.* London: E. H. P.
1968   *The Church and Christian Union.* London: Oxford University Press.

Neuner, Joseph, ed.
1967   *Christian Revelation and World Religions.* London: Burns & Oates.

Neuner, Joseph and J. Dupuis
1973   *The Christian Faith in the Doctrinal Documents of the Catholic Church.* Dublin: The Mercier Press.

Newbigin, L.
1954   *The Household of God.* New York: Friendship Press.

Nicol, W.
1990   "The Cross and the Hammer: Comparing Bosch and Nolan on the Role of the Church in Social Change," in J. N. J. Kritzinger and W. A. Saayman, eds. *Mission in Creative Tension: A Dialogue with David Bosch.* Pretoria: SAMS, 86–98.

Nketia, J. H.
1962   "The Contribution of African Culture to Christian Worship," in Ram Desai, ed. *Christianity in Africa As Seen by Africans.* Denver: A. Swallow, 109–23.

Nolan, Albert
1988   *God in South Africa: The Challenge of the Gospel.* Cape Town and Johannesburg: David Philip; Grand Rapids, MI: Wm. Eerdmans; Gweru: Mambo Press; London: CIIR.

Nürnberger, Klaus
1977   Response to Bosch's Paper, "The Church as the Liberation of Peoples?" *Missionalia,* vol. 5 (August): 43–6.
1991   "De-Ideologizing Confrontations in the Church," in Klaus Nürnberger, ed. *A Democratic Vision for South Africa,* NIR Reader no. 3. Pietermaritzburg: Encounter Publications, 297–300.

Ogden, Schubert M.
1992   *Is There Only One True Religion or Are There Many?* Dallas: Southern Methodist University Press.

Oosterwal, Gottfried
1973   *Modern Messianic Movements as a Theological and Missionary Challenge.* Elkhart, IN: Institute of Mennonite Studies.

Padilla, C. René
1982 "The Unity of the Church and the Homogeneous Unit Principle," *International Bulletin of Missionary Research* 6 (January): 24–30.

Padilla, C. and Chris Sugden
1986 *How Evangelicals Addressed Evangelism and Social Responsibility.* Bramcote, Nottingham: Grove Booklets.

Panikkar, Raimon
1993 *The Cosmotheandric Experience: Emerging Religious Consciousness,* edited, with an introduction by, Scott Eastham. Maryknoll, NY: Orbis Books.

Forthcoming *The Rhythm of Being* (Gifford Lectures, 1989). Maryknoll, NY: Orbis Books.

Perrin, Norman
1963 *The Kingdom of God in the Teaching of Jesus.* Philadelphia: Westminster Press.

Pieris, Aloysius
1988a *An Asian Theology of Liberation.* Maryknoll, NY: Orbis Books.
1988b *Love Meets Wisdom: A Christian Understanding of Buddhism.* Maryknoll, NY: Orbis Books.
1993 "Does Christ Have a Place in Asia? A Panoramic View," *Concilium,* no. 2: 33–47.
1996 *Fire and Water: Women, Society, and Spirituality in Buddhism and Christianity.* Maryknoll, NY: Orbis Books.

Pillay, G. J.
1990 "Text, Paradigms and Context: An Examination of David Bosch's Use of Paradigms in the Reading of Christian History," in J. N. J. Kritzinger and W. A. Saayman, eds. *Mission in Creative Tension: A Dialogue with David Bosch.* Pretoria: SAMS, 109–23.

Pobee, John S.
1985 *Persecution and Martyrdom in the Theology of Paul.* Sheffield: Society of New Testament Studies Monograph Scenes, Chapter 3.
1989 "Oral Tradition and Christian Oral Theology: Challenge to Our Traditional Archival Concept," *Mission Studies* 6 (1), 87–93.
1992a "In Memoriam, David J. Bosch," *Mission Studies* 9: 252.
1992b *Skenosis: Christian Faith in an African Context.* Zimbabwe: Mambo Press.

Pomerville, P. A.
1985 *The Third Force in Missions: A Pentecostal Contribution to Contemporary Mission Theology.* Peabody, MA: Hendrickson Publishers.

Race, Allan
1982 *Christians and Religious Pluralism: Patterns in the Christian Theology of Religions.* Maryknoll, NY: Orbis Books.

Resales G. and C. G. Arevalo
1992   *For All the Peoples of Asia: Federation of Asian Bishops' Conferences Documents from 1970 to 1991.* Quezon City: Claretian Publications.

Ricca, Paolo
1986   "The Mission of the Churches in a Secularized Europe: A Protestant View," in Theo Tschuy, ed. *The Churches' Mission in Europe Today.*

Ridderbos, Herman
1962   *The Coming of the Kingdom.* Philadelphia: Presbyterian and Reformed.

Robert, Dana
1993   "Mount Holyoke Women and the Dutch Reformed Missionary Movement, 1874–1904," *Missionalia* 21(2): 103–23.
Forthcoming "The Woman's Foreign Missionary Society of the Methodist Episcopal Church and Holiness, 1869–1894."

Ross, Andrew
1994   *A Vision Betrayed: The Jesuits in Japan and China 1542–1742.* Edinburgh: Edinburgh University Press; Maryknoll, NY: Orbis Books.

Saayman, Willem A.
1991a   *Christian Mission in South Africa: Political and Ecumenical.* Pretoria: Unisa.
1991b   "Some Reflections on AIDS, Ethics and the Community in Southern and Central Africa," *Theologia Evangelica.*
1992   "*Transforming Mission* by David Bosch: A Review Article from a South African Perspective," *Theologia Evangelica* 25 (June): 37–47.

Saayman, Willem A. and J. R. Kriel
1991   "Towards a Christian Response to AIDS in Africa," *Missionalia* 19:2 (Aug.), 154–67.

Samuel, Vinay and Chris Sugden, eds.
1984   *Sharing Jesus in the Two-Thirds World.* Partnership in Asia.
1991   "What Is Good about Good News to the Poor?" in *AD 2000 and Beyond.* Oxford: Regnum.

Sanneh, Lamin
1989   *Translating the Message: The Missionary Impact on Culture.* Maryknoll, NY: Orbis Books.
1993   *Encountering the West: Christianity and the Global Cultural Process: The African Dimension.* London: Marshall Pickering.

Schaller, Lyle E.
1993   "What Will the Twenty-first Century Bring?" *Circuit Rider* 17, no. 7: 10.

Schnackenburg, Rudolf
1963   *God's Rule and Kingdom.* New York: Herder and Herder.

Schoeman, S.
1990   "AIDS — The International Malady." Paper read at Africa Studies Forum, Unisa, June 21. ASF no. 30.

Schreiter, Robert J.
1985   *Constructing Local Theologies.* Maryknoll, NY: Orbis Books.

Scott, James C.
1990   *Domination and the Arts of Resistance: Hidden Transcripts.* New Haven, CT: Yale University Press.

Segundo, Juan Luis
1976   *Liberation of Theology.* Maryknoll, NY: Orbis Books (Spanish original, Buenos Aires, 1975).

Shank, David A.
1993   "Jesus the Messiah: Messianic Foundation of Mission," 37–82, and "Consummation of Messiah's Mission," 220–41, in W. R. Shenk, ed.

Shenk, Wilbert R., ed.
1993   *The Transfiguration of Mission.* Scottdale, PA: Herald Press.

Shourie, Arun
1994   *Missionaries in India: Continuities, Changes, Dilemmas.* New Delhi: ASA Publications.

Smit, D. J.
1984   "In a Special Way the God of the Destitute, the Poor and the Wronged," in G. D. Cloete and D. J. Smit, eds. *A Moment of Truth: The Confession of the Dutch Reformed Mission Church 1982.* Grand Rapids, MI: Eerdmans.

Stadion, A.
1949   Letter (Jan. 21). South Hadley, MA: Mount Holyoke College Archives.

Stanley, David
1965   *The Apostolic Church in the New Testament.* Westminster, MD: Newman.

Stow, Sarah D.
1887   *History of Mount Holyoke Seminary, South Hadley, Massachusetts, during its First Half Century, 1837–1887.* South Hadley, MA: Mount Holyoke College.

Thomas, Louise Porter
1937   *Seminary Militant: An Account of the Missionary Movement at Mount Holyoke Seminary and College.* South Hadley, MA: Mount Holyoke College.

Tlhagale, B. and I. Mosala, eds.
1986   *Hammering Swords into Ploughshares: Essays in Honor of Archbishop Mpilo Desmond Tutu.* Johannesburg: Skotaville Publishers.

Torres, Sergio and Virginia Fabella, eds.
1978   *The Emergent Gospel: Theology from the Developing World.* Maryknoll, NY: Orbis Books.

Tracy, David
    1975   *Blessed Rage for Order: The New Pluralism in Theology.* New York: Seabury.
    1981   *The Analogical Imagination: Christian Theology and the Culture of Pluralism.* New York: Crossroad.

Troeltsch, Ernst
    1960   *The Social Teaching of the Christian Churches.* Trans. Olive Wyon. New York: Harper and Row (repr. of 1931 ed).
    1976   *The Social Teaching of the Christian Churches.* Trans. Olive Wyon, 2 vols. Chicago: University of Chicago Press (German original, 1911).

Verkuyl, J.
    1992   "Ter gedachtenis aan prof. dr. David Bosch (1929–1992)" (In memory of Prof. Dr. David Bosch [1929–1992]), *Wereld en Zending,* 21(3): 3–6.

Verstraelen, F. J.
    1976   "Church and Society in Conflict: Manipulation and Movement in Colombia," *Exchange: Bulletin of Third World Literature,* no. 15 (December): 1–27.
    1980   *Missiologie onderweg. Een autobibliografie in kontekst* (Missiology En Route: An Autobibliography in Context). IIMO Research Pamphlet no. 2. Leiden: Interuniversity Institute for Missiological and Ecumenical Research (IIMO).
    1985   "Christen-zijn onder bruut geweld: Contextuele theologie in Zuid-Afrika" (Being Christian under Brute Violence: Contextual Theology in South Africa), *De Bazuin,* 29 (Maart): 2–3.
    1993   "The Christian Bible and African Cultural and Religious Realities, in I. Mukonyora, J. L. Cox, and F. J. Verstraelen, eds. *"Rewriting" the Bible: The Real Issues: Perspectives from within Biblical and Religious Studies in Zimbabwe.* Gweru: Mambo Press, 219–44.

Verstraelen-Gilhuis, Gerdien
    1979   "SACLA en de Zuidafrikaanse 'kerkstrijd'" (SACLA and the South African "Church Struggle"), *Wereld en Zending* 8: 261–72.
    1992   "Apartheid, Churches and Black Theology in South Africa, in *A New Look at Christianity in Africa.* Gweru: Mambo Press, 9–36.

Vicedom, Georg F.
    1965   *The Mission of God: An Introduction to a Theology of Mission.* Trans. G. A. Thiele and D. Hilgendorf (from 1957 German ed.). St. Louis: Concordia.

Viviano, Benedict T., O.P.
    1988   *The Kingdom of God in History.* Wilmington, DE: Michael Glazier.

Walsh, Michael
    1992   *Opus Dei: An Investigation into the Secret Society Struggling for Power within the Roman Catholic Church.* San Francisco: Harper San Francisco.

Waterbury, J. B.
  1870   *Memoir of the Rev. John Scudder, M.D.: Thirty-six Years Missionary in India.* New York: Harper & Brothers.

Welbourn, F. B. and B. A. Ogot
  1968   *A Place to Feel at Home.* London: Oxford University Press.

Willis, Wendell, ed.
  1987   *The Kingdom of God in 20th-Century Interpretation.* Peabody, MA: Hendrickson.

Wilmore, Gayraud S. and James H. Cone
  1979   *Black Theology: A Documentary History, 1966–1979.* Maryknoll, NY: Orbis Books.

Wink, Walter
  1993   *Engaging the Powers.* Minneapolis: Fortress Press.

Witvliet, Theo
  1985   *A Place in the Sun: An Introduction to Liberation Theology in the Third World.* Maryknoll, NY: Orbis Books.

Woody, Thomas
  1966   *A History of Women's Education in the United States.* New York: Octagon Books.

Yinger, J. Milton
  1957   *Religion, Society and the Individual.* New York: Macmillan Co.

Yoder, John H.
  1974   "Exodus and Exile — The Two Faces of Liberation," *Missionalia* 2 (April): 29–41.